# Contents

**Skills:**
Writing & Counting 0–2

# Gone to the Dogs

Trace.

0 0 0 0 0 0

1 1 1 1 1 1

2 2 2 2 2 2

Count the dogs. Write the numbers.

# Numbers 3, 4, 5

**Skills:**

Writing & Counting 3–5

Gone to the Dogs

Trace.

3 3 3 3 3 3

4 4 4 4 4 4

5 5 5 5 5 5

Count the dogs. Match the dogs to their doghouses.

# Numbers 6, 7, 8

**Skills:**

Writing & Counting 6–8

Gone to the Dogs

Trace.

6 6 6 6 6 6

7 7 7 7 7 7

8 8 8 8 8 8

Draw the bones. 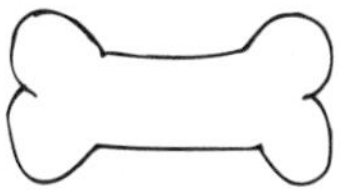

| six bones | eight bones |
| --- | --- |
| | |

Circle the larger number on each bone.

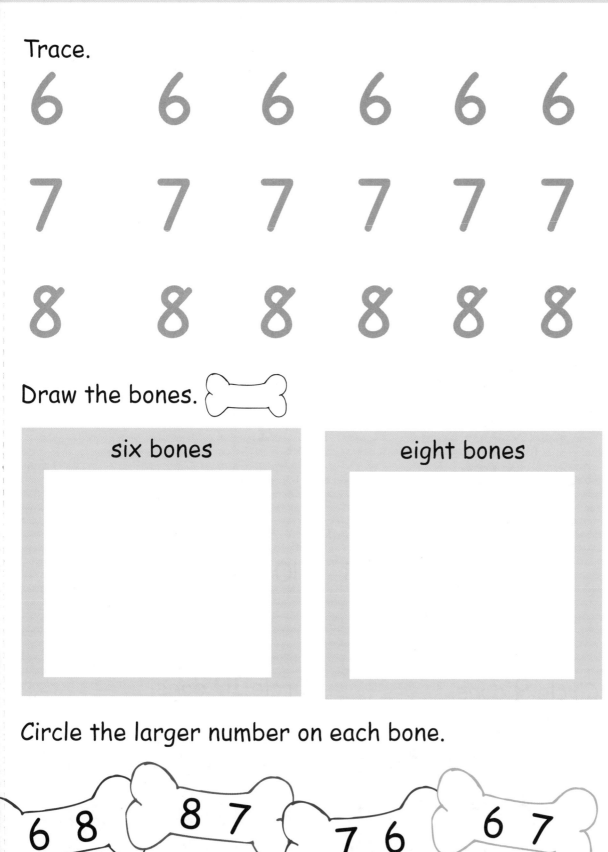

# Numbers 9 and 10

**Skills:**

Writing & Counting 9 and 10

Gone to the Dogs

Trace.

9 9 9 9 9 9

10 10 10 10 10 10

How many dogs?

9 10

9 10

9 10

Circle **9** dogs.

Circle **10** dogs.

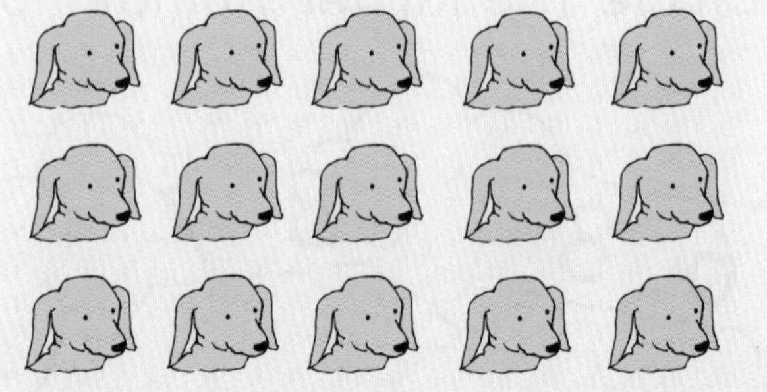

**Skills:**

Counting 0–10

Gone to the Dogs

How many puppies?

8 9 10

4 5 6

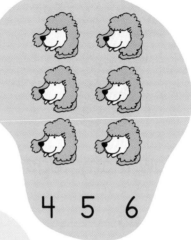

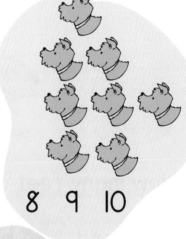

0 1 2

3 4 5

8 9 10

5 6 7

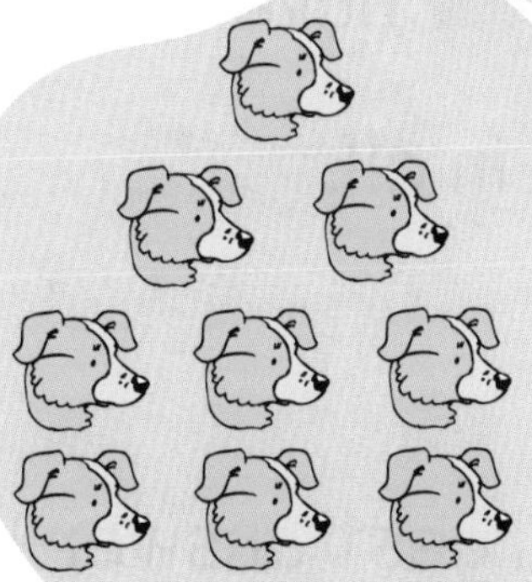

7 8 9

**Skills:**

Counting 0–10

Note: You may need to help your child read the word problems.

**Gone to the Dogs**

How many legs?

 has _____ legs.

How many ears?

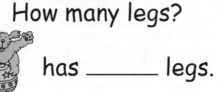

 has _____ ears.

How many feet in all?

 and  have

_____ feet in all.

How many bones?

has _____ bones.

What is the largest answer? _____

What is the smallest answer? _____

Note: You may need to help your child read the word problems.

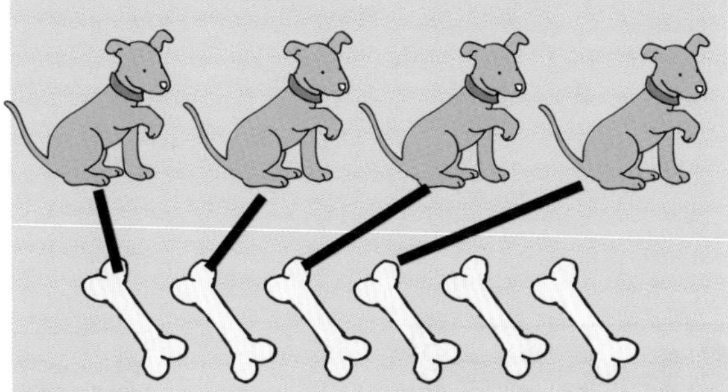

bones
were used.

doghouses
were used.

cans of food
were used.

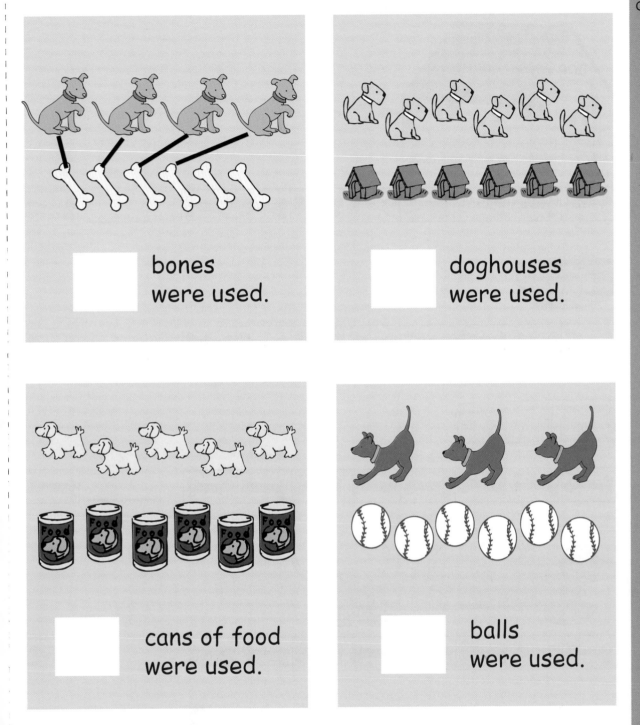

balls
were used.

Gone to the Dogs

What is the largest number of things used? _____

What is the smallest number of things used? _____

**Skills:**

Nonstandard
Measurement

## How long is each thing?

_____

_____

_____

_____

_____

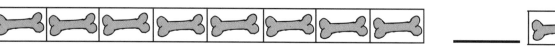

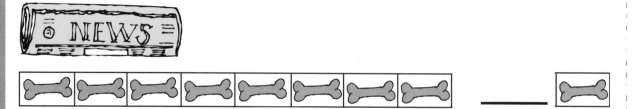

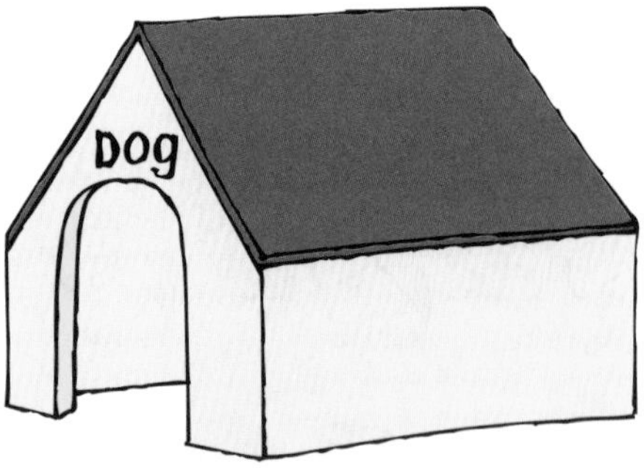

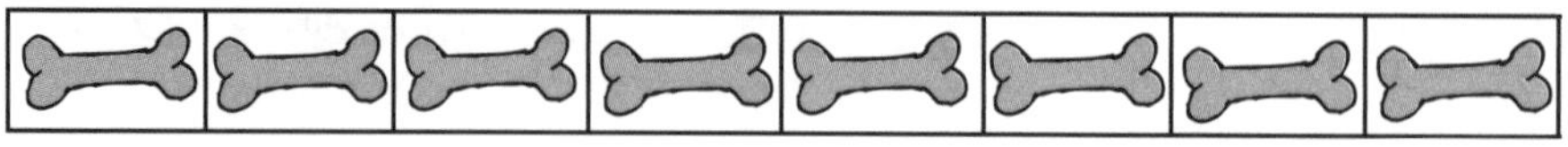

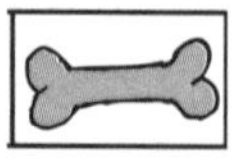

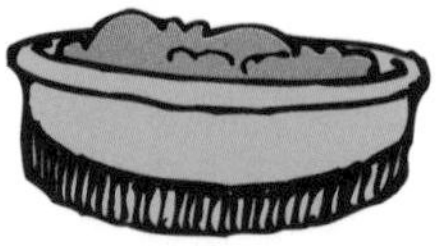

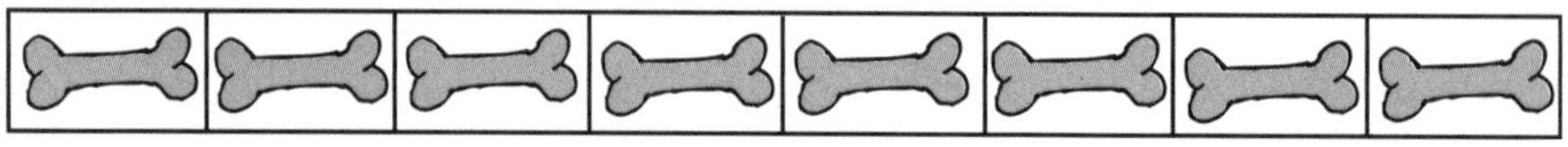

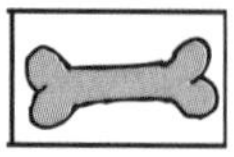

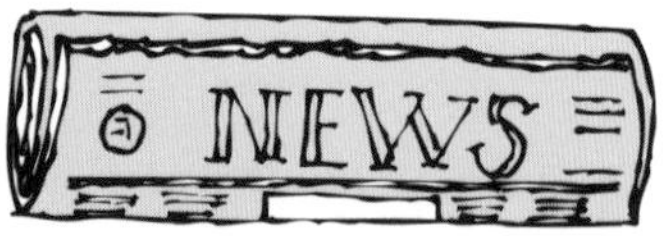

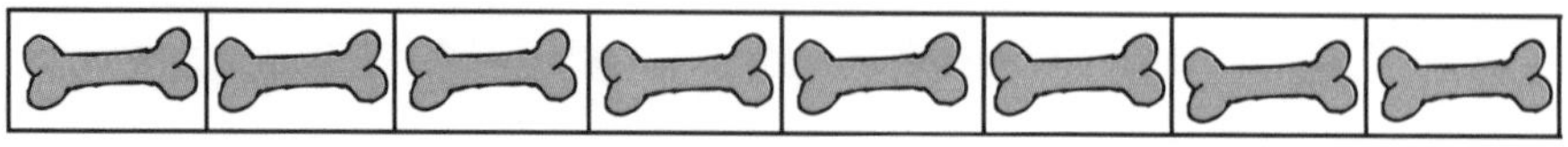

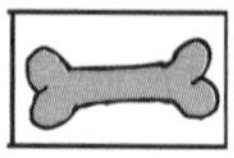

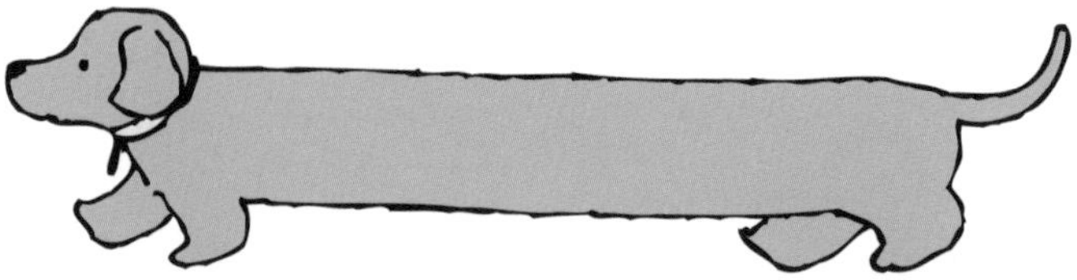

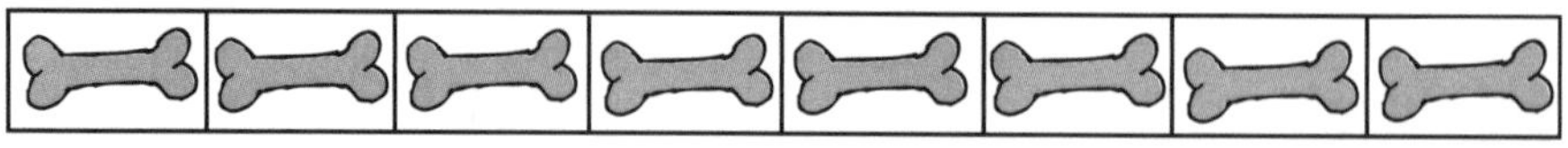

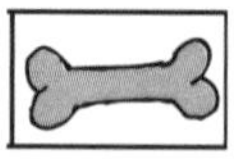

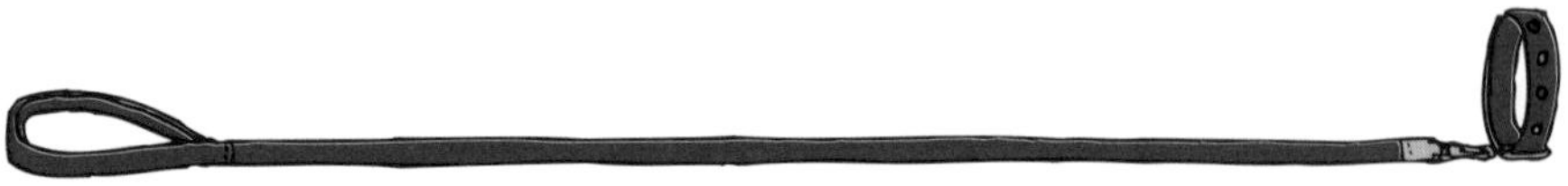

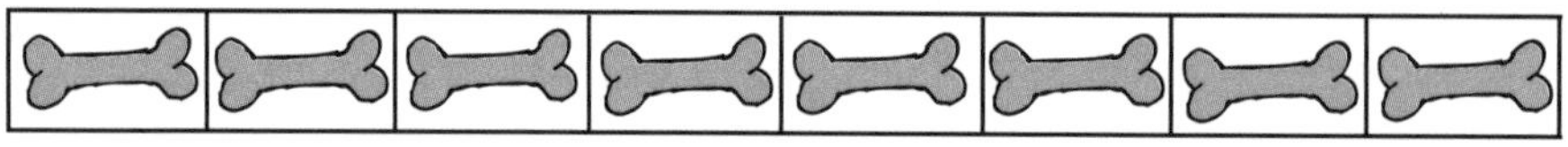

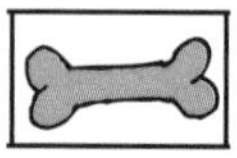

**Skills:**

Reading Graphs

Read the graph. Answer the questions.

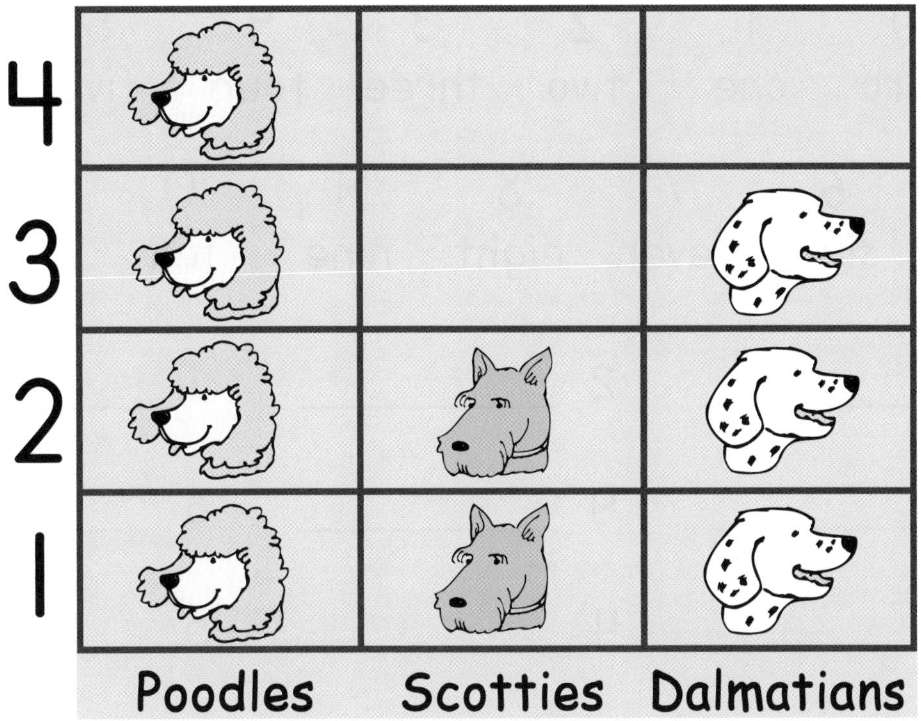


1. How many dogs are in the store?

 ______  ______  ______

2. How many dogs in all? ______

3. Are there more  or ?  

4. Which dog is there the most of?

# Number Words

**Skills:**

Number Words to Ten

Write each number word.

| 0 | 1 | 2 | 3 | 4 | 5 |
|---|---|---|---|---|---|
| zero | one | two | three | four | five |

| 6 | 7 | 8 | 9 | 10 |
|---|---|---|---|---|
| six | seven | eight | nine | ten |

3 ____________ 2 ____________ 1 ____________

10 ____________ 9 ____________ 6 ____________

0 ____________ 4 ____________ 5 ____________

7 ____________ 8 ____________

Count and match.

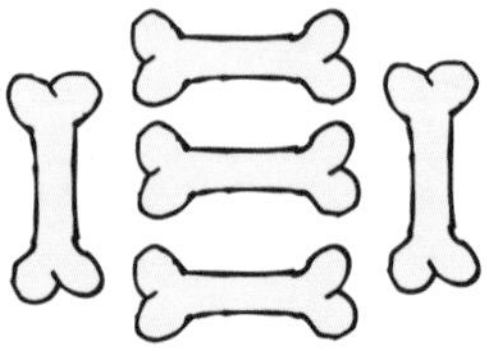

three

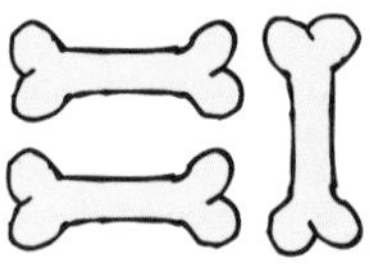

five

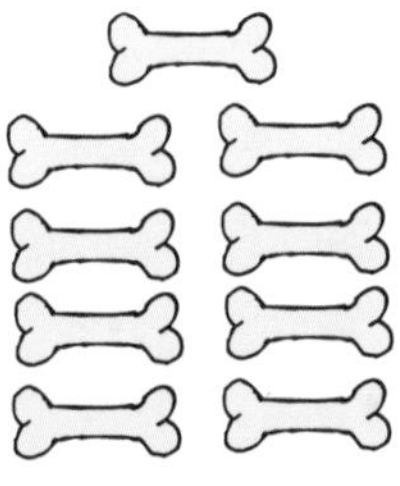

nine

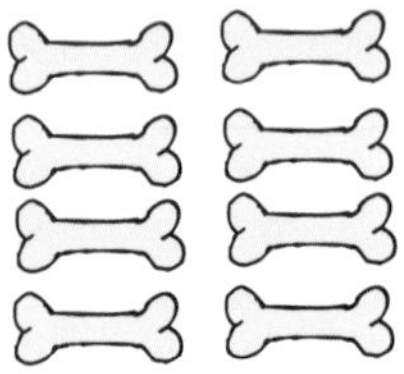

four

one

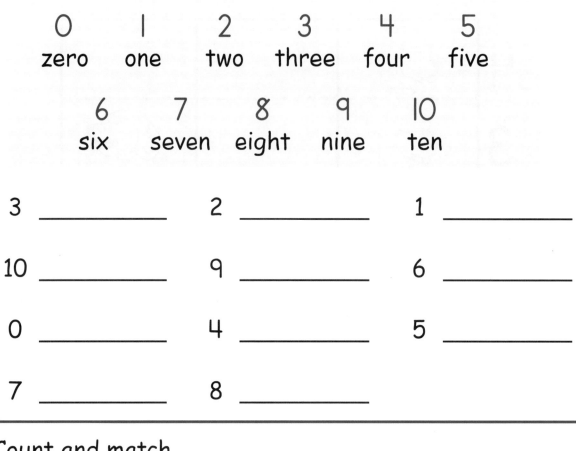

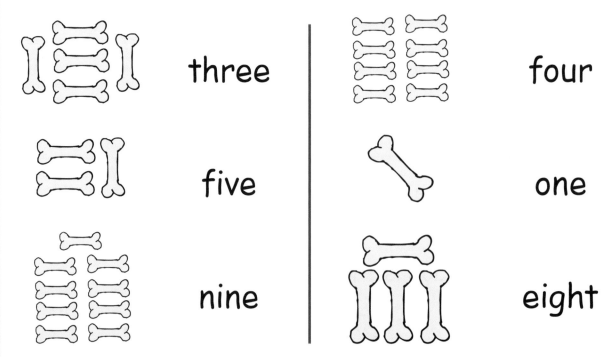

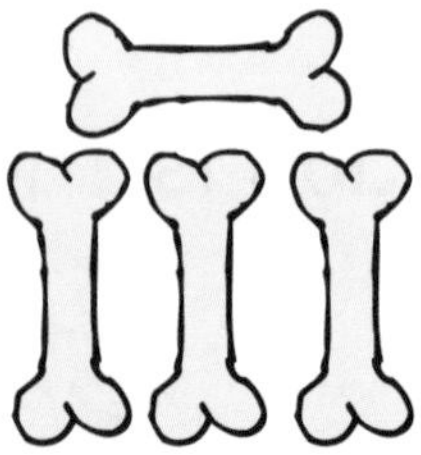

eight

Gone to the Dogs

Write the numbers. Circle the set with more.

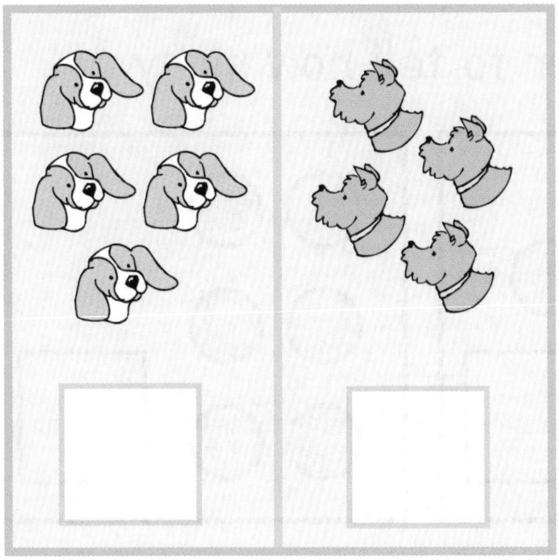

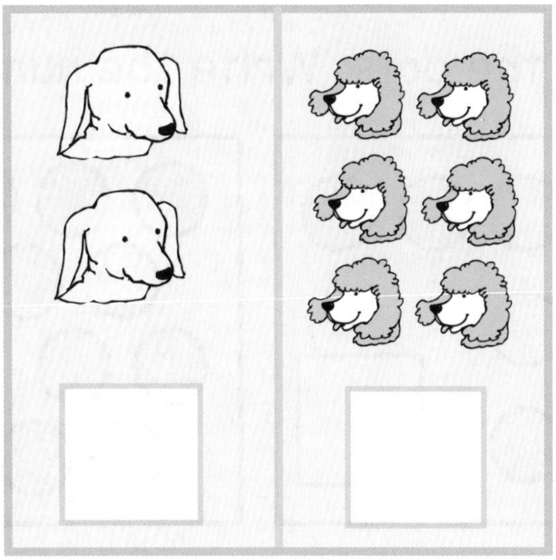

Write the numbers. Circle the set with less.

Which number is larger?      Which number is smaller?

Count the dots. Write the number to tell how many.

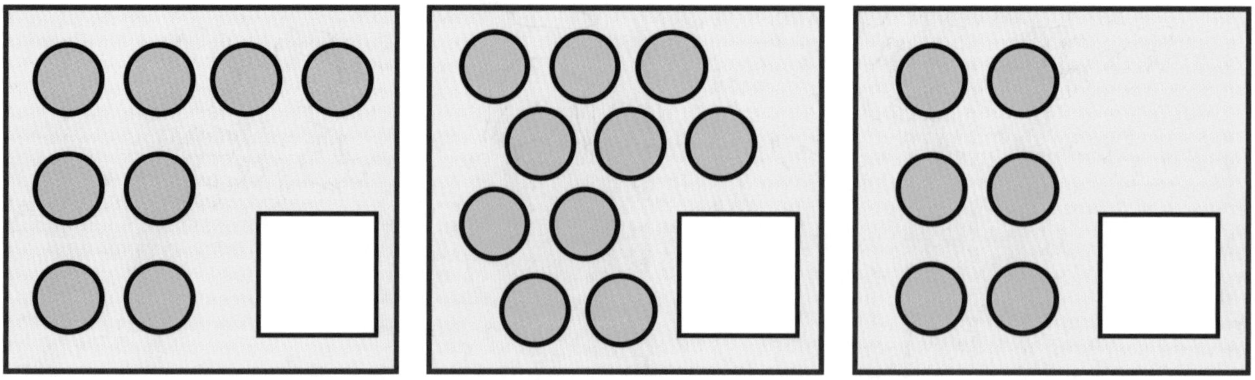

Fill in the circle to show how long it is.

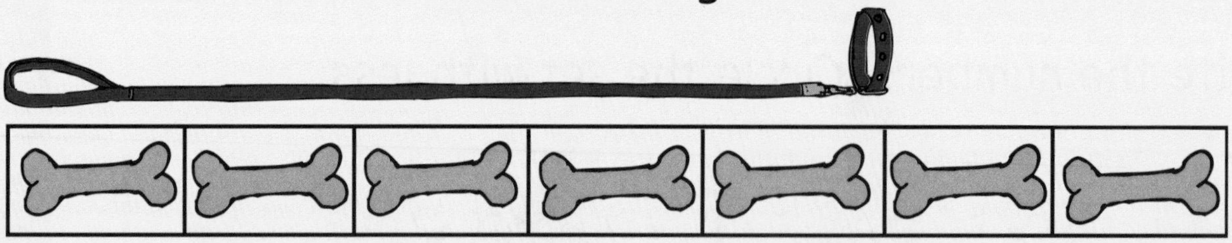

5          7          9
○          ○          ○

Color the shapes.

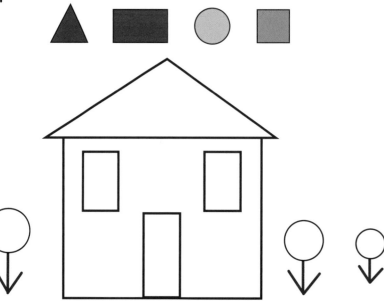

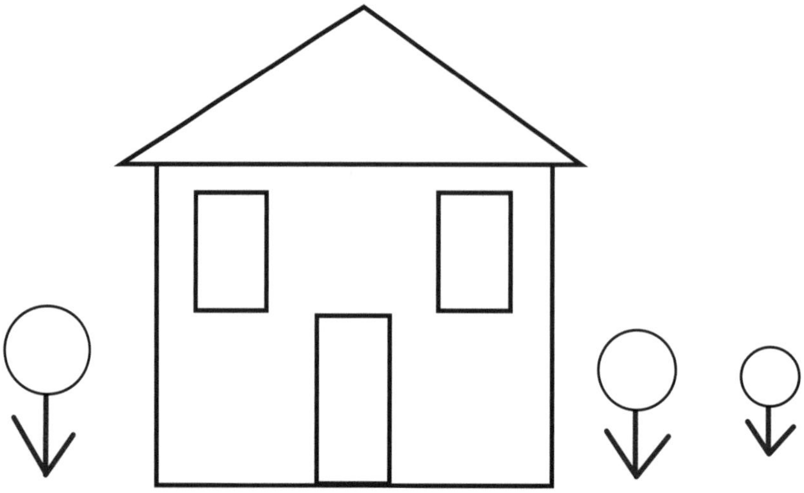

Skills:

Addition to 6

Add.

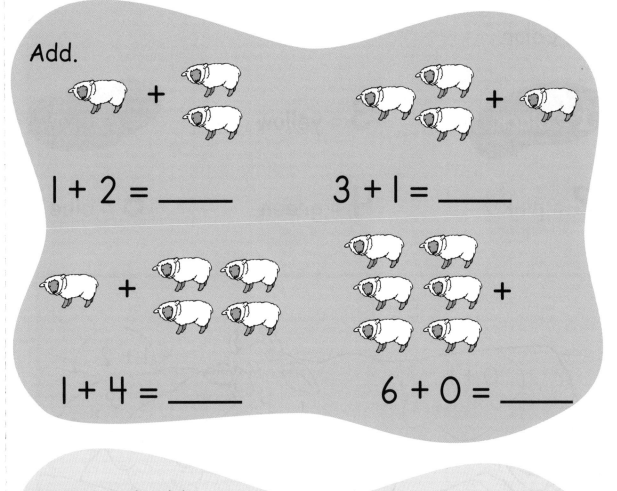

1 + 2 = ____

3 + 1 = ____

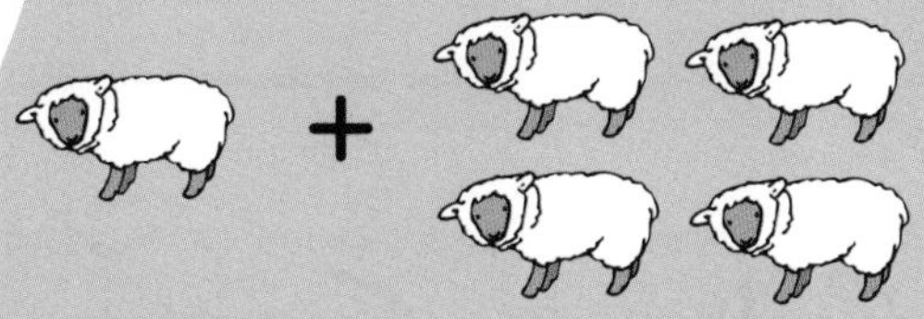

1 + 4 = ____

6 + 0 = ____

Write and add.

1 + 1 = 2

___ + ___ = ___

___ + ___ = ___

___ + ___ = ___

# What Do You See?

**Skills:**
Addition to 6

Add. Color.

1 = black
3 = yellow
5 = brown
2 = pink
4 = green
6 = blue

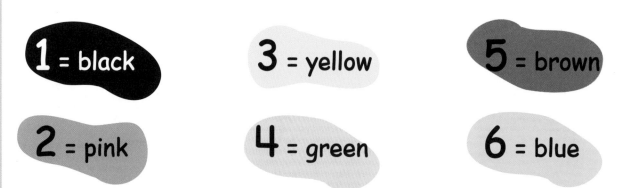

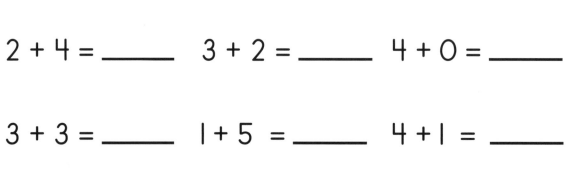

Add.

2 + 4 = ____ 3 + 2 = ____ 4 + 0 = ____

3 + 3 = ____ 1 + 5 = ____ 4 + 1 = ____

On the Farm

Note: You may need to help your child read the word problems.

Add.

2 horses.
2 more horses come.
How many horses?

2 + 2 = 4

4 horses

3 hens.
3 more hens come.
How many hens?

___ + ___ = ___

☐ hens

0 pigs in the pen.
5 pigs jump in.
How many pigs?

___ + ___ = ___

☐ pigs

2 sheep.
1 more sheep comes.
How many sheep?

___ + ___ = ___

☐ sheep

**Skills:**

Word Problems: Addition to 6

On the Farm

**Skills:**

Addition to 6

On the Farm

Add.

2 + 2 = ____ 3 + 2 = ____ 4 + 2 = ____

1 + 2 = ____ 0 + 2 = ____ 1 + 1 = ____

3 + 1 = ____ 1 + 0 = ____ 0 + 3 = ____

0 + 0 = ____ 2 + 3 = ____ 3 + 3 = ____

| | | | | |
|---|---|---|---|---|
| 3 | 2 | 0 | 3 | 0 |
| + 1 | + 3 | + 3 | + 3 | + 0 |
| □ | □ | □ | □ | □ |

| | | | | |
|---|---|---|---|---|
| 1 | 4 | 4 | 2 | 1 |
| + 0 | + 2 | + 1 | + 2 | + 1 |
| □ | □ | □ | □ | □ |

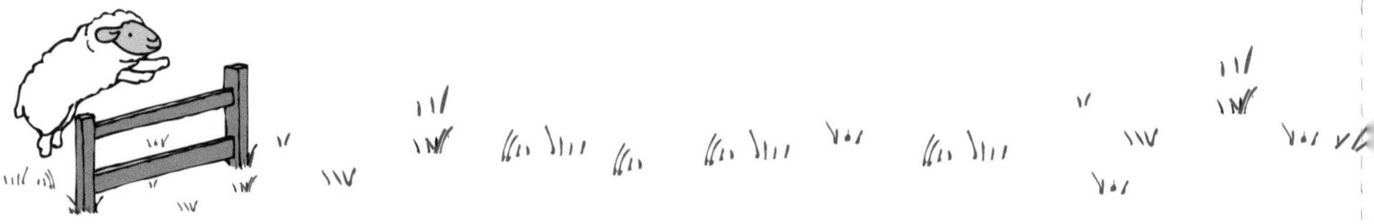

 

# Count the Pennies

**Skills:**

Money—Pennies

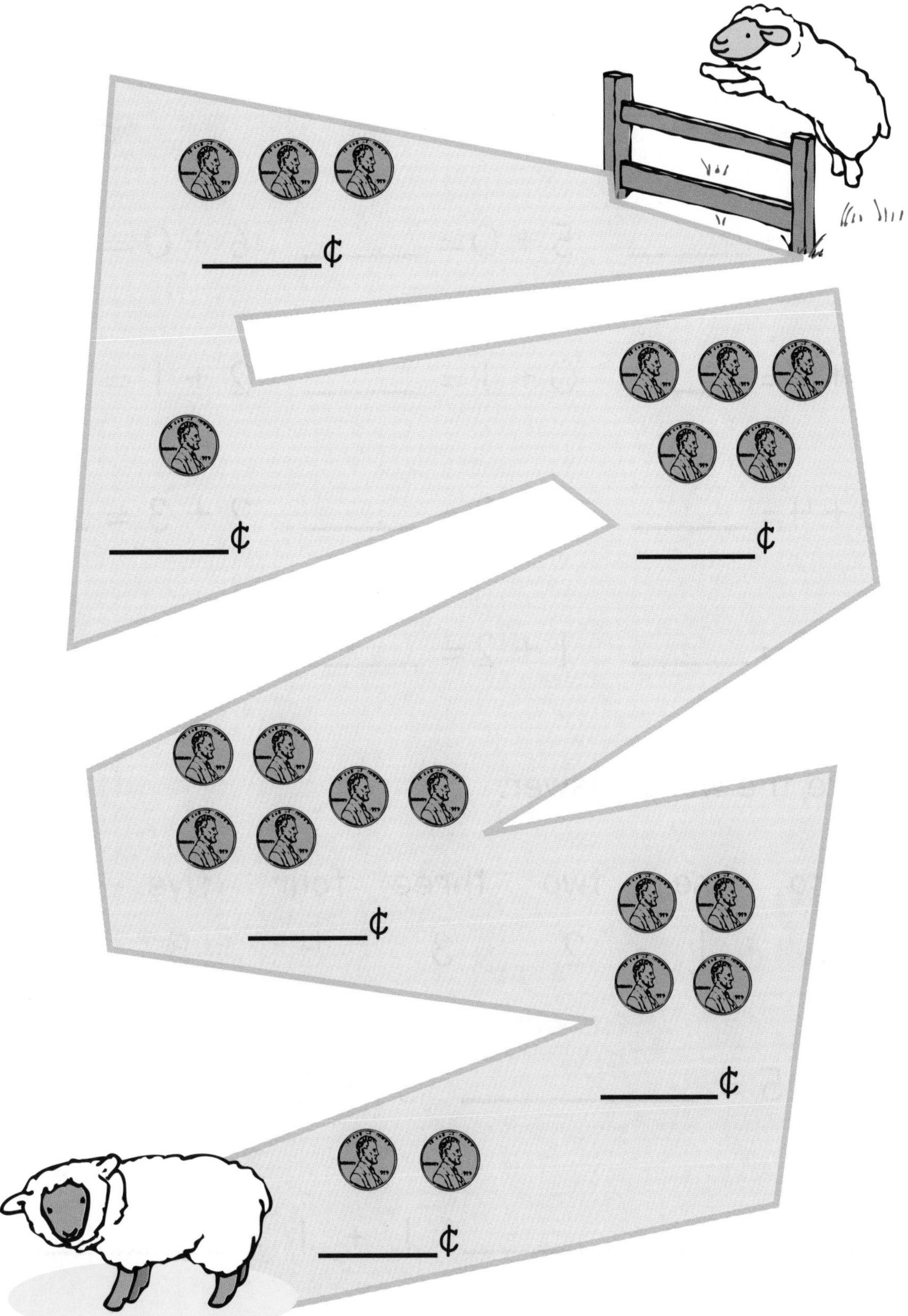

# How Many Pigs?

**Skills:**

Addition to 6

Number Words

On the Farm

Add.

5 + 1 = ______  5 + 0 = ______  6 + 0 = ______

3 + 1 = ______  0 + 1 = ______  2 + 1 = ______

0 + 4 = ______  0 + 2 = ______  2 + 3 = ______

0 + 0 = ______  1 + 2 = ______  0 + 6 = ______

Write the word answer.

| zero | one | two | three | four | five | six |
|---|---|---|---|---|---|---|
| 0 | 1 | 2 | 3 | 4 | 5 | 6 |

1 + 5 = six  3 + 2 = ______

0 + 0 = ______  1 + 1 = ______

1 + 3 = ______  2 + 1 = ______

Skills:

Word Problems: Addition to 6

Note: You may need to help your child read the word problems.

# Add.

4 hens.
1 more hen comes.
How many hens?

___ + ___ = ___

☐ hens

1 cow.
3 more cows come.
How many cows?

___ + ___ = ___

☐ cows

2 chicks.
1 more chick comes.
How many chicks?

___ + ___ = ___

☐ chicks

2 donkeys.
3 more donkeys come.
How many donkeys?

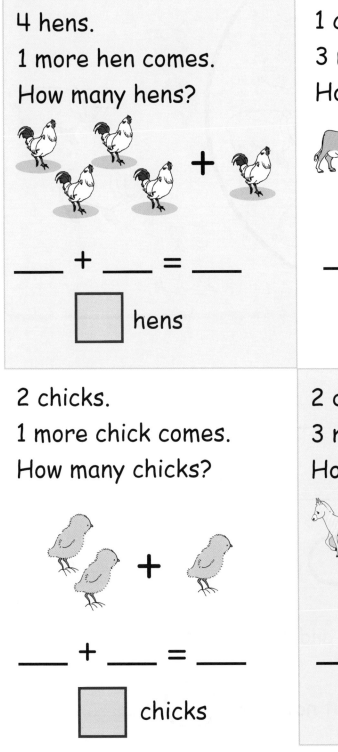

___ + ___ = ___

☐ donkeys

# Pigs and Sheep

**Skills:**

Counting

Venn Diagram

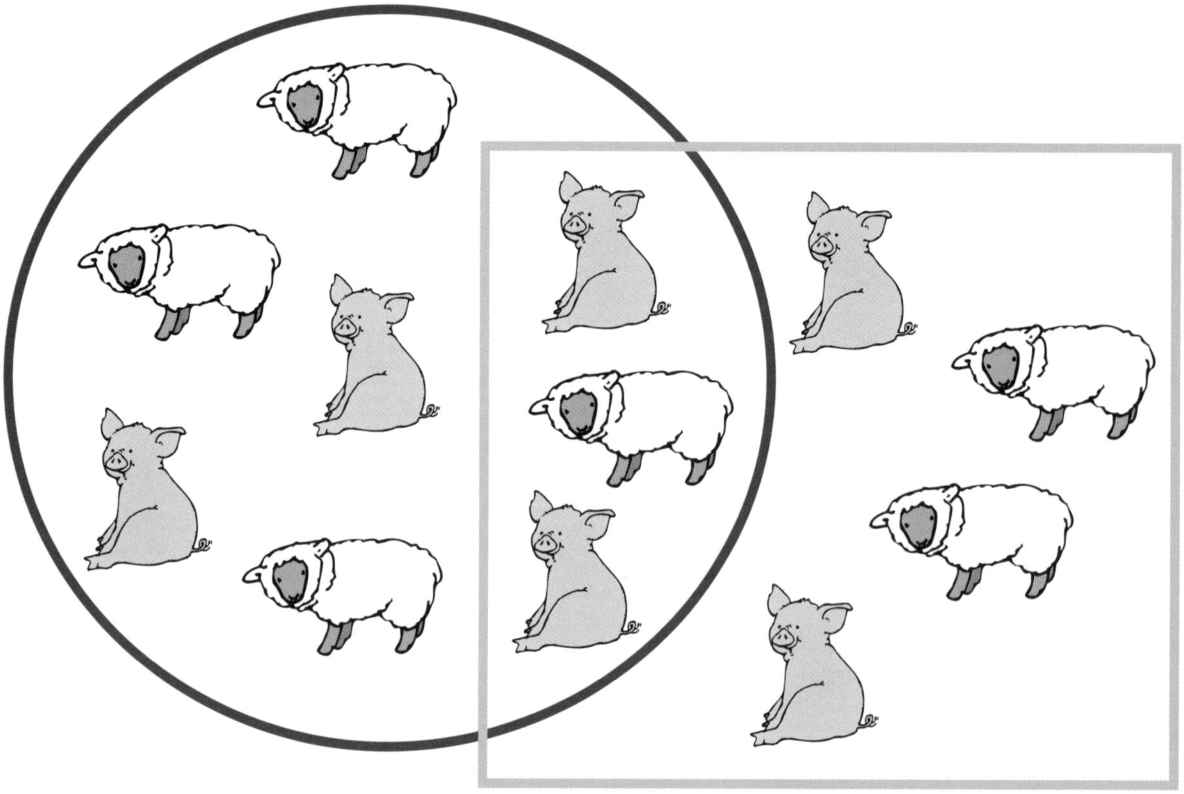

Tell how many.

1.  in the  ? ________

2.  in the  ? ________

3.  in **both** the  and the  ? ________

4.  in **both** the  and the  ? ________

5.  in the  but **not** in the  ? ________

# Name the Place

**Skills:**
Ordinal Numbers

1. Which place is the  in? ______________

2. Which place is the  in? ______________

3. Which place is the  in? ______________

4. Which animal is between the 4th and 6th place?

5. Which animal is between the 2nd and 4th place?

6. Mark the 3rd goat.

7. Mark the 5th dog.

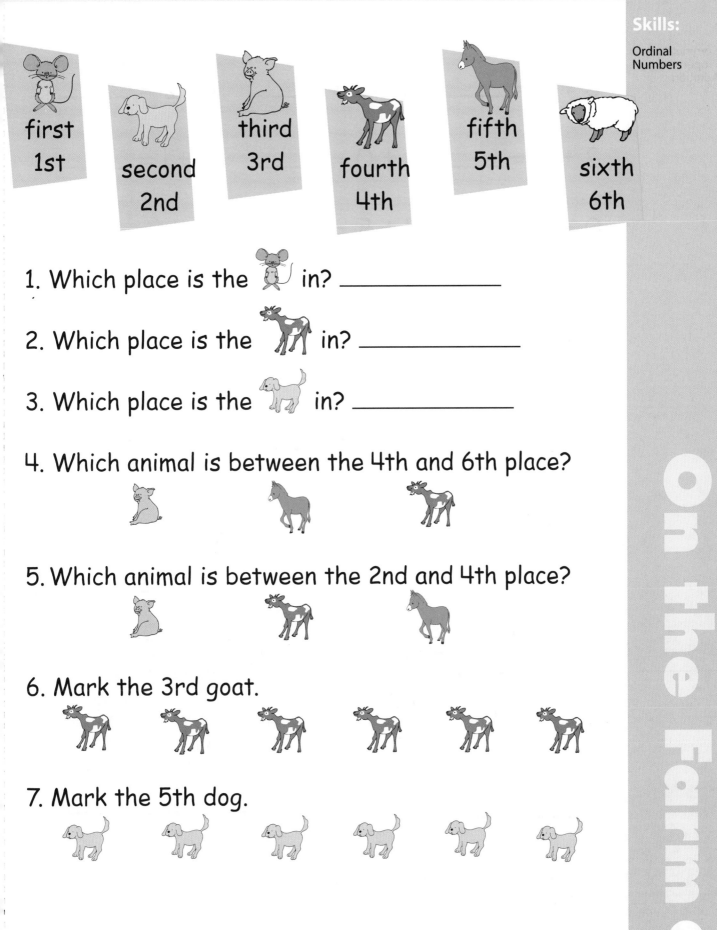

On the Farm

# The Answer Is the Same

**Skills:**

Commutative Property of Addition

Add.

| | | |
|---|---|---|
| 3 + 2 = ____ | 0 + 1 = ____ | 1 + 2 = ____ |
| 2 + 3 = ____ | 1 + 0 = ____ | 2 + 1 = ____ |
| 0 + 4 = ____ | 1 + 5 = ____ | 0 + 6 = ____ |
| 4 + 0 = ____ | 5 + 1 = ____ | 6 + 0 = ____ |
| 3 + 0 = ____ | 3 + 1 = ____ | 4 + 2 = ____ |
| 0 + 3 = ____ | 1 + 3 = ____ | 2 + 4 = ____ |

Make two addition problems.

1 + 2 = 3

2 + 1 = 3

___ + ___ = ___　　___ + ___ = ___

___ + ___ = ___　　___ + ___ = ___

On the Farm

# Who Lives in the Barn?

Skills:
Ordinal Numbers

1. On which floor do the  and  live? ________

2. Which animal lives on the 4th floor?  

3. On which floor does the  live? ________

4. Which animal lives on the 1st floor?  

5. Which floor is below the  ? ________

6. Which floor is above the  ? ________

# Are Both Sides the Same?

**Skills:**

Symmetry

Note: You may need to read the sentence at the bottom of the page to your child.

## Circle **yes** or **no**.

yes no

yes no

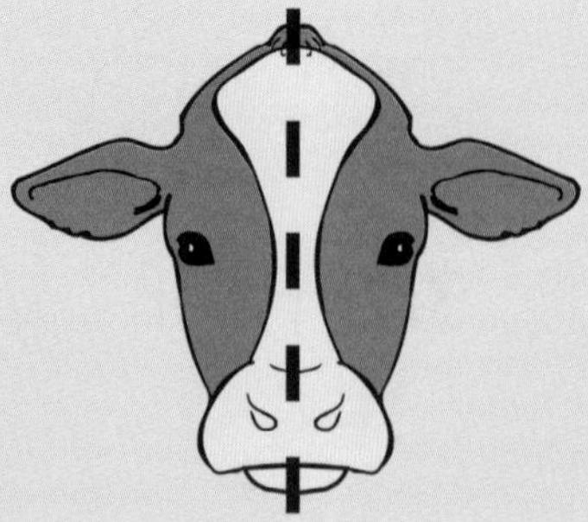

yes no

yes no

yes no

yes no

yes no

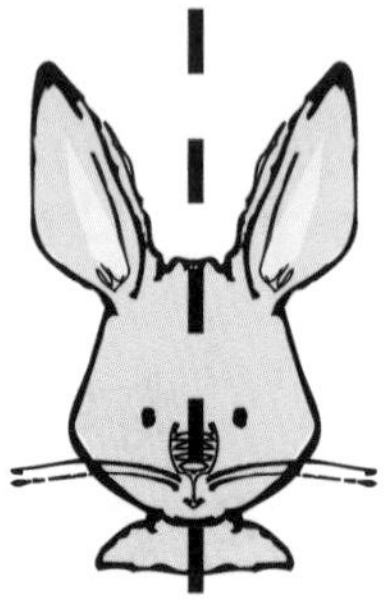

yes no

yes no

When an object is **symmetrical**, both sides are the same in shape and size.

 

Note: Use this assessment after your child has completed through page 26. Help your child read the directions.

# TEST YOUR SKILLS

Count.

Add.

3 + 3 = ____ 4 + 2 = ____ 1 + 2 = ____ 0 + 0 = ____

1 + 0 = ____ 3 + 2 = ____ 4 + 1 = ____ 1 + 1 = ____

Read the graph. Answer the questions.

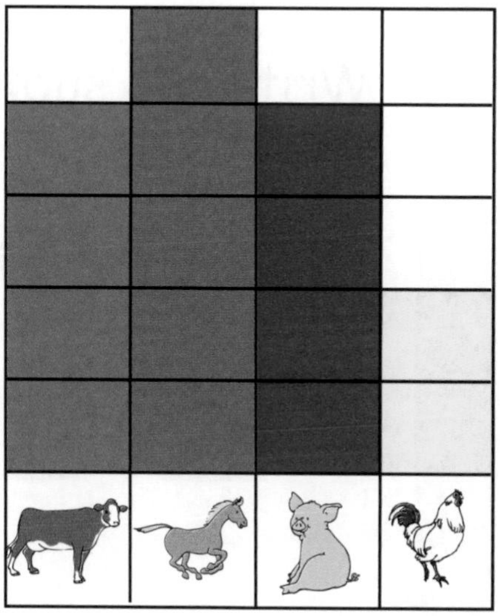

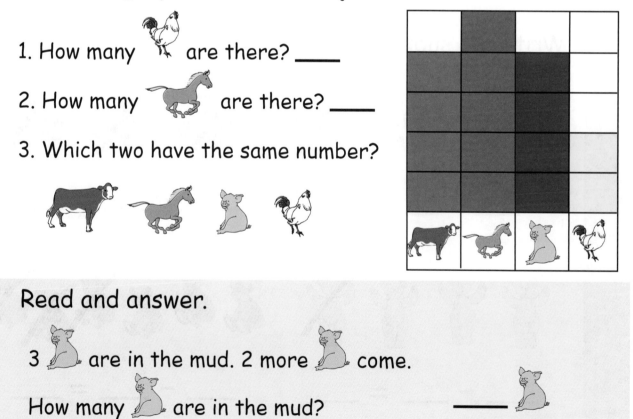

1. How many  are there? ____
2. How many  are there? ____
3. Which two have the same number?

Read and answer.

3  are in the mud. 2 more  come.

How many  are in the mud? ____ 

# How Many Bears?

**Skills:**

Subtraction to 6

Bears Everywhere

Subtract.

3 - 2 = 1

5 - 3 = ___

4 - 0 = ___

6 - 4 = ___

Write and subtract.

5 - 1 = 4

___ - ___ = ___

___ - ___ = ___

___ - ___ = ___

**Skills:**

Greater Than, Less Than

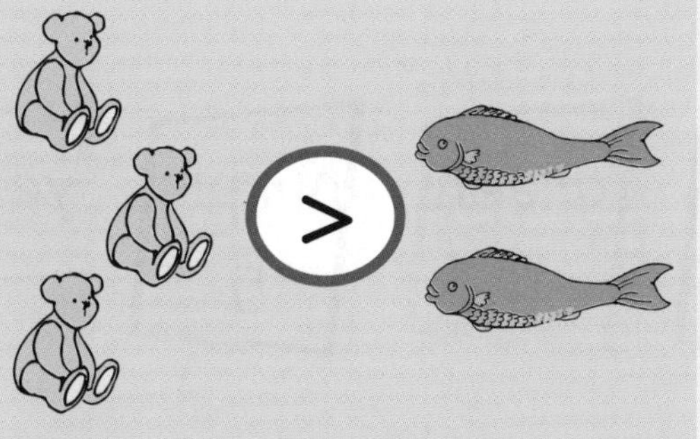


The number of bears is **greater than** the number of fish.

3 > 2

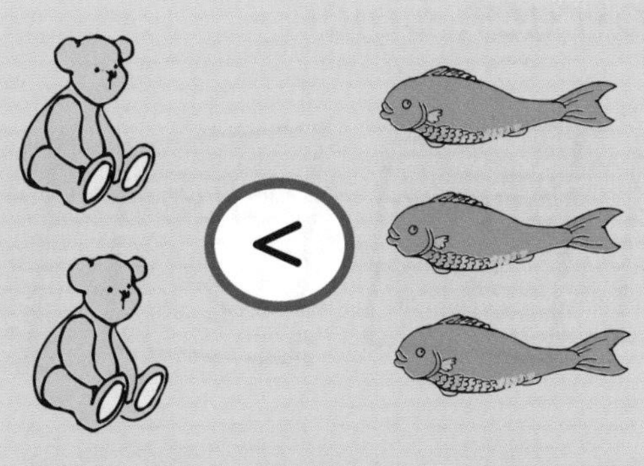


The number of bears is **less than** the number of fish.

2 < 3

Write > or < .

1 ◯ 5

7 ◯ 6

8 ◯ 4

2 ◯ 4

6 ◯ 7

4 ◯ 5

# Color the Bear

**Skills:**

Subtraction to 6

Note: You may need to read the sentence at the bottom of the page to your child.

Subtract. Color.

| orange | brown | blue | red | green | purple | yellow |
|---|---|---|---|---|---|---|
| 0 | 1 | 2 | 3 | 4 | 5 | 6 |

Subtract.

6 – 6 = ___ 3 – 3 = ___ 4 – 4 = ___

1 – 1 = ___ 5 – 5 = ___ 2 – 2 = ___

When you subtract a number from itself, you get ______.

# Bear Stuff

**Skills:**

Measurement to the Nearest Inch

The berry is ____ inch long.

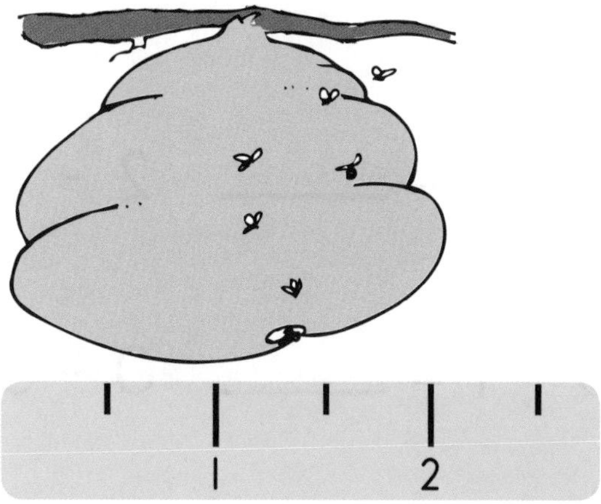


The hive is ____ inches.

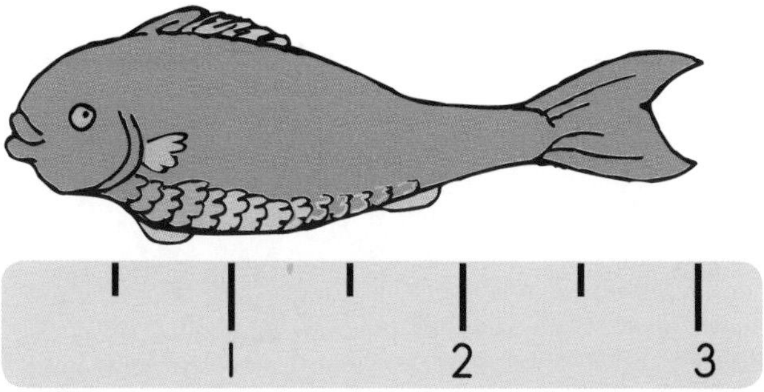


The fish is ____ inches long.

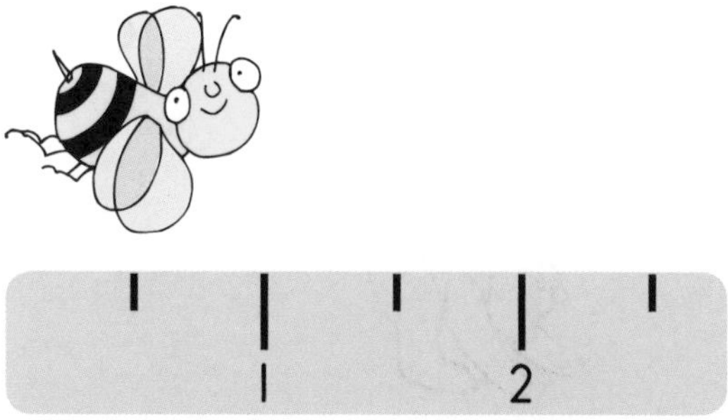


The bee is ____ inch.

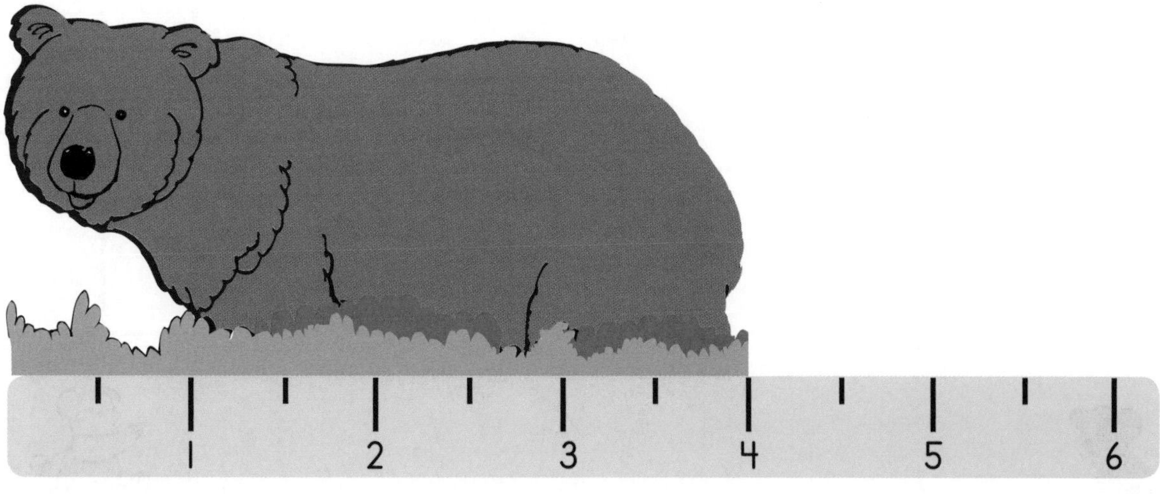


The bear is ____ inches long.

# How Many Bears Are Left?

**Skills:**

Subtraction to 6

Subtract.

5 - 5 = ____ 2 - 1 = ____ 6 - 5 = ____

3 - 1 = ____ 0 - 0 = ____ 4 - 3 = ____

6 - 6 = ____ 5 - 2 = ____ 3 - 0 = ____

5 - 0 = ____ 6 - 2 = ____ 1 - 1 = ____

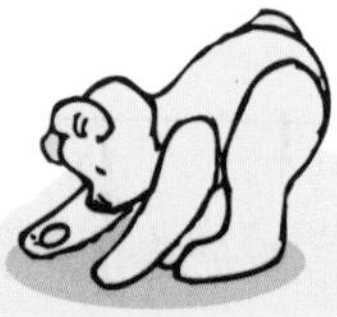

| | | | | |
|---|---|---|---|---|
| 5 | 2 | 4 | 5 | 1 |
| - 0 | - 1 | - 3 | - 5 | - 0 |
| ☐ | ☐ | ☐ | ☐ | ☐ |

| | | | | |
|---|---|---|---|---|
| 6 | 5 | 3 | 5 | 3 |
| - 3 | - 2 | - 0 | - 4 | - 1 |
| ☐ | ☐ | ☐ | ☐ | ☐ |

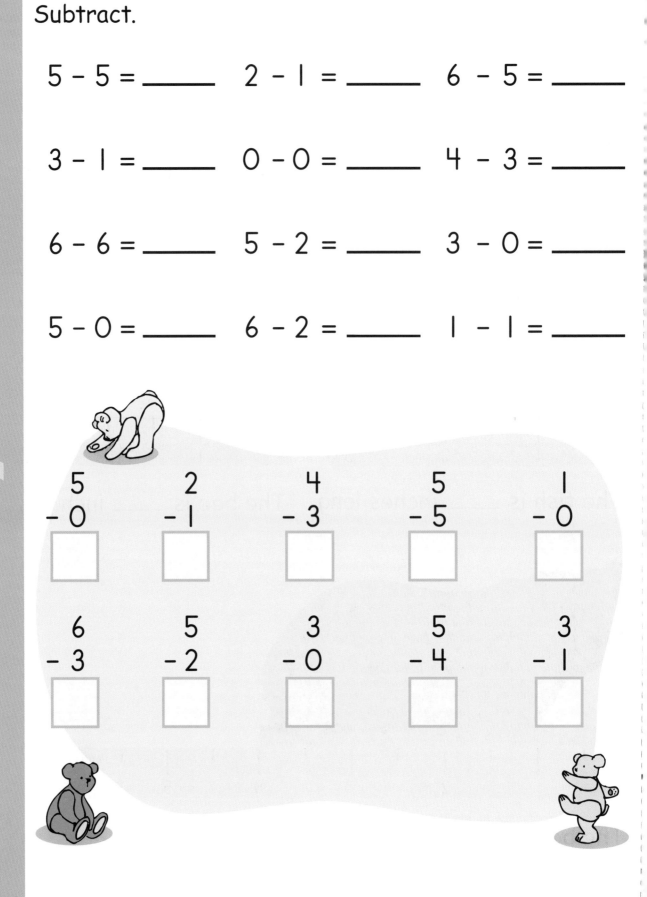

Note: You may need to help your child read the word problems.

**Skills:**

Word Problems: Subtraction to 6

# Write the problems. Answer them.

Black Bear had 5 berries. He ate 3 berries.

How many berries were left?

$$\begin{array}{r} 5 \\ -\ 3 \\ \hline 2 \end{array}$$

2 berries were left.

4 baby bears were in the tree. 1 climbed down.

How many baby bears were still in the tree?

____ baby bears were still in the tree.

Grizzly Bear caught 6 salmon. 1 swam away.

How many salmon were left?

____ salmon were left.

Sun Bear had 3 honeycombs. Sun Bear ate all 3 of them.

How many honeycombs were left?

____ honeycombs were left.

**Skills:**

Subtraction to 6

Number Words

Subtract.

6 - 0 = ____ 4 - 2 = ____ 3 - 3 = ____

5 - 1 = ____ 6 - 3 = ____ 5 - 4 = ____

6 - 1 = ____ 4 - 3 = ____ 3 - 2 = ____

5 - 3 = ____ 4 - 0 = ____ 6 - 6 = ____

Write a word answer.

| zero | one | two | three | four | five | six |
|---|---|---|---|---|---|---|
| 0 | 1 | 2 | 3 | 4 | 5 | 6 |

5 - 5 = zero 3 - 2 = ____

6 - 0 = ____ 6 - 2 = ____

4 - 2 = ____ 4 - 1 = ____

**Skills:**

Reading Graphs



Read the graph.

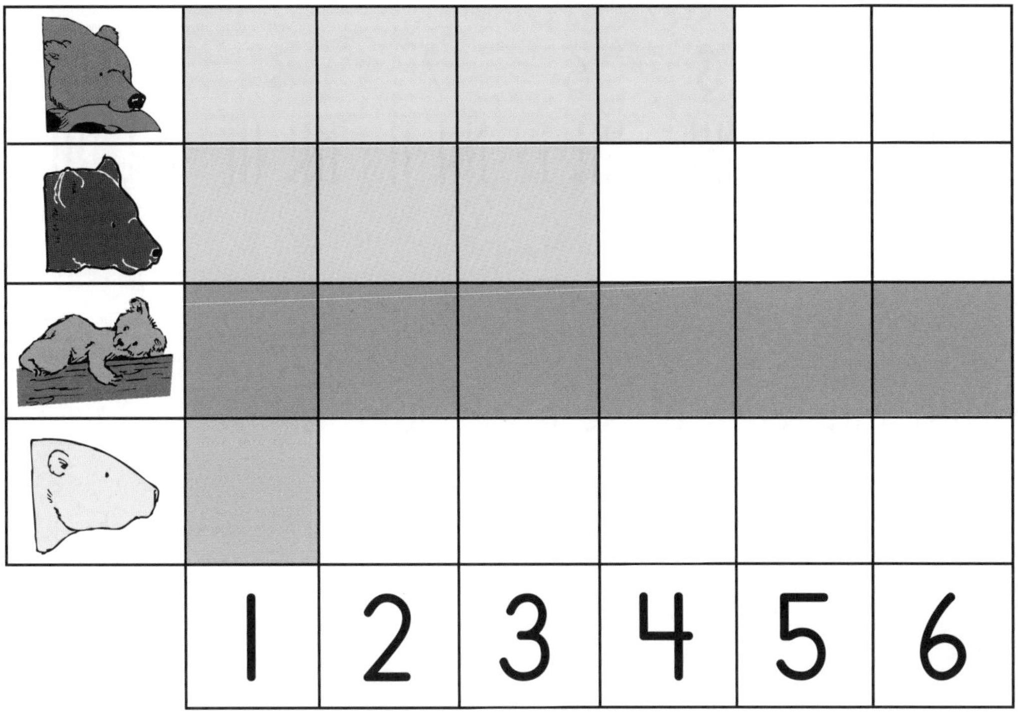

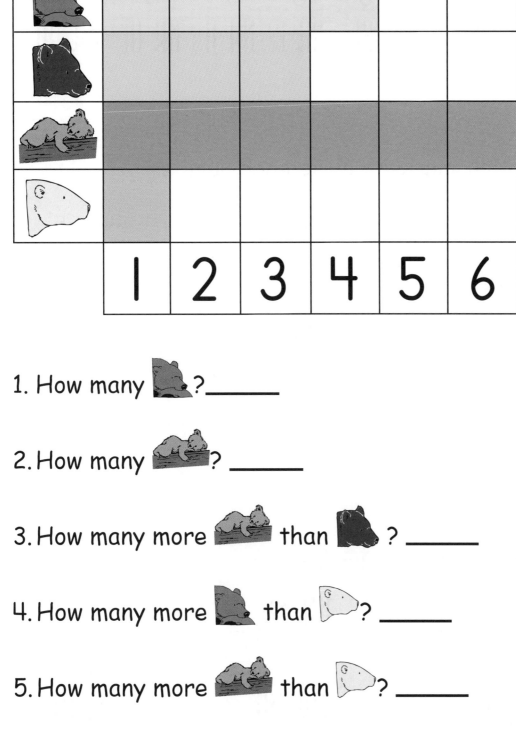

1. How many ? ______

2. How many ? ______

3. How many more  than  ? ______

4. How many more  than 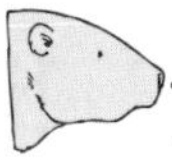? ______

5. How many more  than 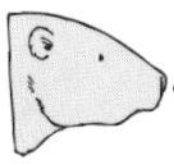? ______

# Tally Marks

Tally marks can tell how many.

| 1 | 2 | 3 | 4 | 5 | 6 | 7 | 8 | 9 | 10 |
|---|---|---|---|---|---|---|---|---|---|
| I | II | III | IIII | ̶I̶I̶I̶I̶I | ̶I̶I̶I̶I̶I I | ̶I̶I̶I̶I̶I II | ̶I̶I̶I̶I̶I III | ̶I̶I̶I̶I̶I IIII | ̶I̶I̶I̶I̶I ̶I̶I̶I̶I̶I |

Use tally marks to make each number.

| Show 3 | Show 10 | Show 5 |
|--------|---------|--------|
| Show 1 | Show 7 | Show 2 |
| Show 8 | Show 4 | Show 6 |

Count. Write the number.

III _____        ̶I̶I̶I̶I̶I ̶I̶I̶I̶I̶I _____        I _____

̶I̶I̶I̶I̶I _____        ̶I̶I̶I̶I̶I IIII _____        ̶I̶I̶I̶I̶I III _____

Skills:

Subtraction to 6

Subtract.

6 − 6 = ____
6 − 0 = ____

5 − 4 = ____
5 − 1 = ____

3 − 1 = ____
3 − 2 = ____

2 − 2 = ____
2 − 0 = ____

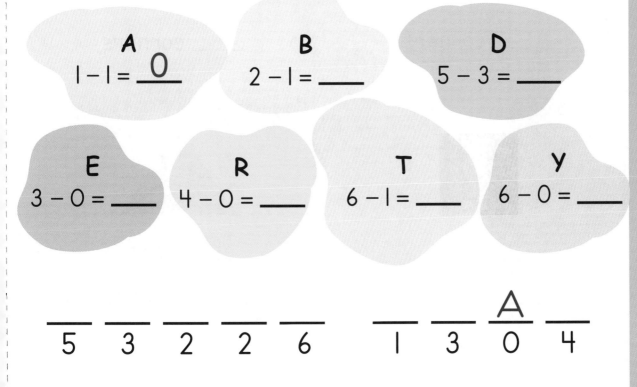

Who is the mystery bear?
Write the letter that goes with each answer.

A
1 − 1 = __0__

B
2 − 1 = ____

D
5 − 3 = ____

E
3 − 0 = ____

R
4 − 0 = ____

T
6 − 1 = ____

Y
6 − 0 = ____

___ ___ ___ ___ ___        ___ ___ _A_ ___
 5   3   2   2   6          1   3   0   4

# Corners and Sides

**Skills:**
Geometric Shapes

Bears Everywhere

Count the number of sides and corners.
Write the number.

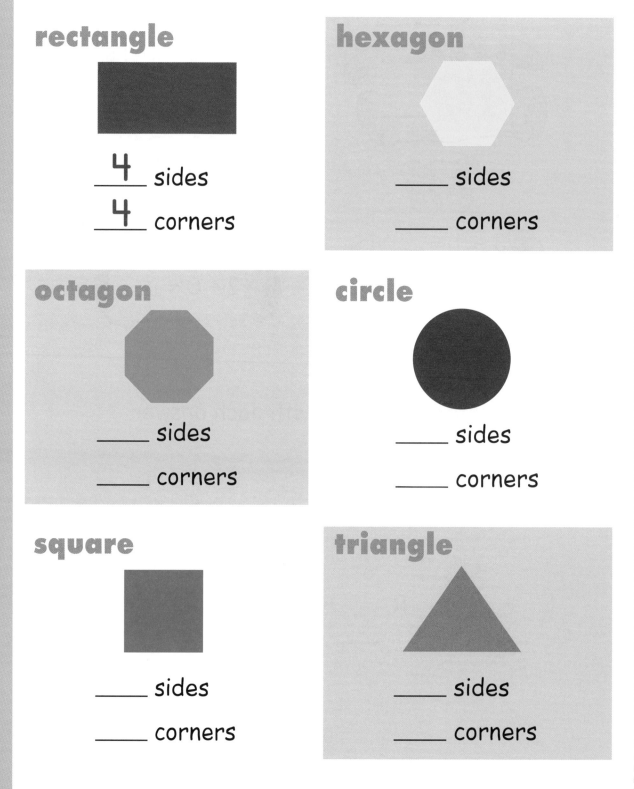

## rectangle

4 sides
4 corners

## hexagon

_____ sides
_____ corners

## octagon

_____ sides
_____ corners

## circle

_____ sides
_____ corners

## square

_____ sides
_____ corners

## triangle

_____ sides
_____ corners

Note: Use this assessment after your child has completed through page 38.

# TEST YOUR SKILLS

Count. Write the number.

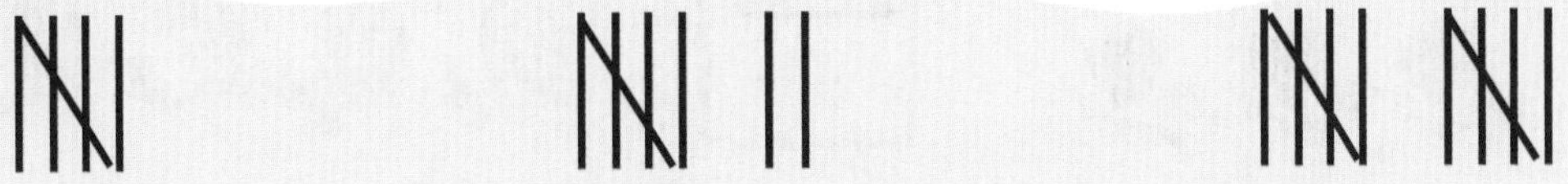

________ ________ ________

Fill in the circle for the answer.

| | 0 | 1 | 2 |
|---|---|---|---|
| 5 - 5 = | ○ | ○ | ○ |
| 2 - 0 = | ○ | ○ | ○ |
| 4 - 2 = | ○ | ○ | ○ |
| 3 - 1 = | ○ | ○ | ○ |

Count the sides and corners.

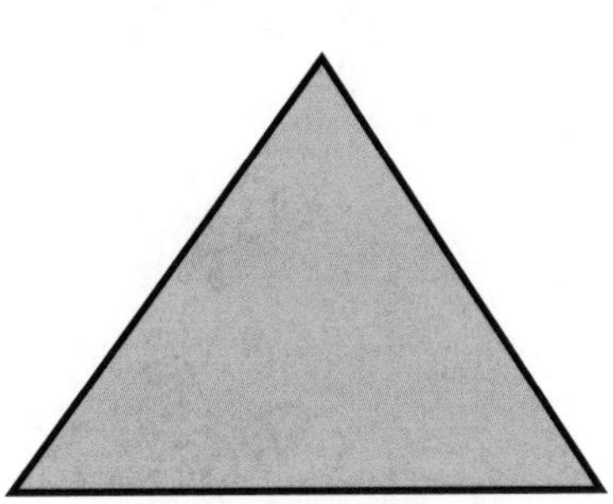

______ sides

______ corners

# How Many Butterflies?

**Skills:**

Addition & Subtraction to 8

Creepy Crawlies

Add.

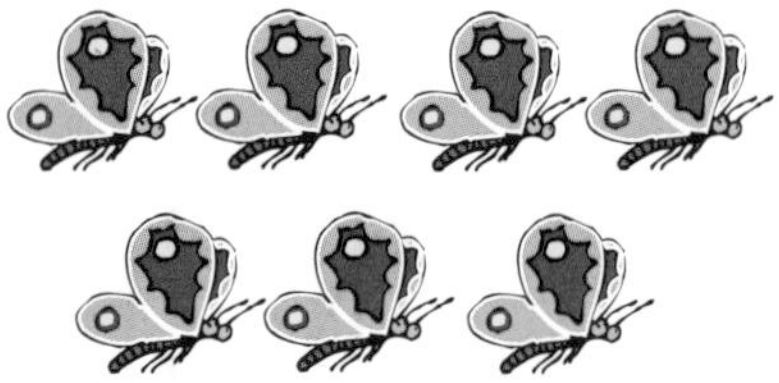

$$\begin{array}{r} 4 \\ +\ 3 \\ \hline \end{array}$$

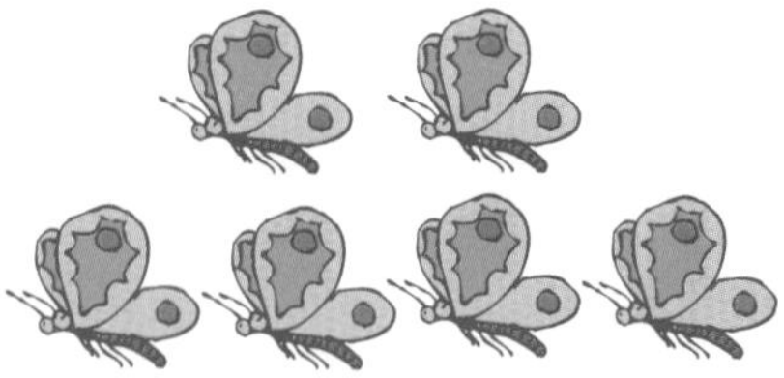

$$\begin{array}{r} 2 \\ +\ 4 \\ \hline \end{array}$$

$$\begin{array}{r} 8 \\ +\ 0 \\ \hline \end{array}$$

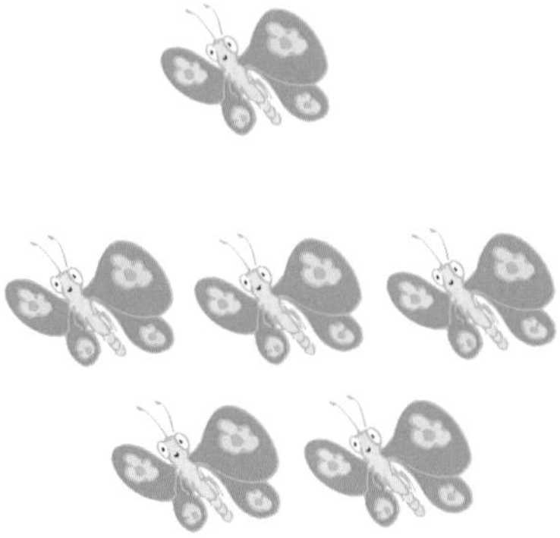

$$\begin{array}{r} 1 \\ +\ 5 \\ \hline \end{array}$$

Subtract.

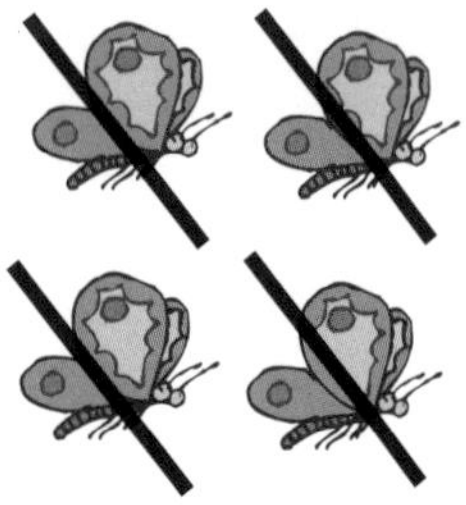

$$\begin{array}{r} 4 \\ -\ 4 \\ \hline 0 \end{array}$$

$$\begin{array}{r} 6 \\ -\ 2 \\ \hline \end{array}$$

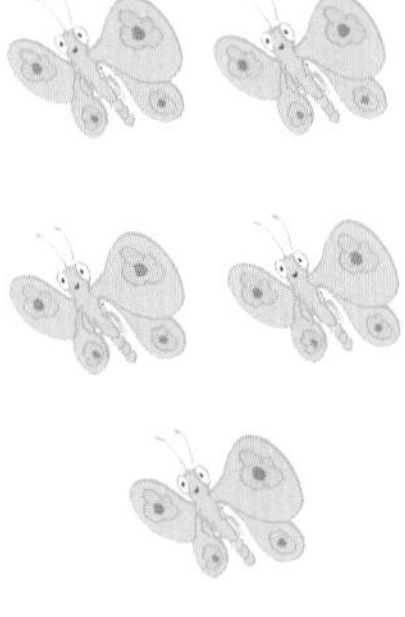

$$\begin{array}{r} 5 \\ -\ 3 \\ \hline \end{array}$$

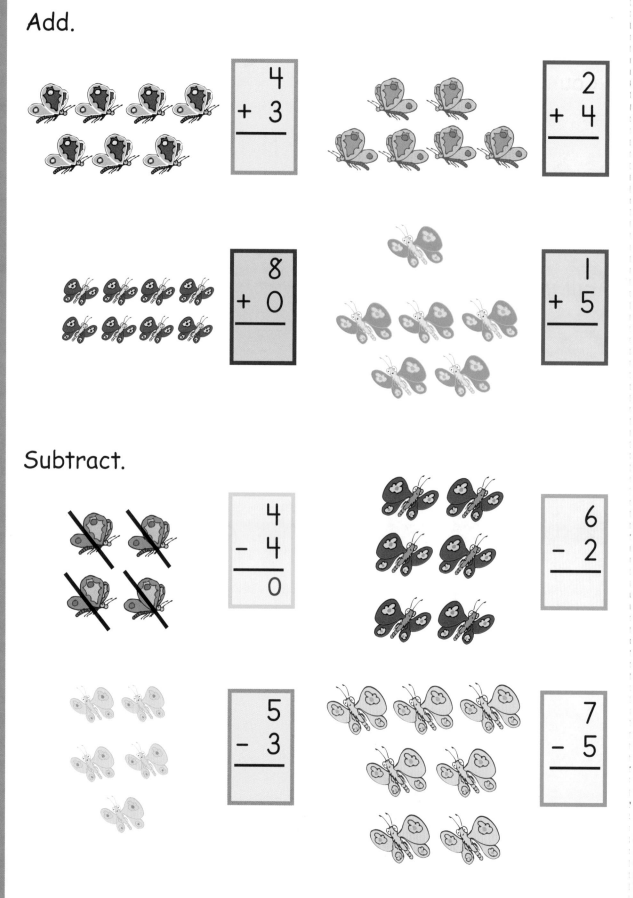

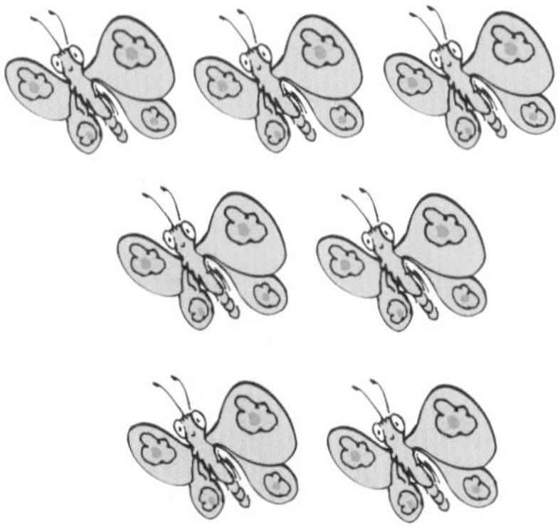

$$\begin{array}{r} 7 \\ -\ 5 \\ \hline \end{array}$$

**Skills:**
Patterns

Circle the shape that comes next in each pattern. Label the patterns.

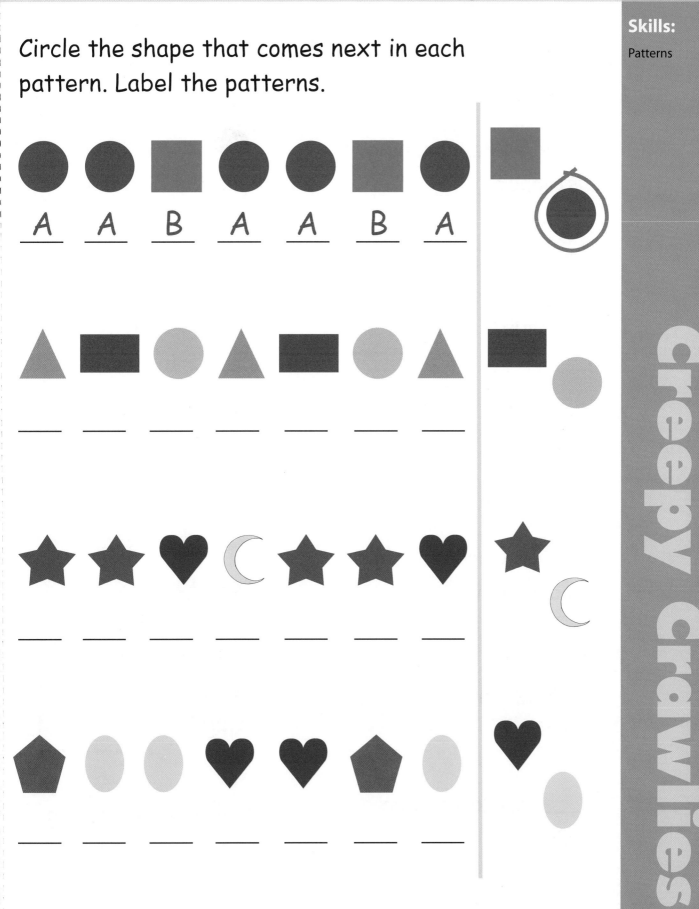

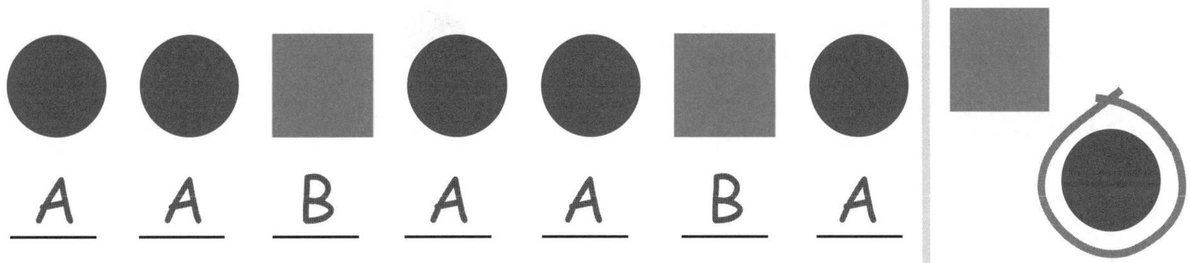

# Bug Problems

**Skills:**

Addition & Subtraction to 8

Note: You may need to help your child read the word problems.

Write the problems. Answer them.

8  were marching.
3 stopped.

How many ants were still marching?

_____ ants were still marching.

4  were looking for aphids. 3 more ladybugs came.

How many ladybugs in all?

There were _____ ladybugs in all.

6  were chirping.
2 more came.

How many crickets were chirping?

_____ crickets were chirping.

5  were buzzing.
4 stopped.

How many bees were buzzing?

_____ bee was buzzing.

**Skills:**

Telling Time to the Hour

Note: You may need to read the information to your child.

There are 2 hands on a clock.

- The shorter hand is the **hour hand.**
  It points to the hour.
- The longer hand is the **minute hand.**
  It points to 12 when the time is "on the hour."

Write the time.

# The Ant Families

**Skills:**

Addition & Subtraction to 8

Make 2 addition problems and 2 subtraction problems.

1 + 3 = 4

3 + 1 = 4

4 - 1 = 3

4 - 3 = 1

___ + ___ = ___

___ + ___ = ___

___ − ___ = ___

___ − ___ = ___

___ + ___ = ___

___ + ___ = ___

___ − ___ = ___

___ − ___ = ___

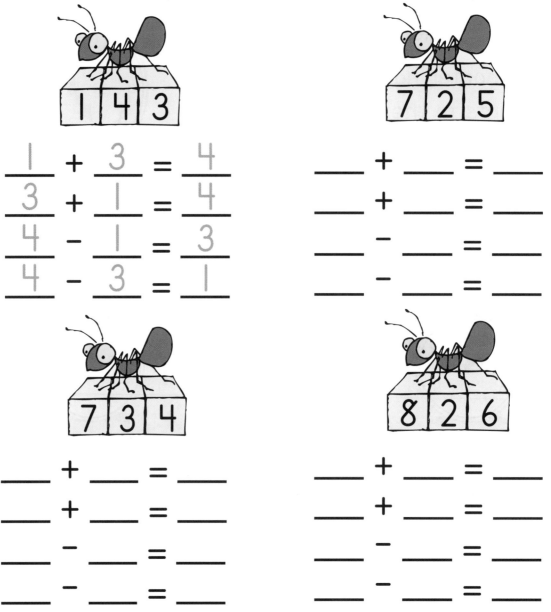

___ + ___ = ___

___ + ___ = ___

___ − ___ = ___

___ − ___ = ___

Circle the one that does **not** belong in this "family."

1 + 6 = 7    6 + 1 = 7    7 − 1 = 6    6 − 1 = 5

Which 3 numbers are "family members"?    ___ ___ ___

**Skills:**

Completing and Reading a Graph

Color the graph to show how many.

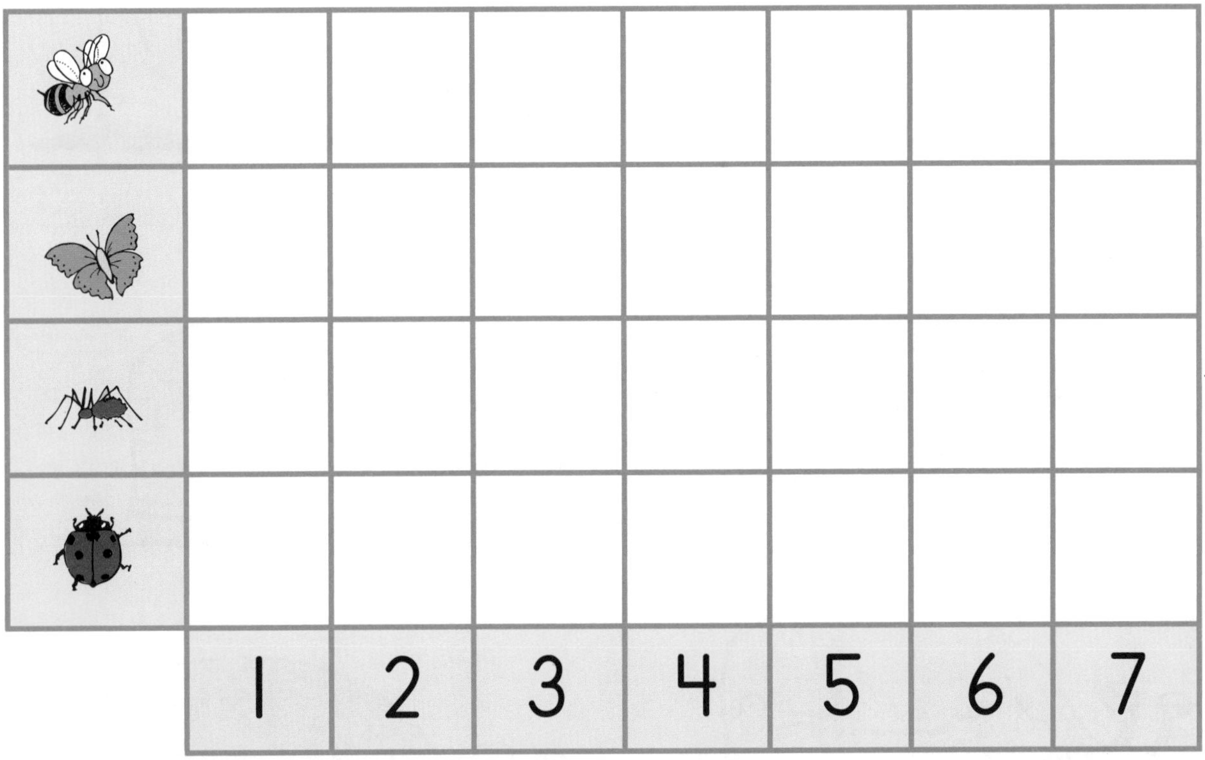


1. There were the most

2. There were the least

3. Which 2 bugs had the same number?

# What's Missing?

Fill in the numbers.

$2 + 3 = \underline{\hspace{1cm}}$

$7 + \underline{\hspace{1cm}} = 7$

$1 + \underline{\hspace{1cm}} = 7$

$4 + \underline{\hspace{1cm}} = 8$

$4 - \underline{\hspace{1cm}} = 1$

$8 - \underline{\hspace{1cm}} = 0$

$4 + 3 = \underline{\hspace{1cm}}$

$7 - 6 = \underline{\hspace{1cm}}$

$6 - \underline{\hspace{1cm}} = 4$

Creepy Crawlies

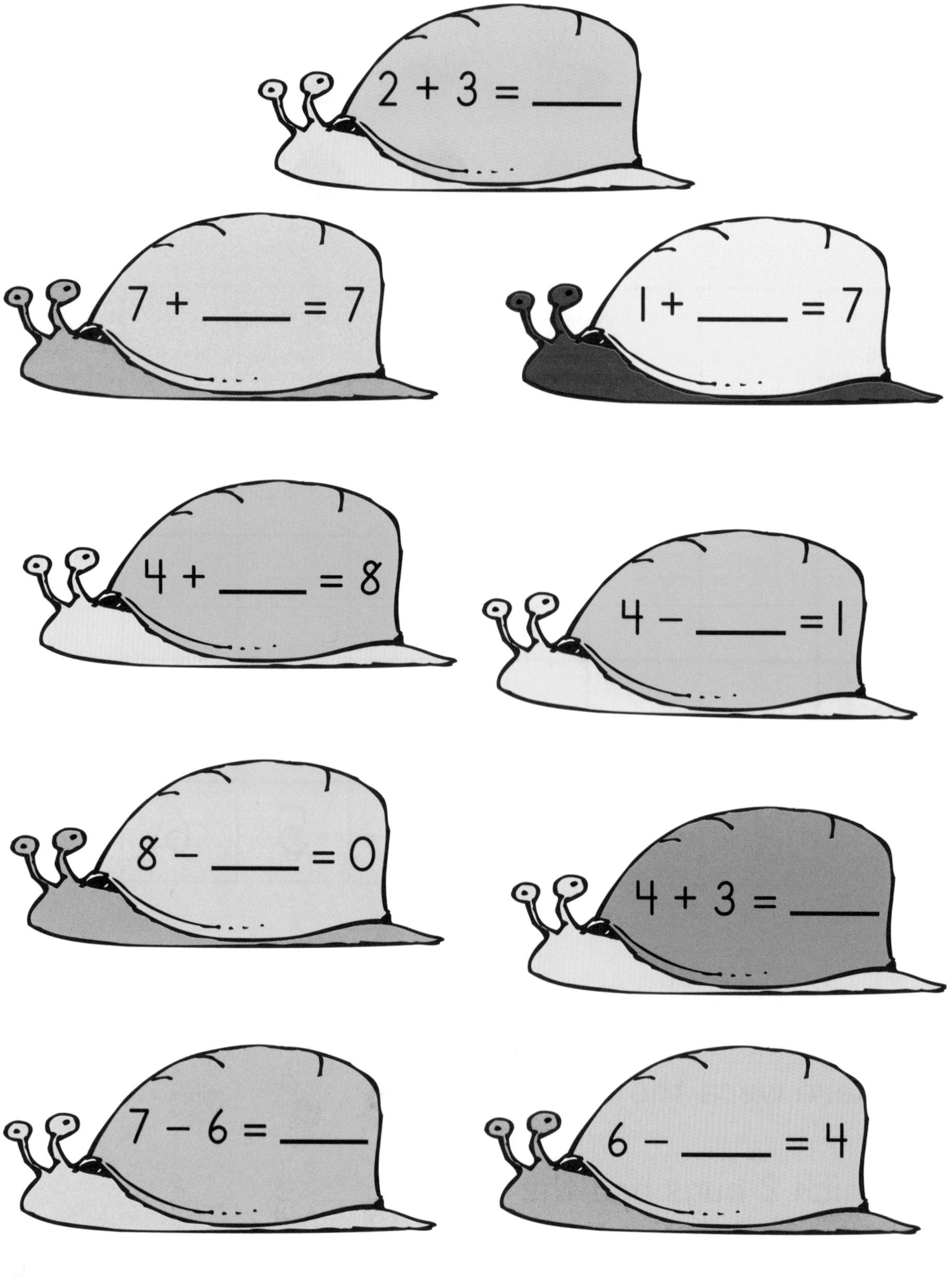

# Equal Parts

**Skills:**

Fractions

How many parts?

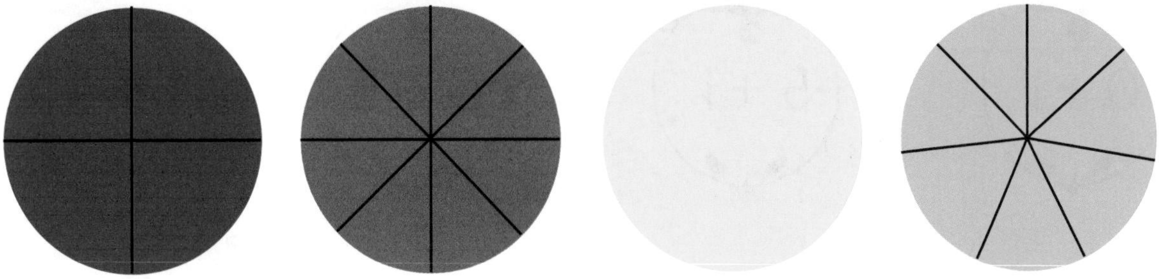

4 parts ____ parts ____ part ____ parts

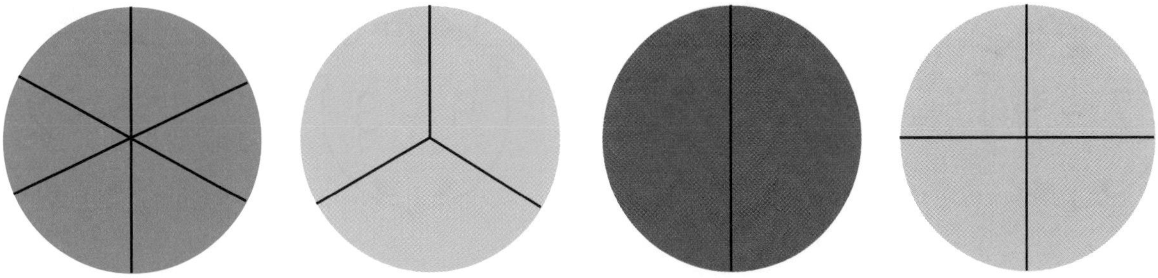

____ parts ____ parts ____ parts ____ parts

Which ones have **2 equal parts**? Circle them.

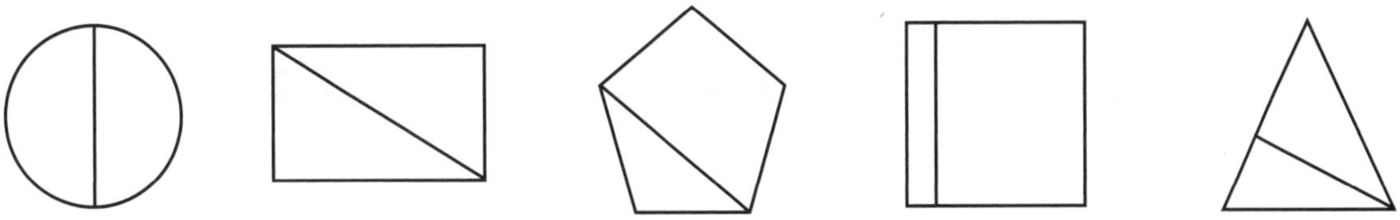

Which ones have **3 equal parts**? Circle them.

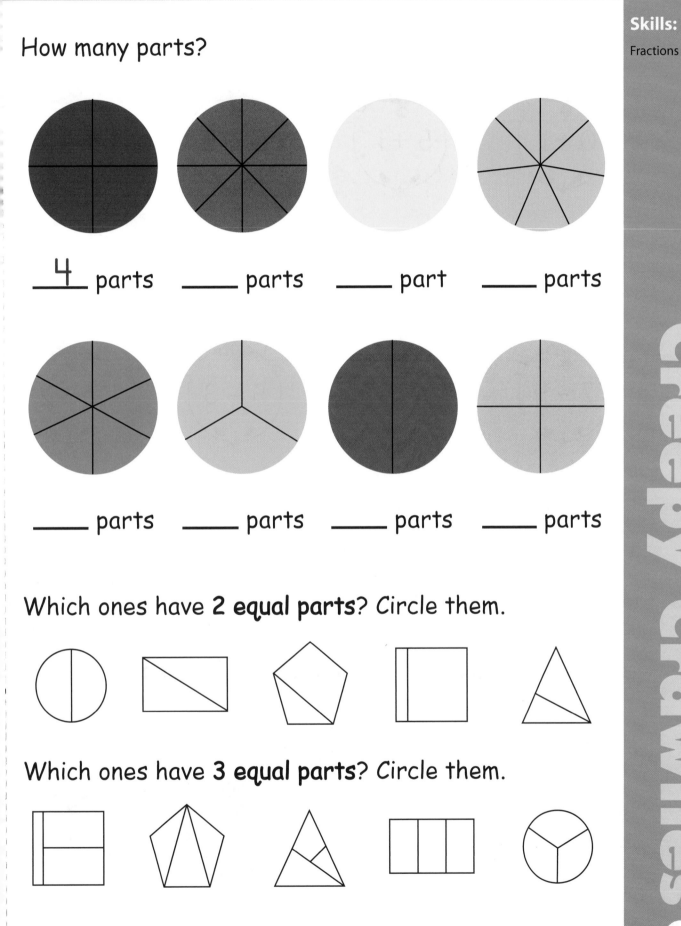

Creepy Crawlies

# Ladybugs Are Everywhere!

**Skills:**

Addition & Subtraction to 8

Creepy Crawlies

Add or subtract. Color the ladybugs that = **6**.

0 + 1 5 + 1 0 + 5 4 − 1

3 − 3 6 − 1 2 + 4

7 − 4 7 + 1 9 − 3 7 − 2

Add or subtract. Color the ladybugs that = **3**.

5 + 1 6 + 2 6 − 3 5 − 2

3 − 0 3 + 3 4 − 0

3 − 2 8 − 5 3 + 5 2 + 6

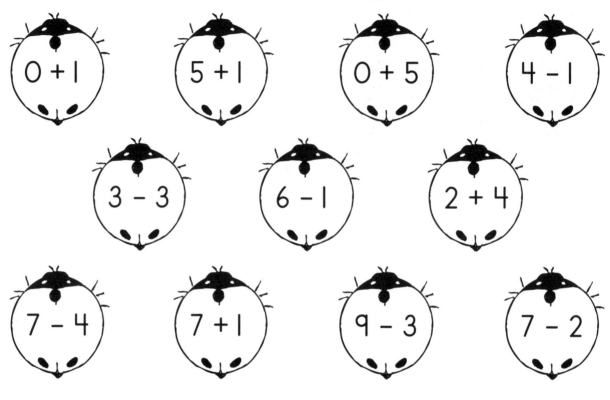

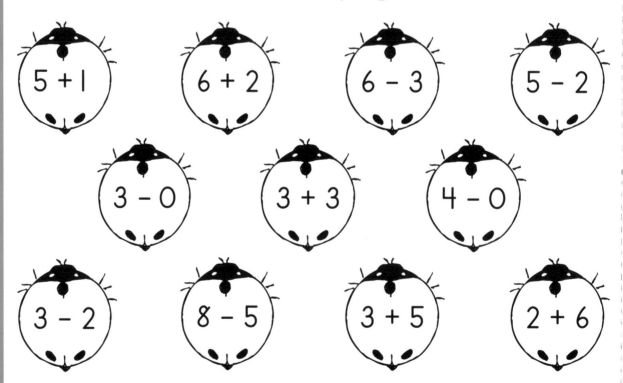

 

# Don’t Bug Me!

**Skills:**

Word Problems: Addition & Subtraction to 6

Note: You may need to help your child read the word problems.

## Write the problems. Answer them.

6  were crawling. 3 stopped to take a nap.

How many snails were still crawling?

_____ snails were still crawling.

1 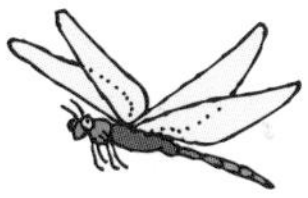 was flying. 3 more dragonflies came.

How many dragonflies were flying?

_____ dragonflies were flying.

6 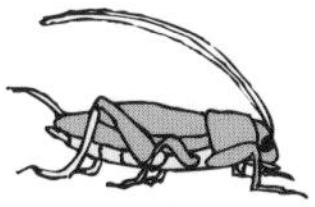 were eating grass. All 6 hopped away.

How many grasshoppers were still eating grass?

_____ grasshoppers were still eating grass.

2  were sipping nectar. 4 more butterflies came.

How many butterflies were sipping nectar?

_____ butterflies were sipping nectar.

Creepy Crawlies

# Fraction Fun

**Skills:**

Fractions

Creepy Crawlies

## Color $\frac{1}{2}$.

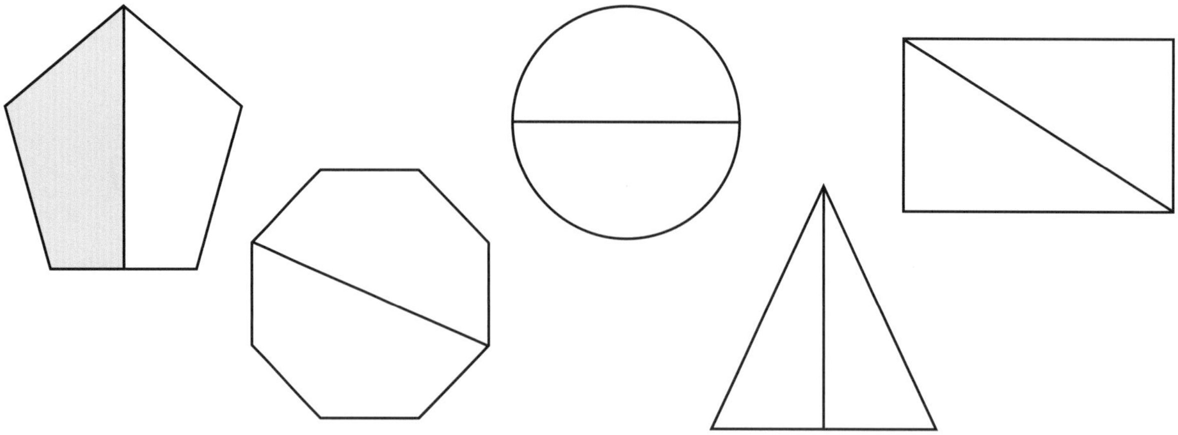

## Color $\frac{1}{3}$.

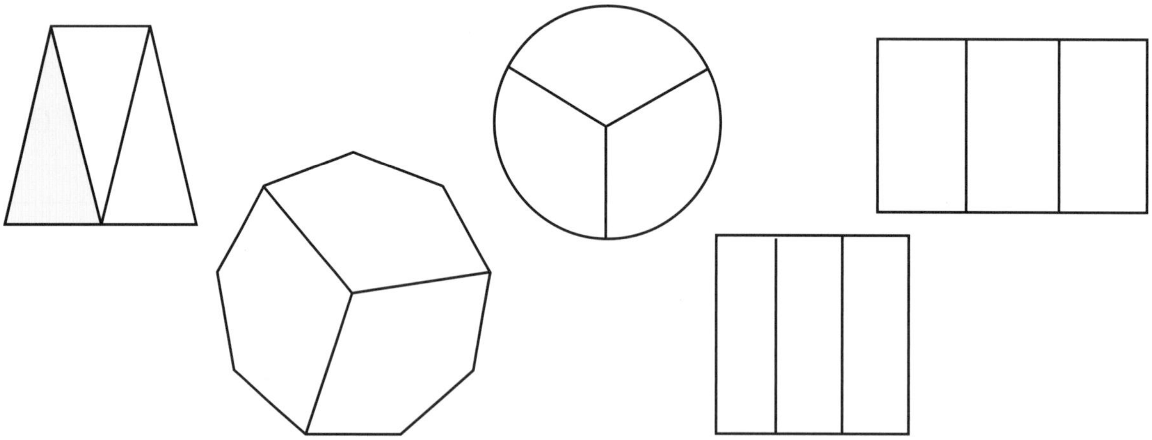

## Color $\frac{1}{4}$.

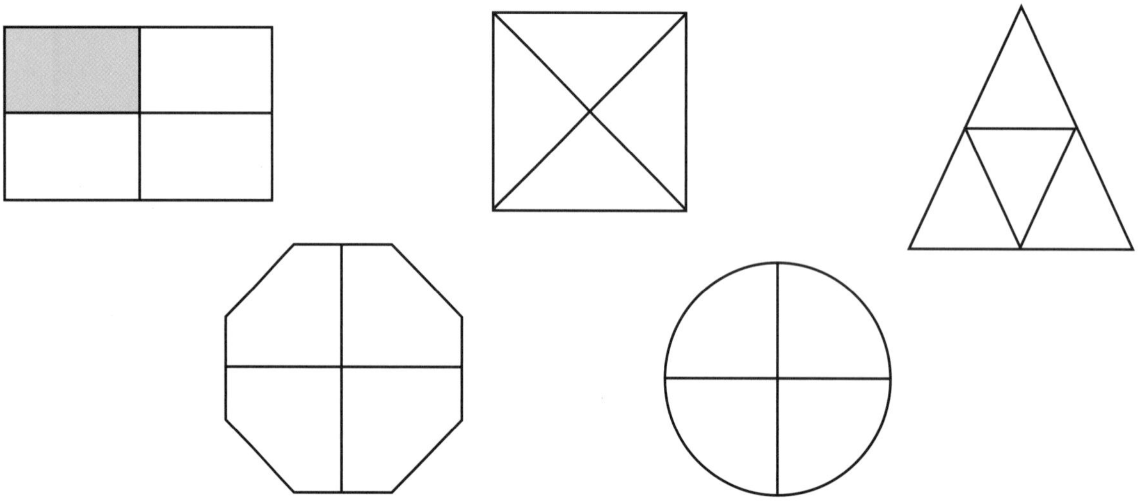

Addition &
Subtraction
to 8

Add and subtract.

5 + 2 = \_\_\_\_\_

5 − 2 = \_\_\_\_\_

8 + 0 = \_\_\_\_\_

8 − 0 = \_\_\_\_\_

6 + 2 = \_\_\_\_\_

6 − 2 = \_\_\_\_\_

4 + 4 = \_\_\_\_\_

4 − 4 = \_\_\_\_\_

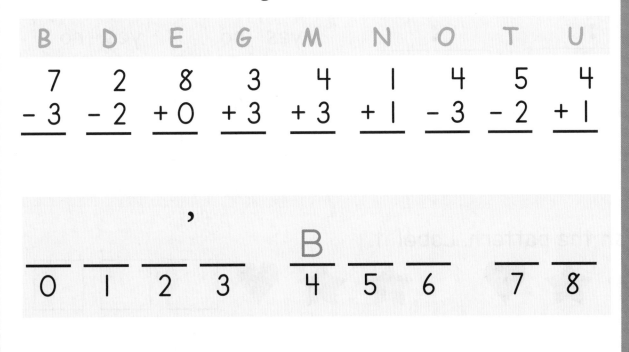

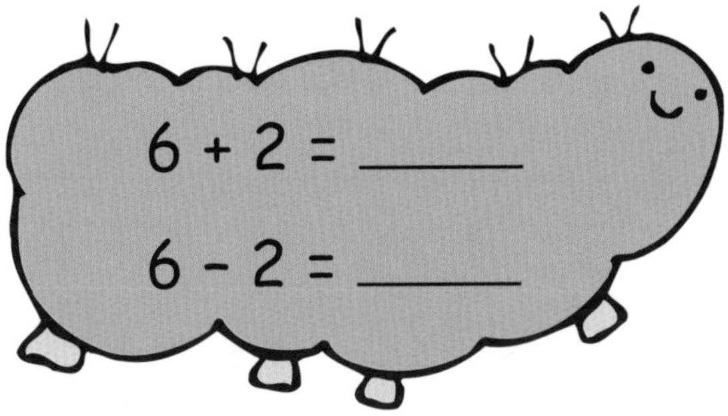

## What Does It Say?

Write the letter that goes with each answer.

| B | D | E | G | M | N | O | T | U |
|---|---|---|---|---|---|---|---|---|
| 7 | 2 | 8 | 3 | 4 | 1 | 4 | 5 | 4 |
| − 3 | − 2 | + 0 | + 3 | + 3 | + 1 | − 3 | − 2 | + 1 |

\_\_\_ \_\_\_ \_\_\_ \_\_\_ , B \_\_\_ \_\_\_ \_\_\_ \_\_\_

0    1    2    3    4    5    6    7    8

Note: Use this assessment after your child has completed through page 51. Help your child read the directions.

# TEST YOUR SKILLS

Add or subtract.

3 + 5 = _____ 6 + 2 = _____ 8 − 1 = _____ 8 − 5 = _____

8 + 0 = _____ 3 + 2 = _____ 7 − 4 = _____ 7 − 7 = _____

Measure.

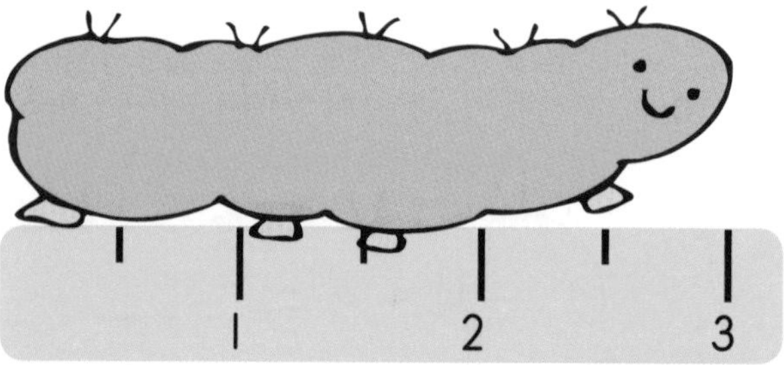


The caterpillar is _____ inches long.

Write the time.

___ : ___

___ : ___

Symmetrical?

yes no

yes no

> or < ?

7 ◯ 4 2 ◯ 8

What is colored?

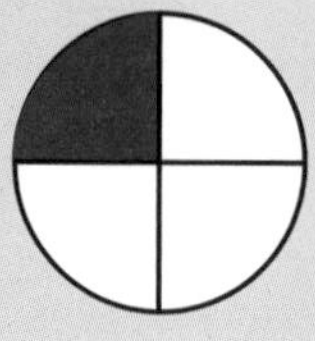

$\frac{1}{4}$ $\frac{1}{2}$ $\frac{1}{3}$

Finish the pattern. Label it.

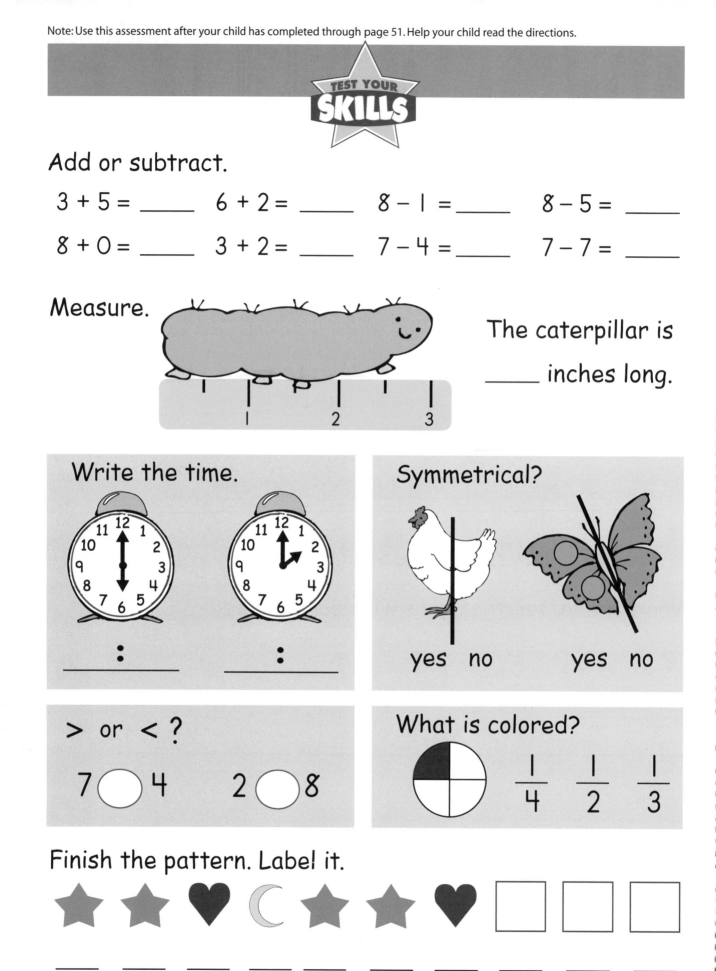

___ ___ ___ ___ ___ ___ ___ ___ ___ ___

# Counting On

**Skills:**

Addition to 10

A number line can help you add.

4 + 5 = ?

Put a 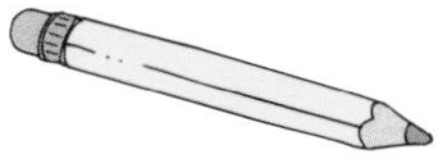 on 4.

Count forward 5 spaces. The answer is 9.

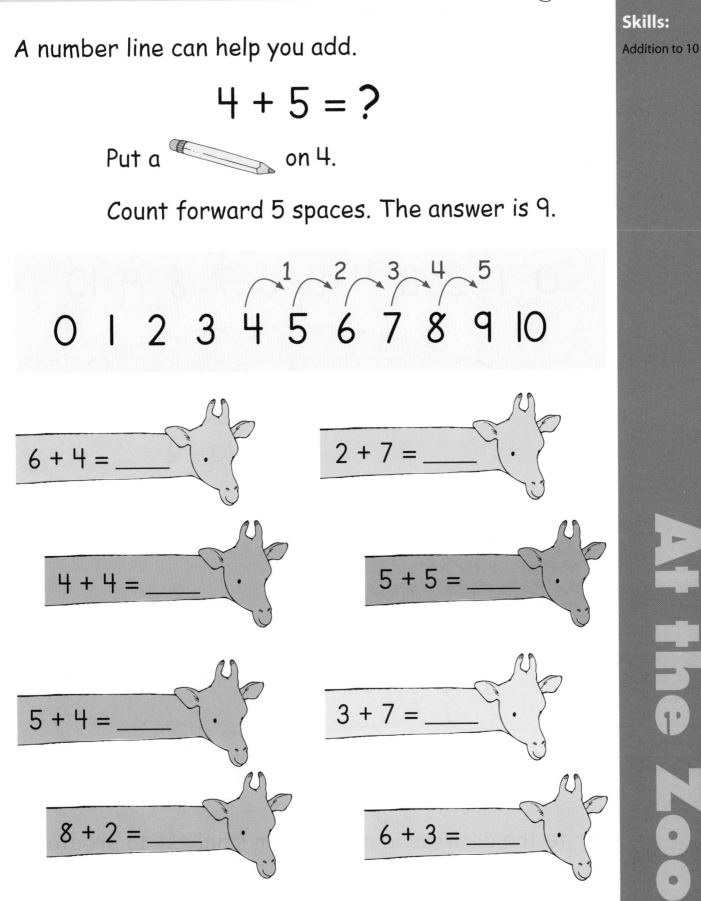

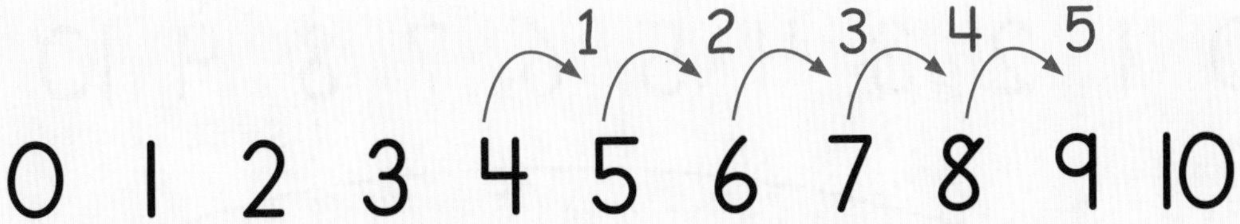


6 + 4 = _____

2 + 7 = _____

4 + 4 = _____

5 + 5 = _____

5 + 4 = _____

3 + 7 = _____

8 + 2 = _____

6 + 3 = _____

At the Zoo

# Counting Back

**Skills:**

Subtraction to 10

A number line can help you subtract.

9 − 3 = ?

Put a 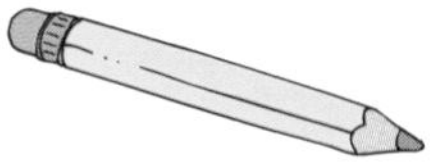 on 9.

Count back 3 spaces. The answer is 6.

3 2 1

0 1 2 3 4 5 6 7 8 9 10

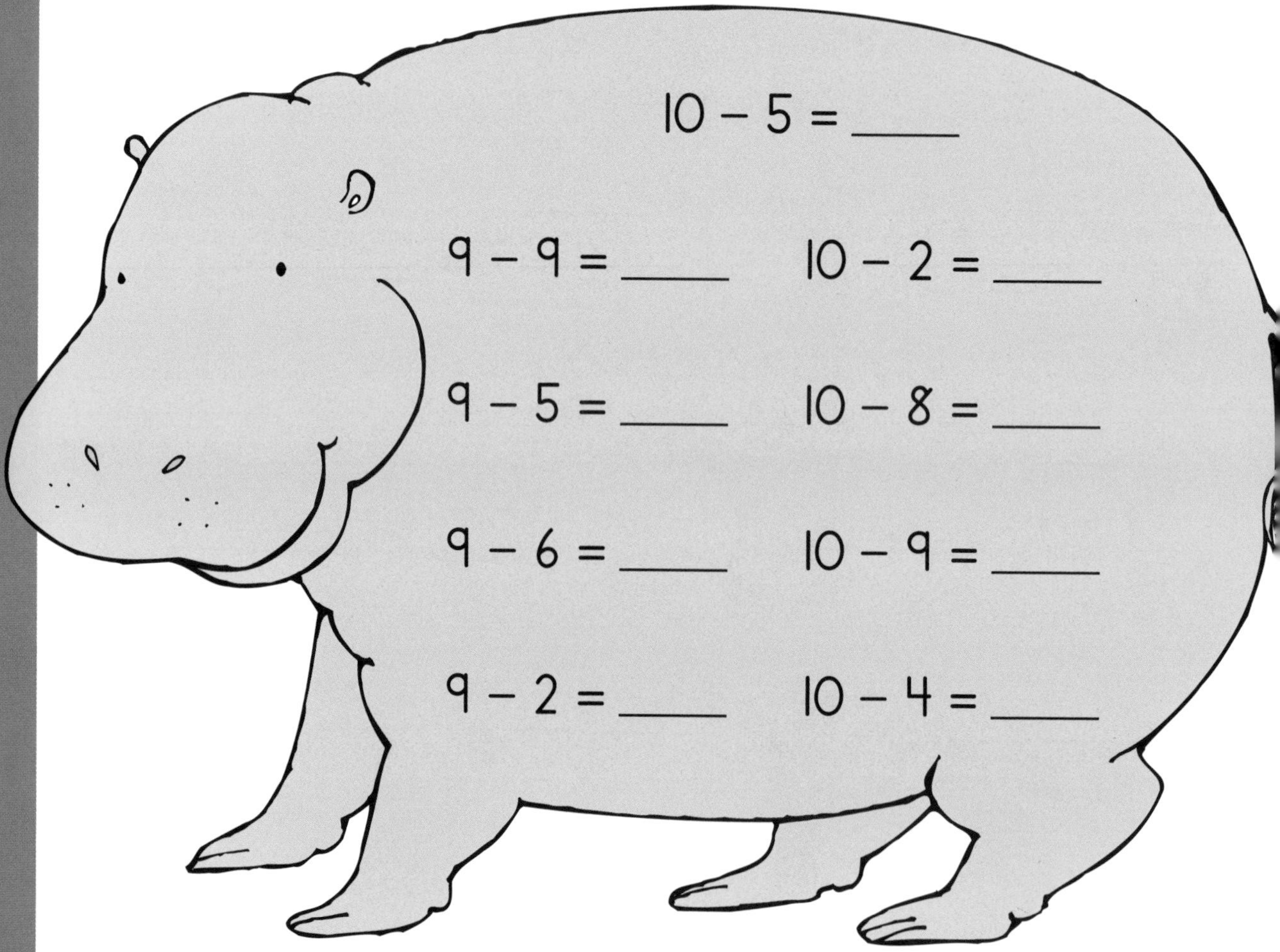

10 − 5 = ____

9 − 9 = ____ 10 − 2 = ____

9 − 5 = ____ 10 − 8 = ____

9 − 6 = ____ 10 − 9 = ____

9 − 2 = ____ 10 − 4 = ____

Write the answers in order from smallest to greatest.

____, ____, ____, ____, ____, ____, ____, ____, ____

At the Zoo

 

# Weighing In

**Skills:**

Measurement—Weight

Which animal weighs more?

Which animal weighs less?

At the Zoo

# At the Zoo

**Skills:**

Word Problems: Addition & Subtraction to 10

Note: You may need to help your child read the word problems.

## Write the problems. Answer them.

10 seals were juggling balls. 7 seals dropped their balls. How many seals were still juggling?

10 - 7 = 3

[ 3 ] seals were still juggling.

9 elephants were eating hay. 8 elephants ran away. How many elephants were left?

___ - ___ = ___

[   ] elephant was left.

5 walruses jumped into the pool. 4 more walruses jumped into the pool. How many walruses jumped into the pool?

___ + ___ = ___

[   ] walruses jumped into the pool.

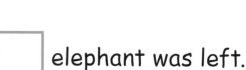

A flamingo caught 5 shrimp. Then the flamingo caught 5 more shrimp. How many shrimp did the flamingo catch in all?

___ + ___ = ___

The flamingo caught [   ] shrimp in all.

# Count by Tens

**Skills:**

Counting by 10s

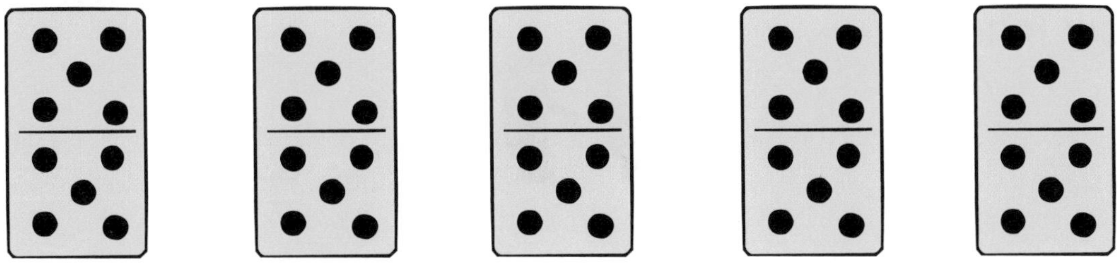

10 20 ___ ___ ___

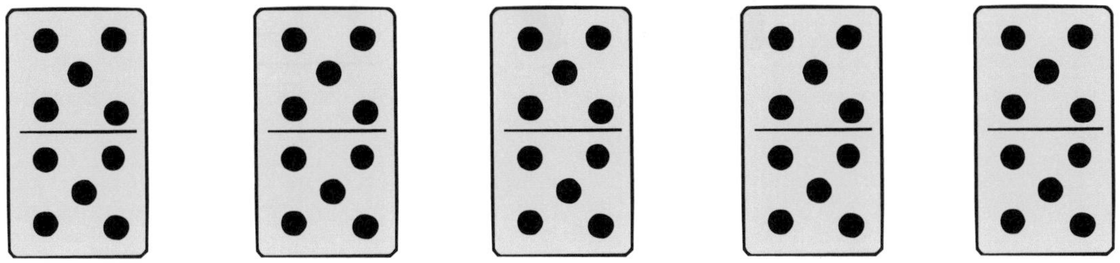

___ ___ ___ ___ ___

Connect the dots. Start at 10.

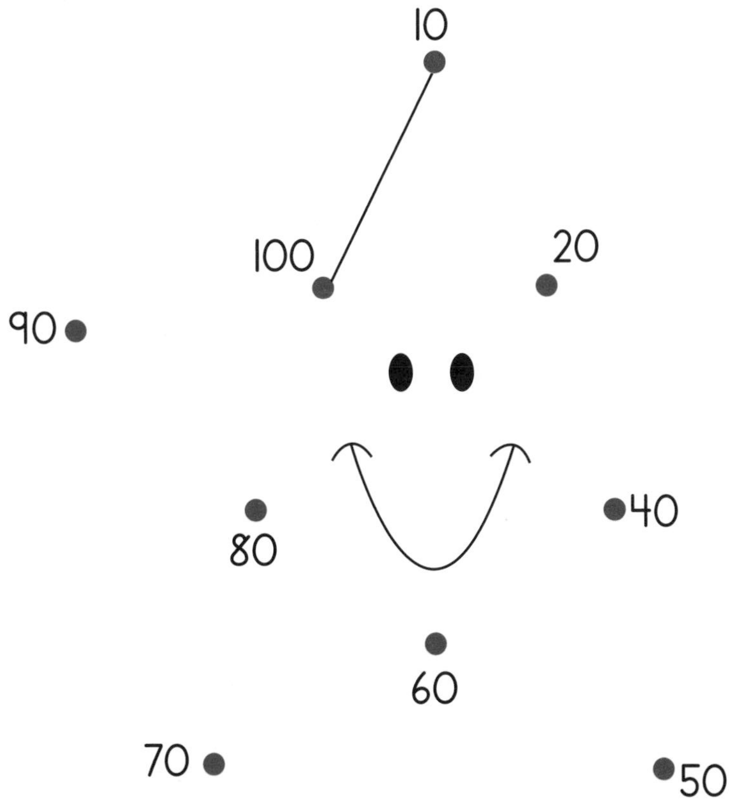


At the Zoo

# Add Three Numbers

**Skills:**

Column Addition

How many?

| | | | | |
|---|---|---|---|---|
| 2 | 3 | 6 | 4 | 8 |
| 3 | 5 | 1 | 3 | 0 |
| + 4 | + 1 | + 2 | + 1 | + 2 |
| | | | | |
| 1 | 1 | 2 | 3 | 4 |
| 7 | 6 | 5 | 4 | 3 |
| + 1 | + 3 | + 2 | + 3 | + 2 |
| | | | | |
| 5 | 6 | 3 | 5 | 7 |
| 2 | 1 | 4 | 2 | 0 |
| + 3 | + 2 | + 2 | + 1 | + 2 |
| | | | | |

# How Many Tens?

**Skills:**

Place Value—Tens, Ones

Circle groups of 10 animals. How many tens did you make? How many were left?

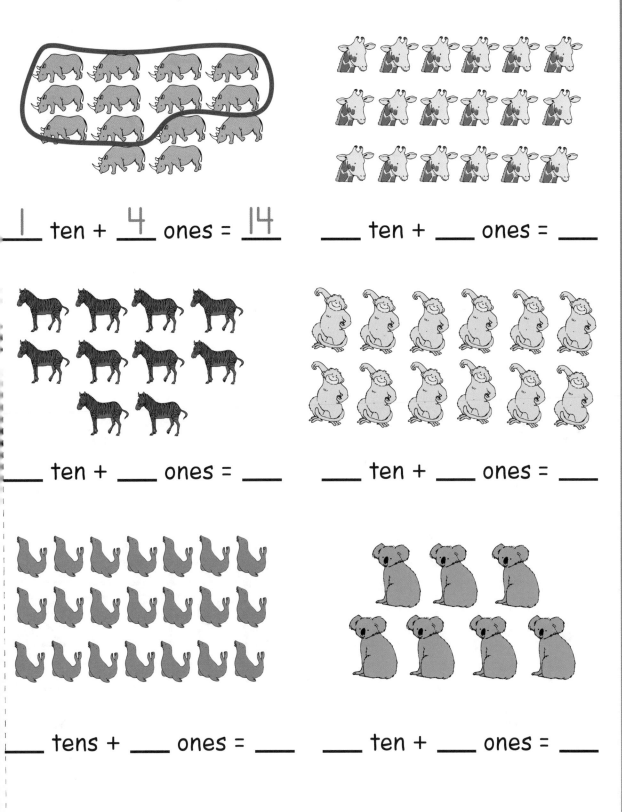

1 ten + 4 ones = 14

___ ten + ___ ones = ___

___ ten + ___ ones = ___

___ ten + ___ ones = ___

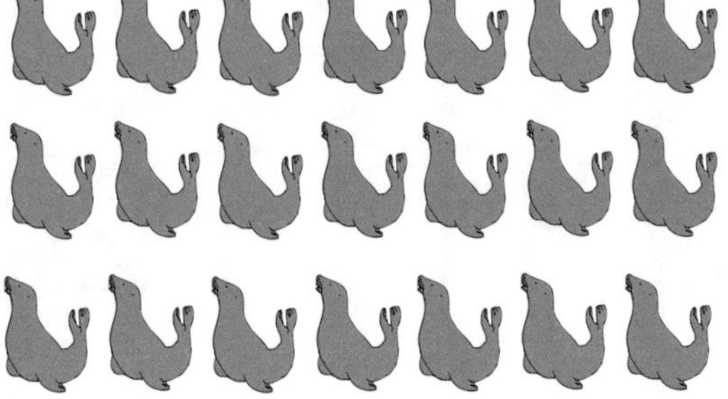

___ tens + ___ ones = ___

___ ten + ___ ones = ___

At the Zoo

# Mystery Boxes

**Skills:**

Addition to 10

Write the missing numbers.

**Make 7**

7 →

↓

| | | | |
|---|---|---|---|
| 2 | 3 | 2 | 2 + 3 + 2 = 7 |
| 3 | 4 | 0 | 3 + 4 + 0 = 7 |
| 2 | 0 | 5 | 2 + 0 + 5 = 7 |
| 2 + 3 + 2 = 7 | 3 + 4 + 0 = 7 | 2 + 0 + 5 = 7 | |

**Make 8**

8 →

↓

| | | |
|---|---|---|
| | 2 | 3 |
| | 5 | |
| 3 | | |

**Make 9**

9 →

↓

| | | |
|---|---|---|
| | 3 | 4 |
| | | 2 |
| 5 | 1 | |

**Make 10**

10 →

↓

| | | |
|---|---|---|
| | 3 | |
| 4 | | 2 |
| | 3 | 3 |

At the Zoo

**Skills:**

Money—Penny, Nickel

Match.

5¢

1¢

nickel

penny

# Feed the Elephant

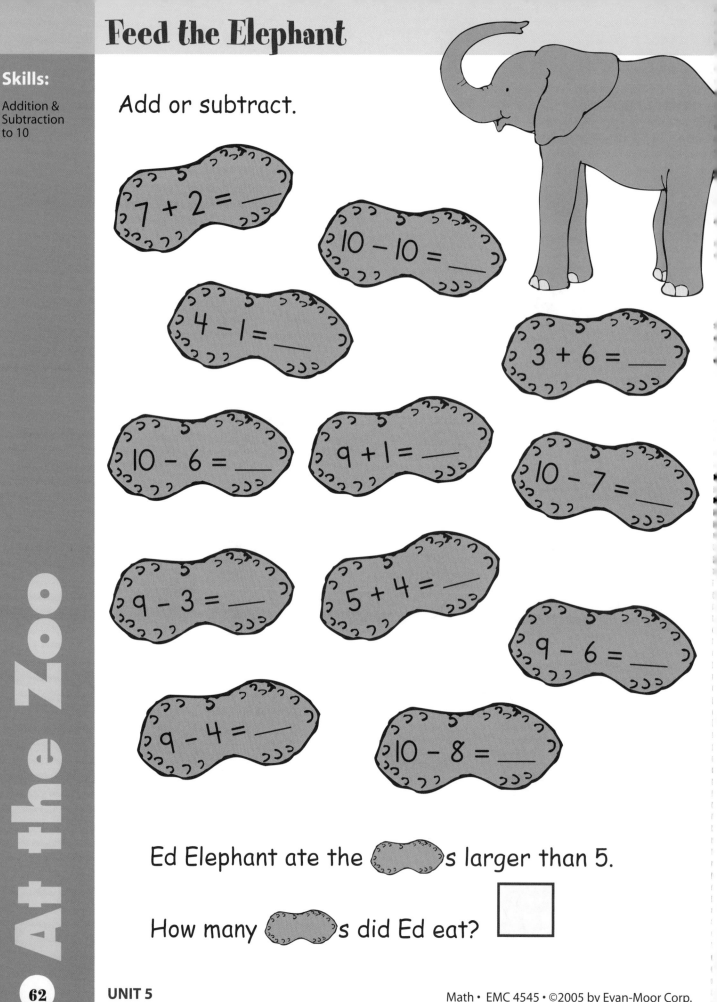

**Skills:**

Addition & Subtraction to 10

Add or subtract.

7 + 2 = ___

10 − 10 = ___

4 − 1 = ___

3 + 6 = ___

10 − 6 = ___

9 + 1 = ___

10 − 7 = ___

9 − 3 = ___

5 + 4 = ___

9 − 6 = ___

9 − 4 = ___

10 − 8 = ___

Ed Elephant ate the peanuts larger than 5.

How many peanuts did Ed eat? ☐

# Tens and Ones

**Skills:**

Place Value—Tens, Ones

Each block is one. Here are **3 ones.**

There are 10 blocks in this set. This is **1 ten.**

How many?

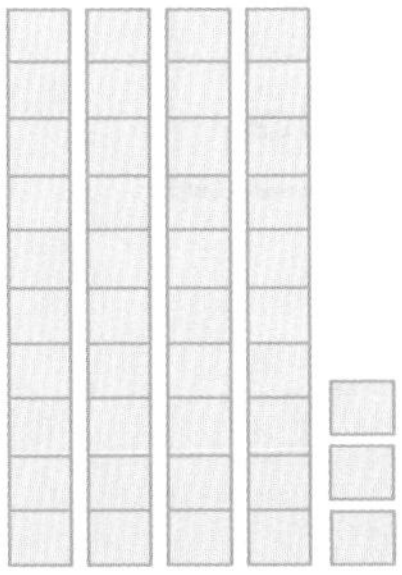

| Tens | Ones |
|---|---|
| | |

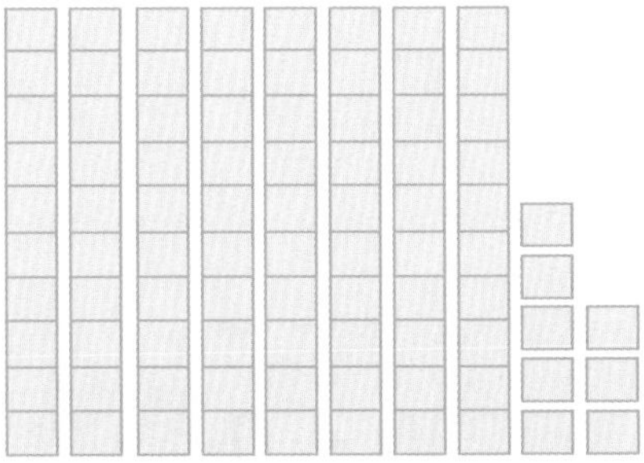

| Tens | Ones |
|---|---|
| | |

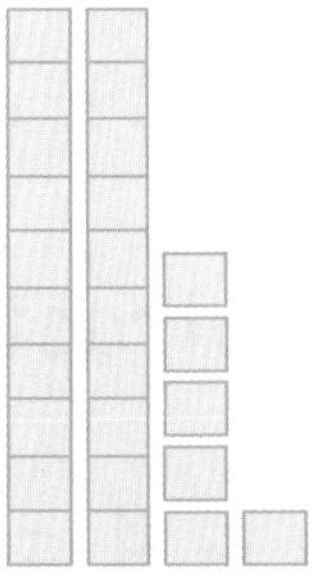

| Tens | Ones |
|---|---|
| | |

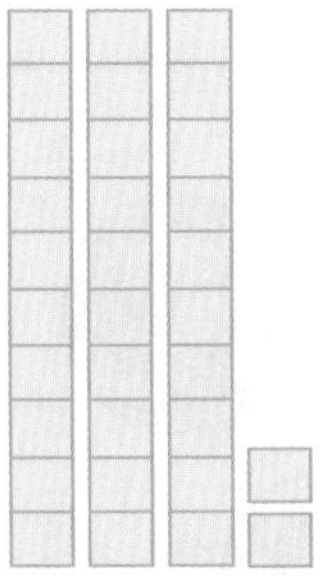

| Tens | Ones |
|---|---|
| | |

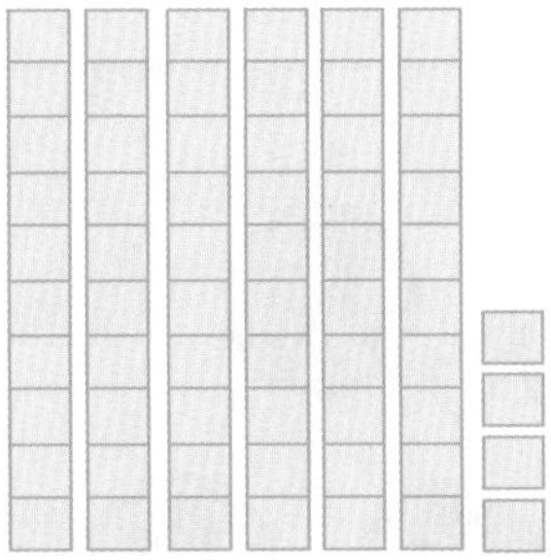

| Tens | Ones |
|---|---|
| | |

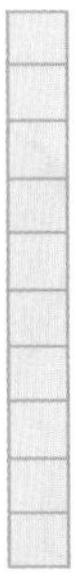

| Ten | Ones |
|---|---|
| | |

At the Zoo

Note: Use this assessment after your child has completed through page 63.

# TEST YOUR SKILLS

## How many?

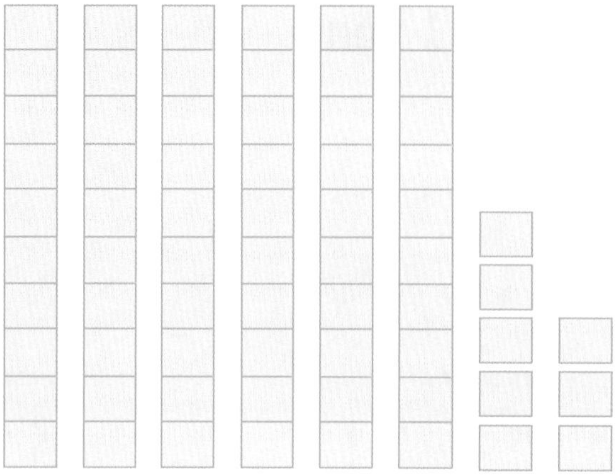

Tens

Ones

## Add or subtract.

6 + 4 = ______ 10 – 0 = ______

8 + 2 = ______ 9 – 4 = ______

## Fill in the circle to show how much.

7¢ ○ 12¢ ○ 15¢ ○

8¢ ○ 9¢ ○ 11¢ ○

10¢ ○ 15¢ ○ 20¢ ○

**Skills:**

Addition & Subtraction to 12

Match each problem to its answer.

6 + 5

10 – 0

9 + 2

12 – 3

9 + 3

12 – 4

4 + 8

11 – 2

8 + 3

12 – 5

7 + 4

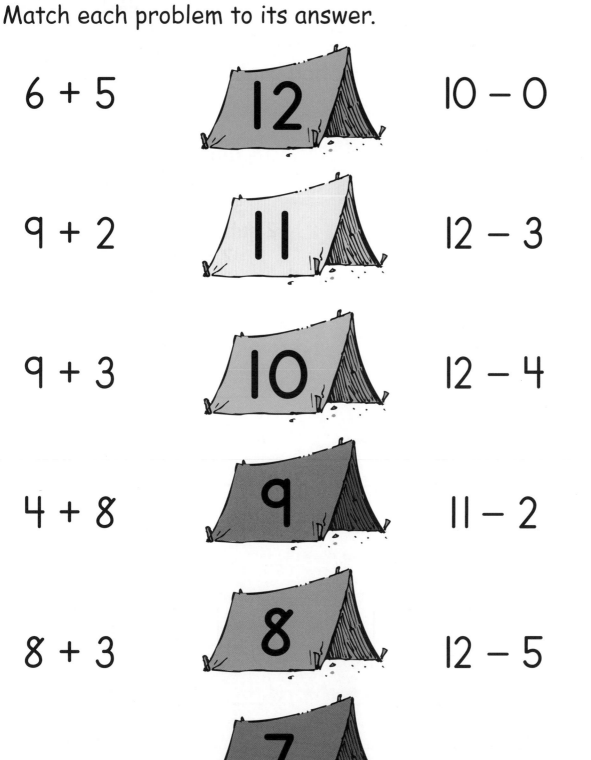

11 – 4

# Number Families

**Skills:**

Addition & Subtraction to 12

Number families have 2 addition problems and 2 subtraction problems made from 3 numbers.

3 numbers: 7, 5, 12

2 addition problems

$7 + 5 = 12$

$5 + 7 = 12$

2 subtraction problems

$12 - 7 = 5$

$12 - 5 = 7$

Complete each number family.

**8, 3, 11**

___ + ___ = ___

___ + ___ = ___

___ − ___ = ___

___ − ___ = ___

**9, 2, 11**

___ + ___ = ___

___ + ___ = ___

___ − ___ = ___

___ − ___ = ___

**8, 4, 12**

___ + ___ = ___

___ + ___ = ___

___ − ___ = ___

___ − ___ = ___

**9, 3, 12**

___ + ___ = ___

___ + ___ = ___

___ − ___ = ___

___ − ___ = ___

Camping

**Skills:**

Addition to 12

How to:

1. Put the larger number in your head.
2. Count on. Write each number on a boot.

9 + 3 = ?

Put 9 in your head.

Add the 3 by counting on.

9 + 3 = 12

8 + 4 = ___

7 + 4 = ___

7 + 5 = ___

6 + 6 = ___

# Counting Back

**Skills:**

Subtraction to 12

Use the sleeping bags to help you find the answers.

11 − 9 = ___ 11 − 5 = ___

11 − 7 = ___ 11 − 4 = ___

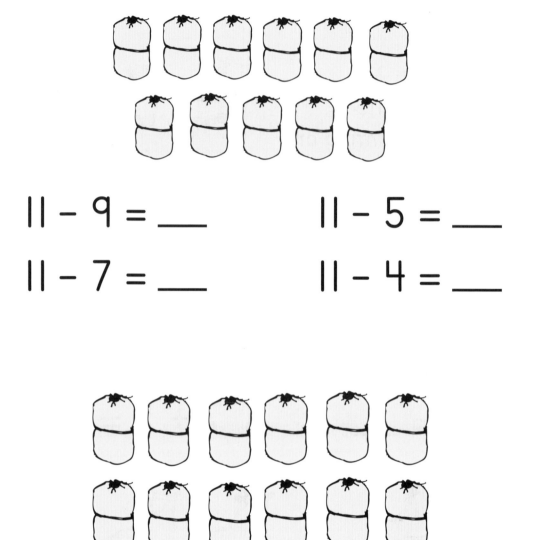

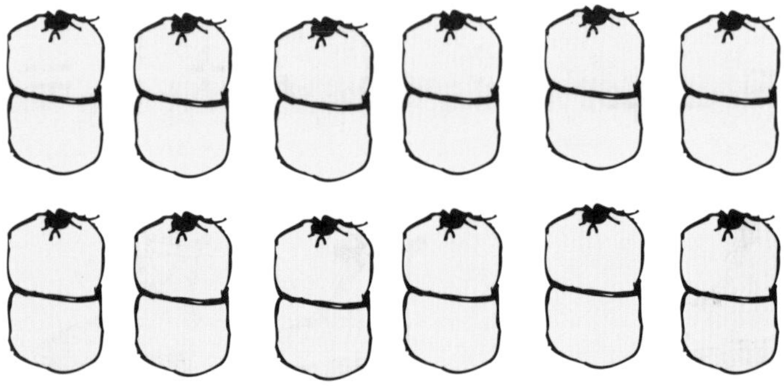

12 − 4 = ___ 12 − 6 = ___

12 − 9 = ___ 12 − 3 = ___

Camping

Skills:
Reading Graphs

Read the graph. Answer the questions.

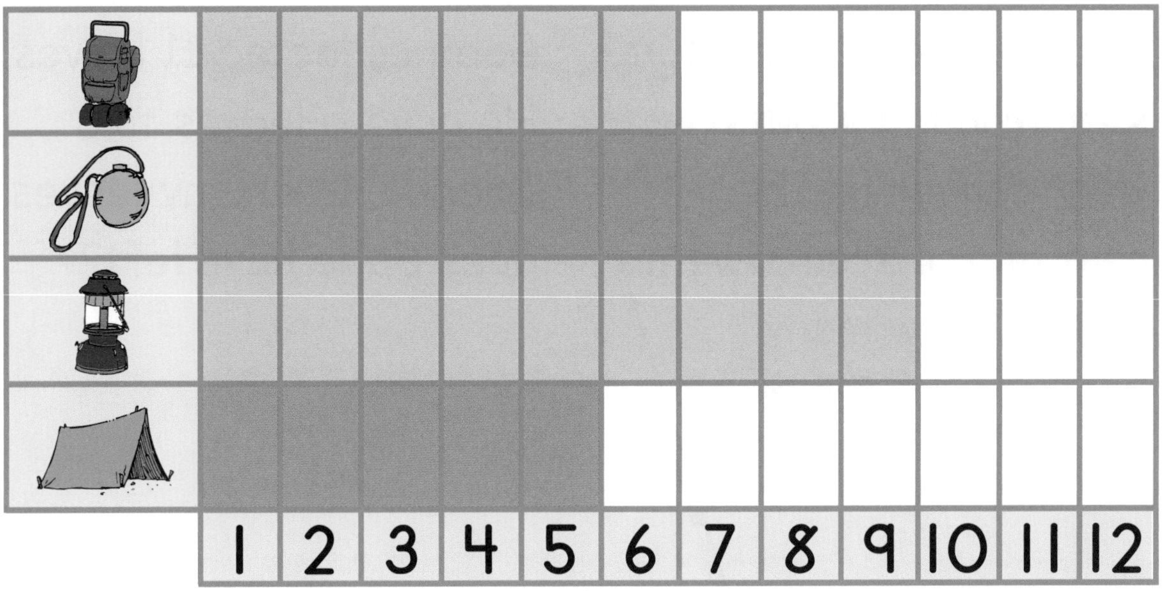


1. How many  are there?

2. How many 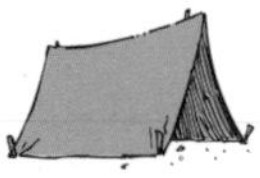 are there?

3. Are there more  or more  ?  

Write the problems. Answer them.

How many more  than  are there?

How many 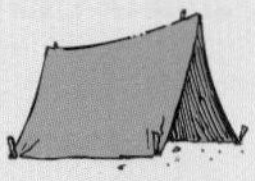 and  are there in all?

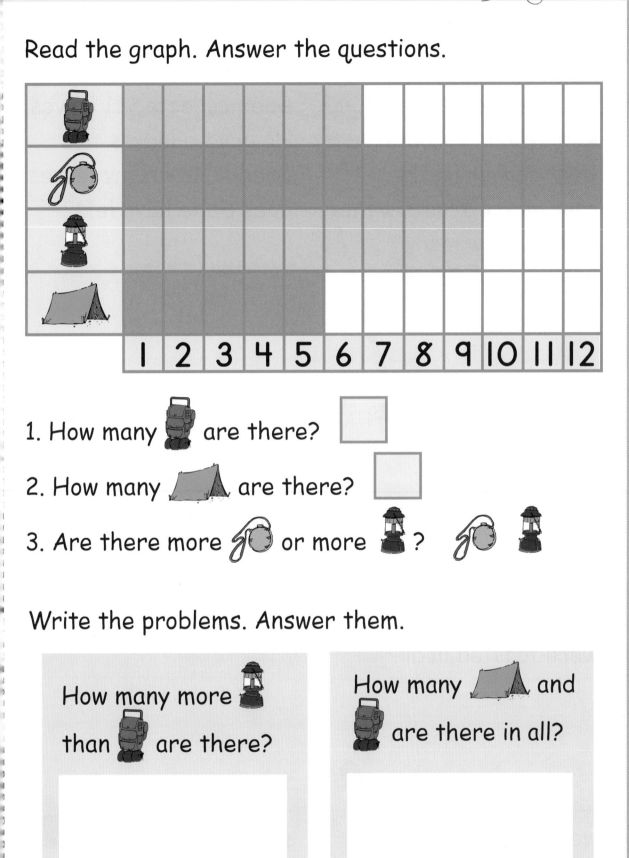

Camping

# A Week at Camp

**Skills:**

Word Problems: Addition & Subtraction to 12

Write the problems. Answer them.

There were 12 scouts in Red Troop. 9 scouts went canoeing. The rest of the scouts went fishing. How many scouts went fishing?

____ scouts went fishing.

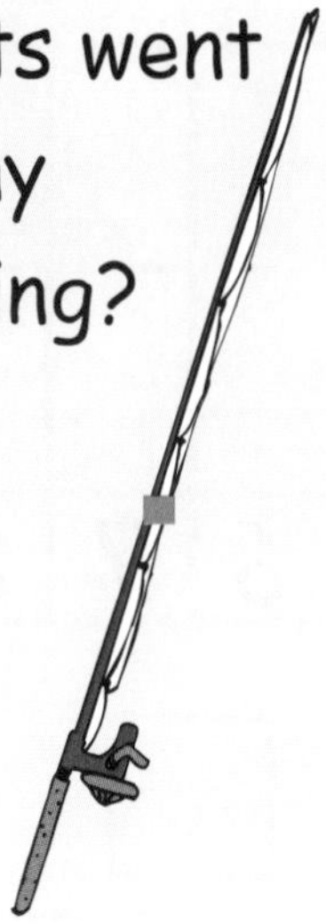

Gabe collected 11 leaves. He gave 5 leaves to a friend. How many leaves does Gabe have left?

Gabe has ____ leaves left.

Katherine toasted 5 marshmallows. Mary toasted 6 marshmallows. How many marshmallows were toasted in all?

____ marshmallows were toasted in all.

Blue Troop put up 12 tents. The wind blew down 8 tents. How many tents were still standing?

____ tents were still standing.

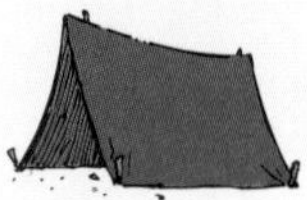

Camping

Skills:
Addition & Subtraction to 12

Write the letter that goes with each number.

| Letter | Problem | Answer |
|---|---|---|
| A | 12 − 7 | 5 |
| F | 12 − 11 | |
| K | 8 + 3 | |
| M | 2 + 1 | |
| N | 10 − 6 | |
| O | 7 − 7 | |
| R | 3 + 9 | |
| S | 7 + 1 | |
| T | 12 − 2 | |
| U | 11 − 9 | |
| W | 0 + 6 | |
| Y | 11 − 4 | |

__ __ A __   A __ A __
8 10 5 7   5 6 5 7

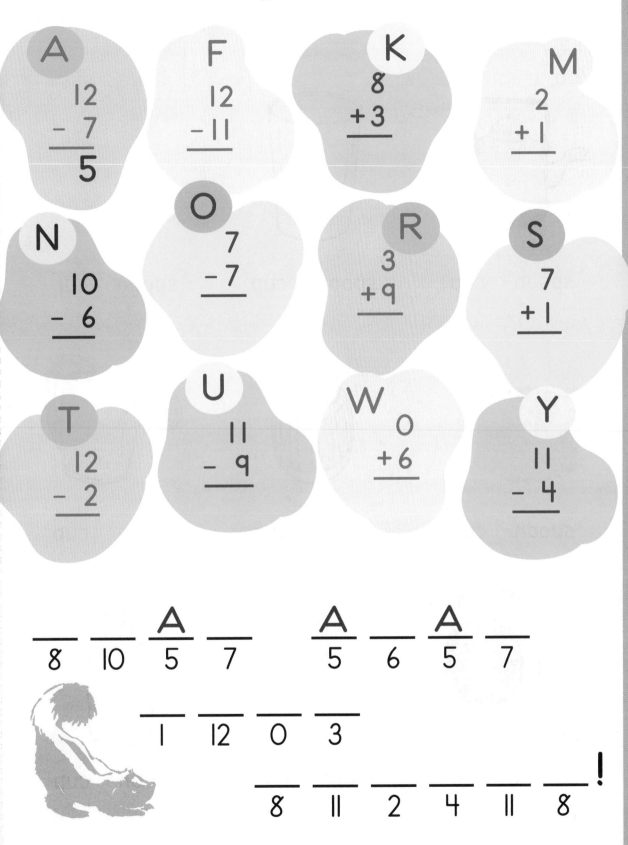

__ __ __ __
1 12 0 3

__ __ __ __ __ __!
8 11 2 4 11 8

Camping

# Fill Them Up!

**Skills:**

Liquid Measurement

Would you use a spoon or a cup to fill the containers?

spoon cup

spoon cup

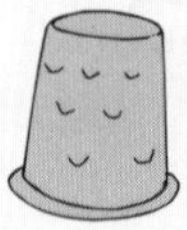

spoon cup

spoon cup

spoon cup

spoon cup

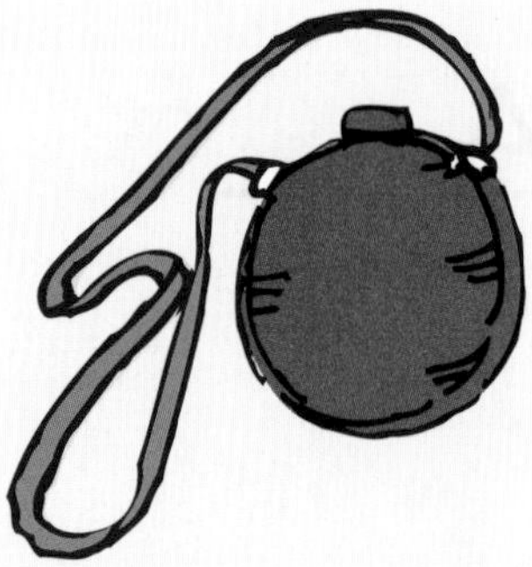

spoon cup

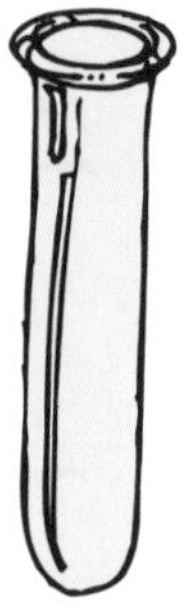

spoon cup

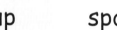

spoon cup

**Skills:**

Adding & Subtracting Two-Digit Numbers

Add or subtract the **ones** first.

Then add or subtract the **tens**.

| tens | ones |
|---|---|
| 2 | 7 |
| +3 | 0 |
| 5 | 7 |

Start on the ones side.

| tens | ones |
|---|---|
| 9 | 8 |
| −2 | 5 |
| | |

| tens | ones |
|---|---|
| 1 | 3 |
| +3 | 1 |
| | |

| tens | ones |
|---|---|
| 6 | 4 |
| −3 | 0 |
| | |

| tens | ones |
|---|---|
| 6 | 0 |
| +2 | 5 |
| | |

| tens | ones |
|---|---|
| 3 | 7 |
| −2 | 7 |
| | |

| tens | ones |
|---|---|
| 8 | 6 |
| −7 | 5 |
| | |

| tens | ones |
|---|---|
| 7 | 1 |
| −5 | 1 |
| | |

| tens | ones |
|---|---|
| 5 | 1 |
| +4 | 4 |
| | |

Camping

# Jobs at Camp

**Skills:**

Word Problems: Addition & Subtraction to 12

Camping

Write the problems. Answer them.

Cassie planted 7 big pine trees and 5 little pine trees. How many pine trees did Cassie plant in all?

Cassie planted ____

Jayme filled 4 canteens with water and 8 canteens with milk. How many canteens did Jayme fill?

Jayme filled ____ canteens.

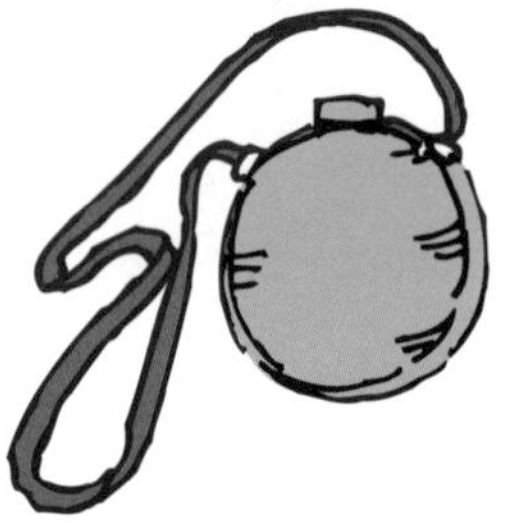

Green Troop made 6 baskets. Orange Troop made the same number. How many baskets were made by both troops?

____ baskets were made.

Jake chopped 12 logs. He used 3 of the logs to make a campfire. How many logs were left?

There were ____ logs left.

# Through the Woods

**Skills:**

Counting by 1s and 10s

Camping

This is a long path.
Count by ones.

This is a short path.
Count by tens.

# Lots of Sticks

**Skills:**

Place Value—Tens & Ones

How many tens and ones in these numbers?

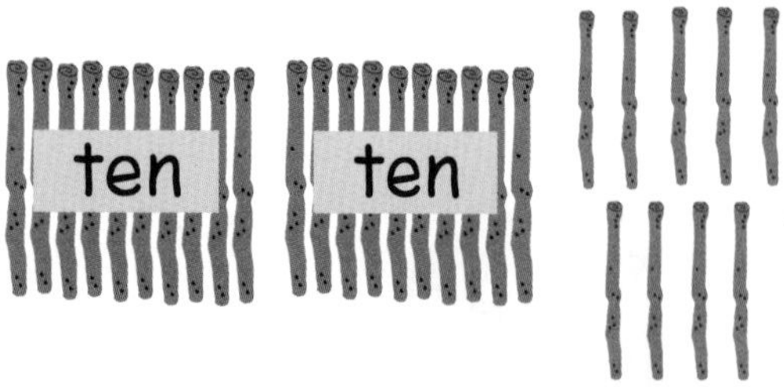


__2__ tens and __9__ ones = 29

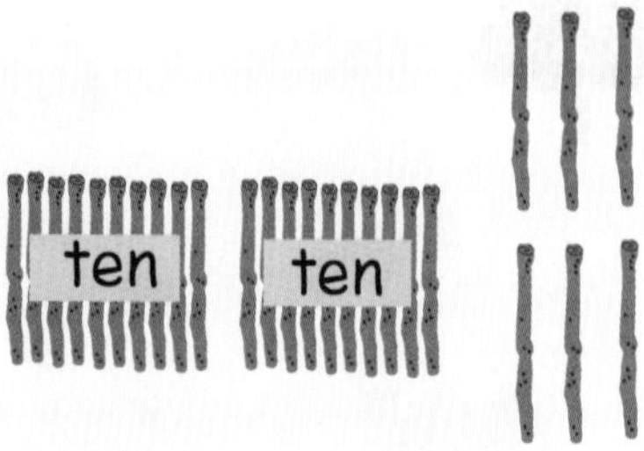


______ tens and ______ ones = 26

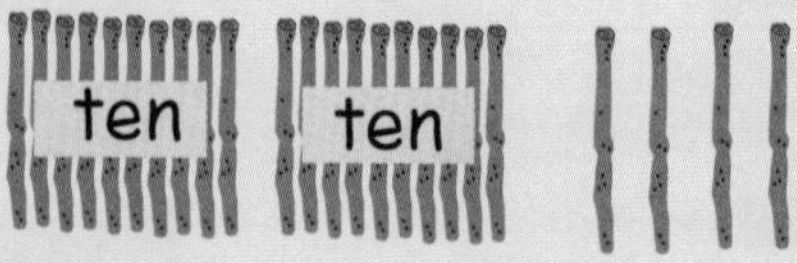


______ tens and ______ ones = 24

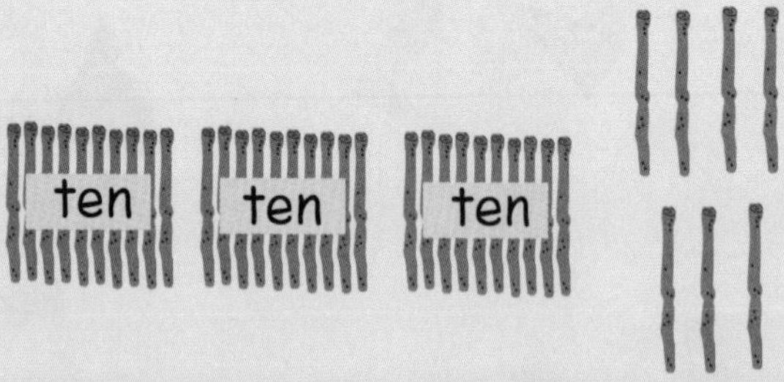


______ tens and ______ ones = 37

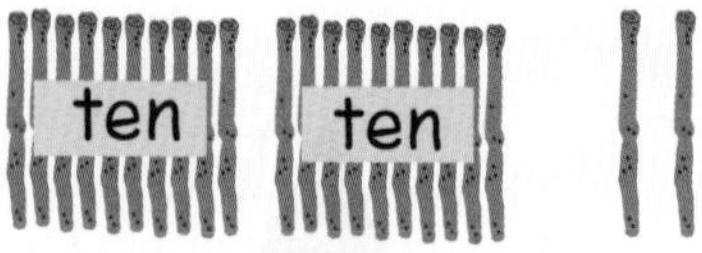


______ tens and ______ ones = 22

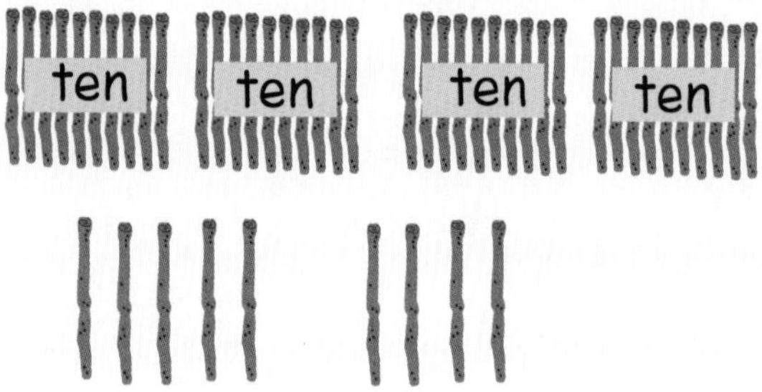


______ tens and ______ ones = 49

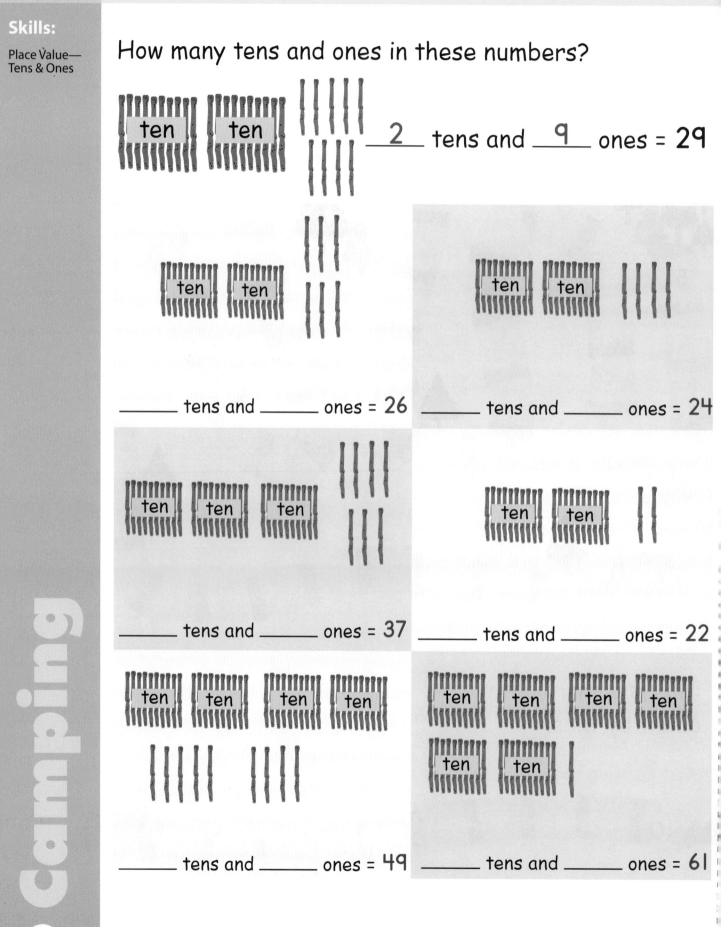

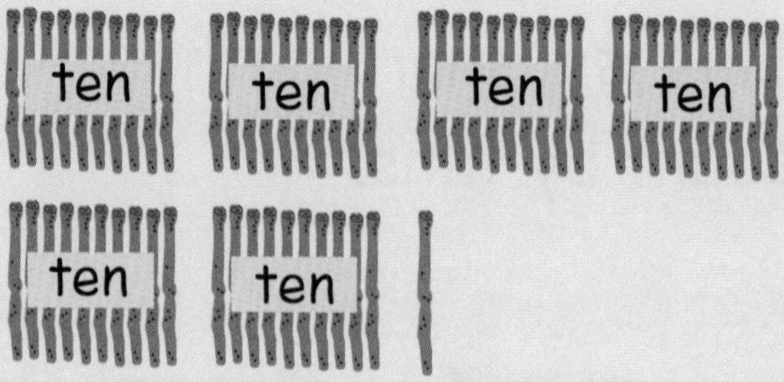


______ tens and ______ ones = 61

Camping

Note: Use this assessment after your child has completed through page 76. Help your child read the directions.

# TEST YOUR SKILLS

Add or subtract.

12 - 8 = ____ 11 - 0 = ____ 9 + 3 = ____

7 + 5 = ____ 12 - 4 = ____ 8 + 4 = ____

Would you use a 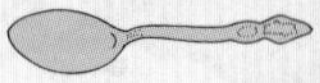 or a  to fill the bucket?

spoon cup

Does a ladybug weigh more than you or less than you?

more less

Does a hippo weigh more than you or less than you?

more less

Count by 1s.

75 ____ ____

____ ____ ____

____ ____ 83

Write the problem and answer it.

Jason had 12 trading cards. He gave 7 to his sister. How many trading cards does Jason have left?

Jason has ____ trading cards left.

Count by 10s to 100.

____, ____, ____, ____, ____, ____, ____, ____, ____, ____

How many tens and ones?

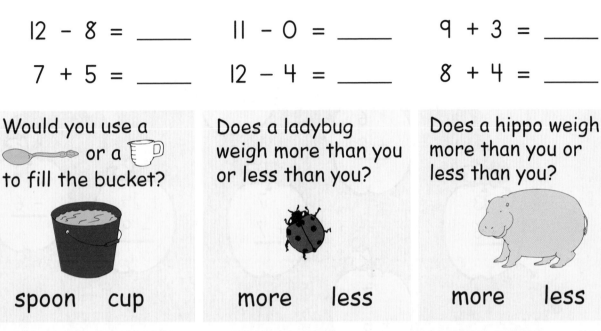

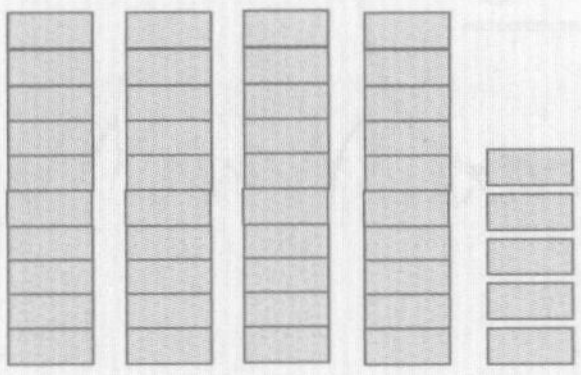

| tens | ones |
|---|---|
| | |

Add or subtract.

$$\begin{array}{r} 22 \\ +45 \\ \hline \end{array} \quad \begin{array}{r} 36 \\ -14 \\ \hline \end{array} \quad \begin{array}{r} 57 \\ -33 \\ \hline \end{array} \quad \begin{array}{r} 61 \\ +28 \\ \hline \end{array}$$

**Skills:**
Addition & Subtraction to 14

Find the answer that is the same as 3 + 3 + 3.
Color that apple red. Color the other apples yellow.

**Skills:**

Column Addition

Number Words to 14

| | | | | |
|---|---|---|---|---|
| 6 | 2 | 5 | 1 | 3 |
| 4 | 8 | 2 | 6 | 8 |
| +3 | +1 | +2 | +5 | +2 |

| | | | | |
|---|---|---|---|---|
| 7 | 4 | 9 | 1 | 3 |
| 0 | 4 | 0 | 5 | 4 |
| +5 | +4 | +4 | +6 | +5 |

## Find the Number Words

| | | | | | | | | | | | |
|---|---|---|---|---|---|---|---|---|---|---|---|
| d | f | o | u | r | t | e | e | n | s | q | f |
| b | s | i | x | e | q | i | i | j | r | u | u |
| n | p | u | x | d | q | k | g | d | w | b | l |
| o | h | z | e | r | o | o | f | i | c | v | d |
| h | e | i | g | h | t | u | x | u | t | p | j |
| w | f | w | f | g | f | i | v | e | o | z | b |
| t | e | n | c | t | w | e | l | v | e | n | l |
| f | o | u | r | c | s | e | v | e | n | g | x |
| n | i | n | e | g | d | d | t | h | r | e | e |
| t | w | o | y | c | b | b | i | x | o | n | e |
| k | l | y | v | t | h | i | r | t | e | e | n |
| e | l | e | v | e | n | n | v | s | k | g | a |

1. zero
2. one
3. two
4. three
5. four
6. five
7. six
8. seven
9. eight
10. nine
11. ten
12. eleven
13. twelve
14. thirteen
15. fourteen

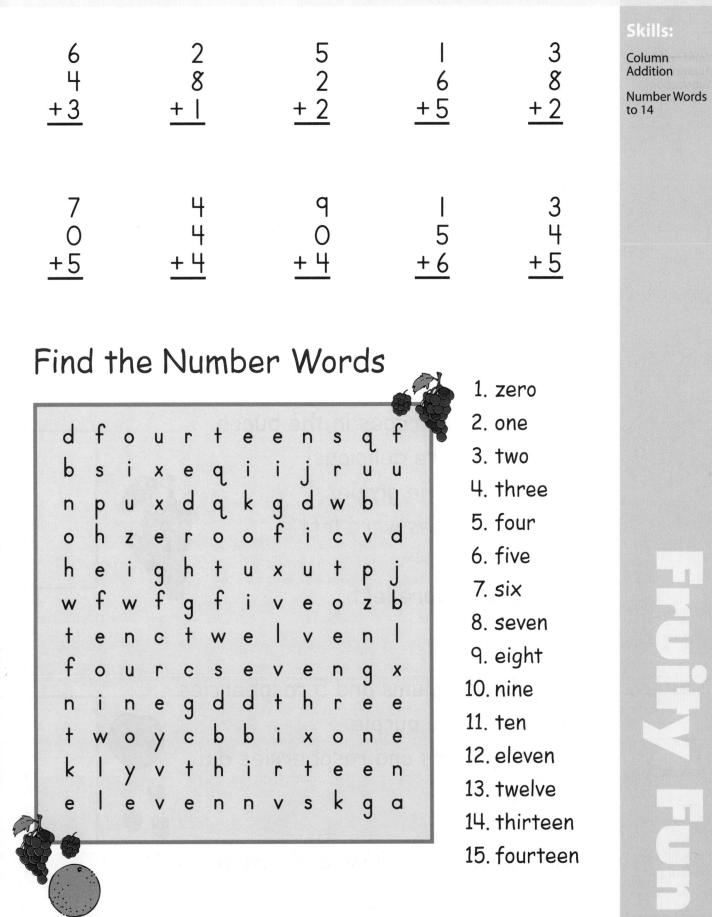

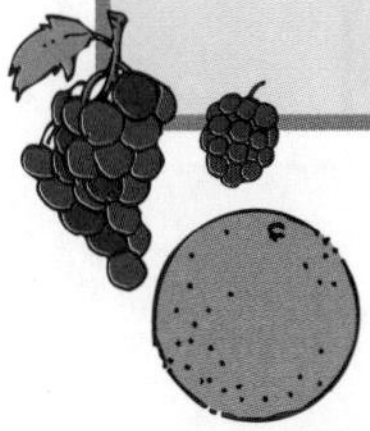

**Skills:**

Word Problems: Addition & Subtraction to 14

Read. Find the sentence that isn't needed. Mark it out. Write the problems. Answer them.

Dana planted 14 watermelon seeds.
9 of the watermelon seeds sprouted.
~~She ate a slice of watermelon.~~
How many watermelon seeds did **not** sprout?

$$\begin{array}{r} 14 \\ -\ 9 \\ \hline 5 \end{array}$$

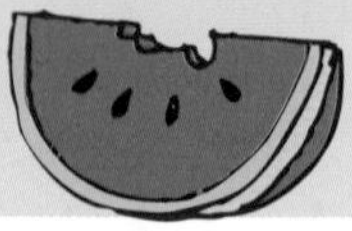

__5__ seeds did not sprout.

There were 12 grapes in the bunch.
The grapes were delicious!
Gary ate 6 of the grapes.
How many grapes were left?

____ grapes were left.

Bobby grew 7 plums and 5 raspberries.
The plums were purple.
How many plums and raspberries did Bobby grow?

Bobby grew ____ plums and raspberries.

Fruity Fun

**Skills:**

Addition & Subtraction to 14

$6 + 7 =$ ______

$7 + 6 =$ ______

$13 - 7 =$ ______

$13 - 6 =$ ______

$9 + 4 =$ ______

$4 + 9 =$ ______

$13 - 4 =$ ______

$13 - 9 =$ ______

$8 + 5 =$ ______

$5 + 8 =$ ______

$13 - 8 =$ ______

$13 - 5 =$ ______

$9 + 5 =$ ______

$5 + 9 =$ ______

$14 - 9 =$ ______

$14 - 5 =$ ______

$8 + 4 =$ ______

$4 + 8 =$ ______

$12 - 8 =$ ______

$12 - 4 =$ ______

$8 + 6 =$ ______

$6 + 8 =$ ______

$14 - 6 =$ ______

$14 - 8 =$ ______

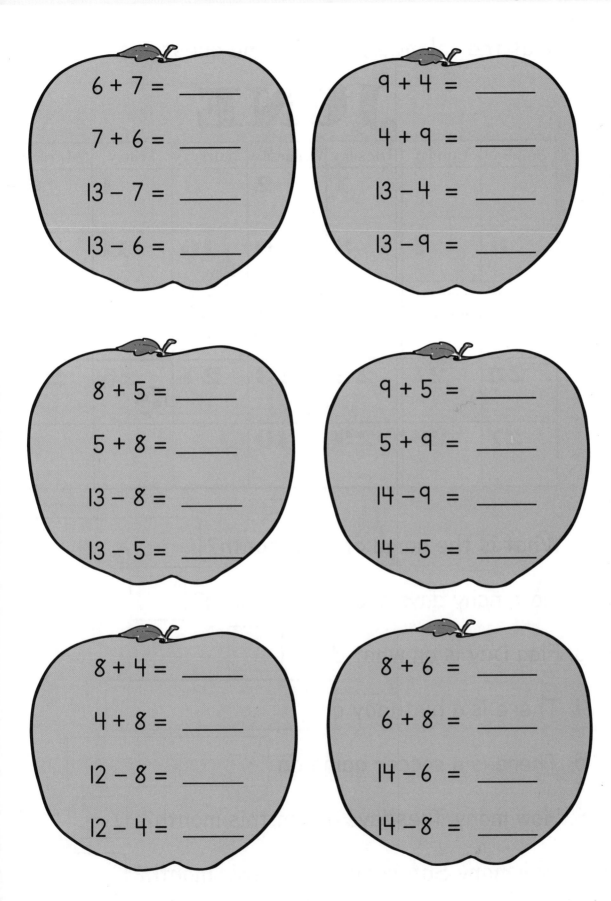

**Skills:**

Reading a Calendar

Look at the calendar. Answer the questions.

# JUNE

| Sunday | Monday | Tuesday | Wednesday | Thursday | Friday | Saturday |
|---|---|---|---|---|---|---|
| | | 1 | 2 | 3 | 4 | 5 |
| 6 | 7 | 8 | 9 | 10  | 11 | 12 |
| 13 | 14  | 15 | 16 | 17 | 18 | 19 |
| 20 | 21 | 22 | 23 | 24 | 25  | 26 |
| 27 | 28 | 29 | 30 | | | |

1. What is the name of this month? ☐
2. How many days are in this month? ☐
3. Flag Day is on what day? ☐
4. There is a birthday on ☐.
5. There is a soccer game on ☐.
6. How many Tuesdays are in this month? ☐
7. How many Saturdays are in this month? ☐

**Skills:**

Counting

Number Order

| after | before | in between |
|---|---|---|
| 21 <u>22</u> | <u>46</u> 47 | 29 <u>30</u> 31 |
| 39 ___ | ___ 50 | 43 ___ 45 |
| 45 ___ | ___ 36 | 38 ___ 40 |
| 50 ___ | ___ 64 | 51 ___ 53 |
| 64 ___ | ___ 21 | 67 ___ 69 |
| 77 ___ | ___ 92 | 80 ___ 82 |
| 99 ___ | ___ 63 | 87 ___ 89 |

Fruity Fun

**Skills:**

Addition & Subtraction to 14

Barry Banana has a message for you.
Write the letter that goes with each number.

| A | D | E | F | I |
|---|---|---|---|---|
| 14 − 9 = ___ | 8 + 5 = ___ | 13 − 7 = ___ | 7 + 7 = ___ | 9 + 3 = ___ |

| R | S | T | U | V | Y |
|---|---|---|---|---|---|
| 11 − 8 = ___ | 13 − 9 = ___ | 13 − 5 = ___ | 14 − 7 = ___ | 14 − 5 = ___ | 7 + 4 = ___ |

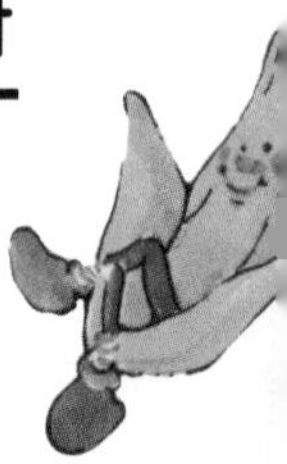

# Farmer Fred's Fruit

**Skills:**
Completing and Reading a Graph

Fruity Fun

Farmer Fred likes to keep track of the fruit he sells at his stand. Here is what he sold last Saturday.

8 bags of cherries  10 watermelons 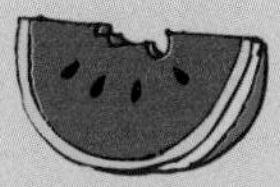

7 baskets of berries  5 pears 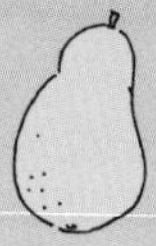

**Color the graph to show what Farmer Fred sold.**

| | | | | | | | | | | |
|---|---|---|---|---|---|---|---|---|---|---|
|  | | | | | | | | | | |
|  | | | | | | | | | | |
|  | | | | | | | | | | |
| 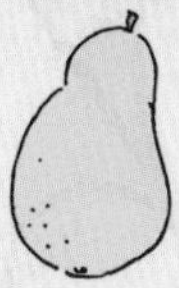 | | | | | | | | | | |
| | 1 | 2 | 3 | 4 | 5 | 6 | 7 | 8 | 9 | 10 |

1. How many more watermelons sold than pears? ______

2. Which fruit sold the smallest amount? ______________

3. How many bags of cherries and baskets of berries? ______

**Skills:**

Addition &
Subtraction
to 14

## Add and subtract. Color.

| red | yellow | blue | green |
|-----|--------|------|-------|
| 7 | 5 | 8 | 10 |

$14 - 6 =$ ___

$9 + 1 =$ ___

$12 - 4 =$ ___

$13 - 6 =$ ___

$14 - 6 =$ ___

$11 - 3 =$ ___

$$\begin{array}{r} 14 \\ -\ 9 \\ \hline \end{array}$$

$$6 + 2 =$$ ___

$13 - 8 =$ ___

$$\begin{array}{r} 11 \\ -\ 6 \\ \hline \end{array}$$

$$\begin{array}{r} 5 \\ +\ 3 \\ \hline \end{array}$$

$7 + 1 =$ ___

## Fruity Fun

Math • EMC 4545 • ©2005 by Evan-Moor Corp.

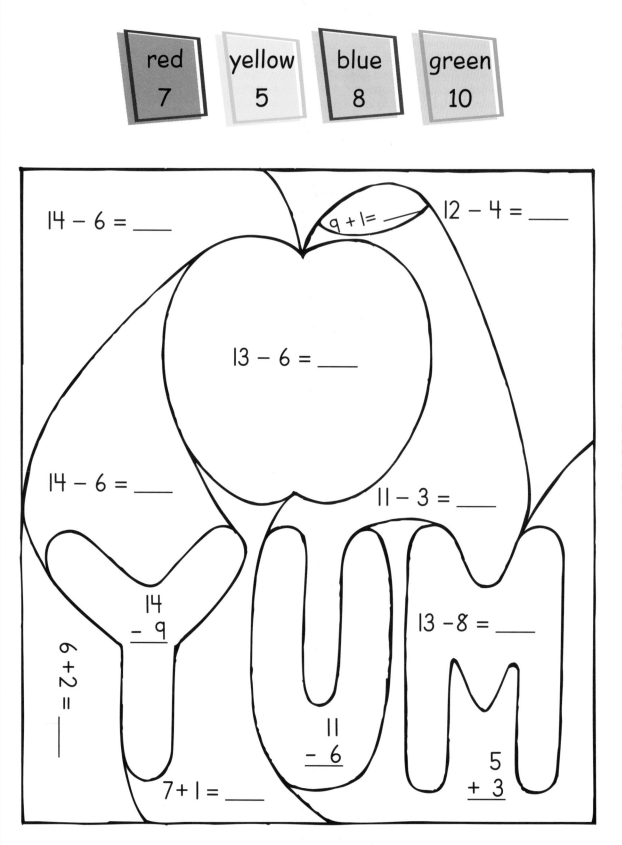

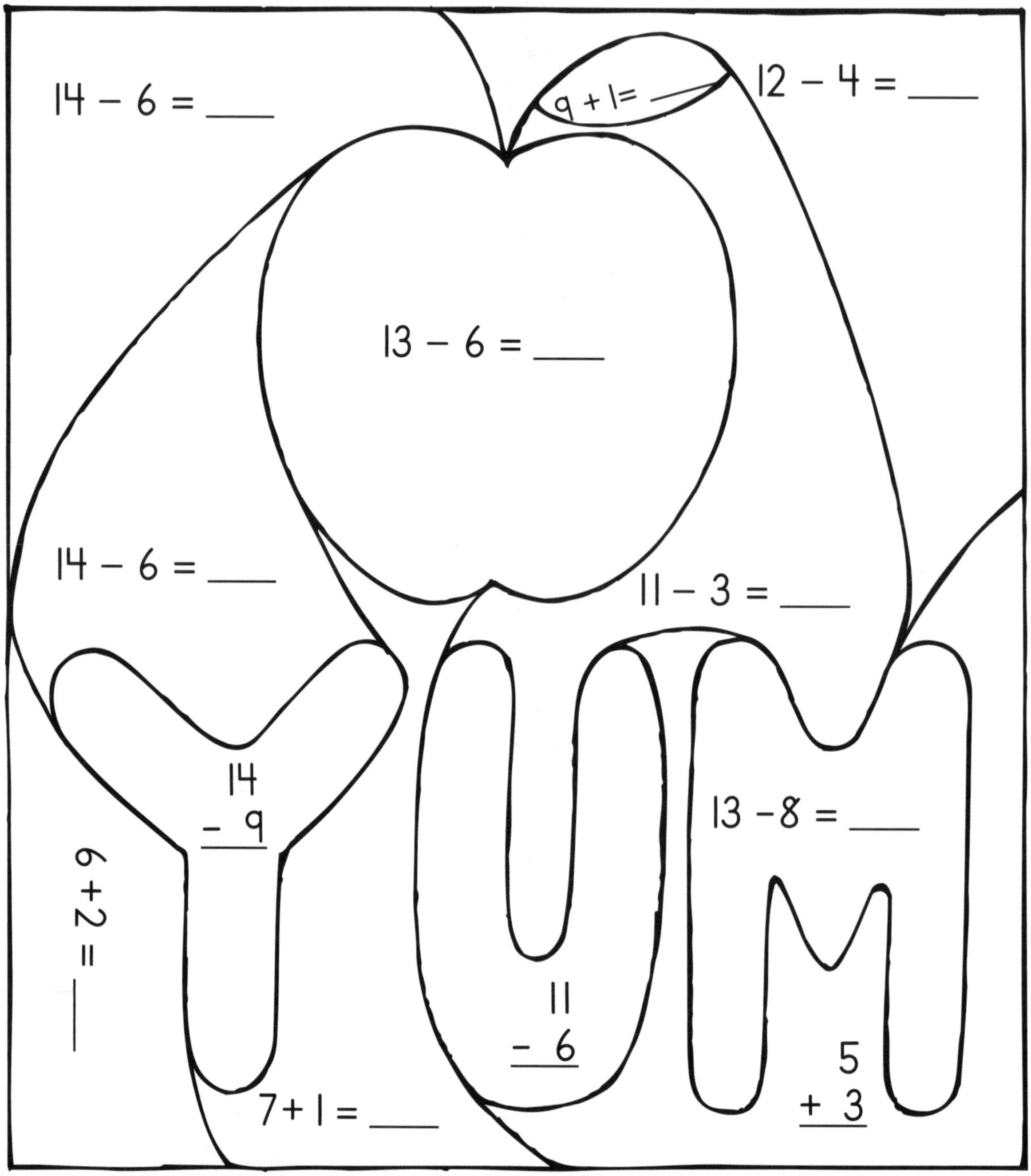

**Skills:**

Counting by 5s

Count by 5s.

5 ______ ______ ______ ______ ______

______ ______ ______ ______ ______

Connect the dots.

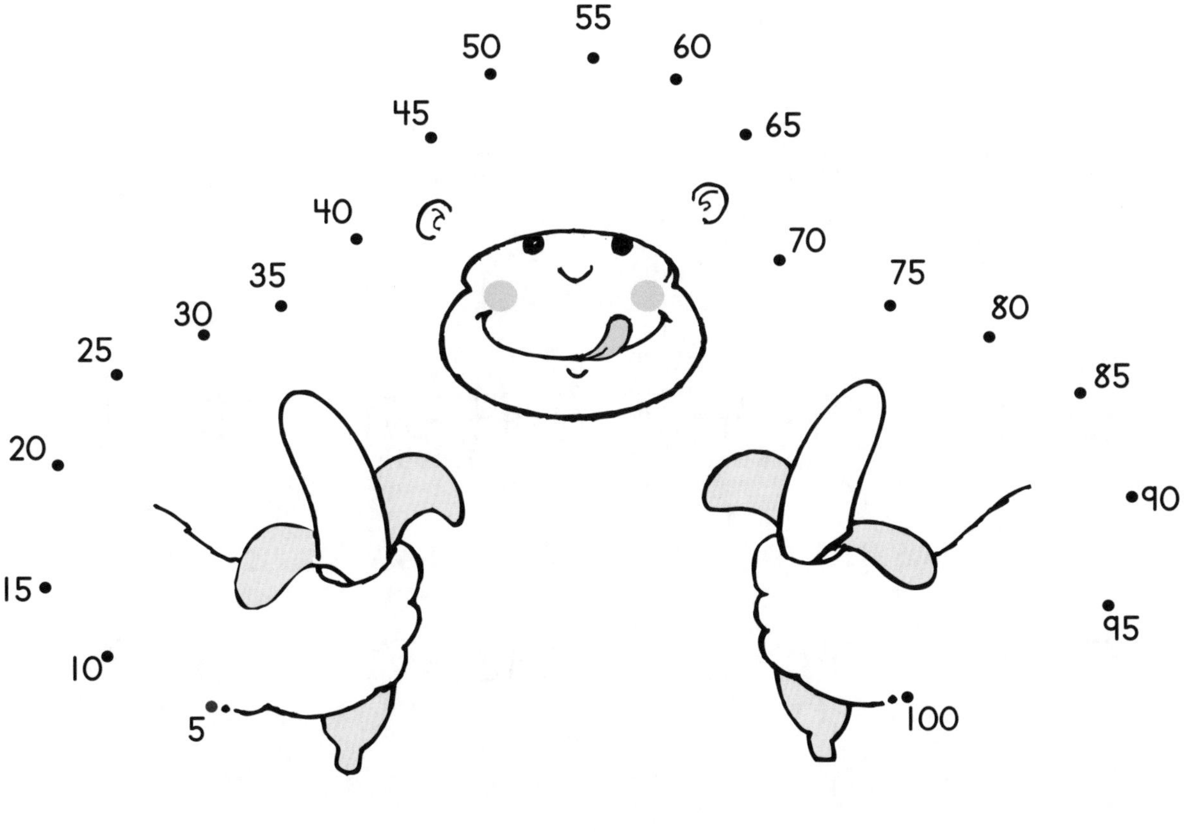


Fruity Fun

**Skills:**

Greater Than, Less Than

> = greater than

< = less than

8 > 7

7 < 8

| | | |
|---|---|---|
| 7 ☐ 12 | 13 ☐ 20 | 18 ☐ 9 |
| 5 ☐ 15 | 14 ☐ 4 | 10 ☐ 0 |

Add or subtract. Write > or < in the ◯.

| | |
|---|---|
| 9 + 5 > 12 + 1<br>14 13 | 8 + 5 ◯ 5 + 6<br>☐ ☐ |
| 3 + 7 ◯ 6 + 6<br>☐ ☐ | 5 + 4 ◯ 8 + 3<br>☐ ☐ |
| 13 − 8 ◯ 11 − 4<br>☐ ☐ | 14 − 7 ◯ 5 + 4<br>☐ ☐ |
| 7 + 6 ◯ 14 − 5<br>☐ ☐ | 12 − 7 ◯ 11 − 7<br>☐ ☐ |

Fruity Fun

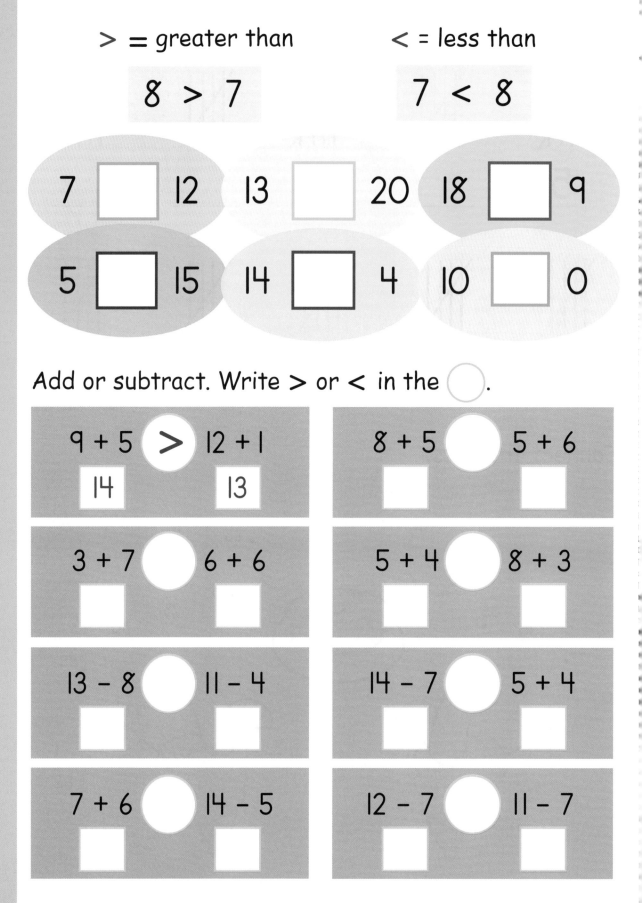

Note: Use this assessment after your child has completed through page 88.

## TEST YOUR SKILLS

Count by 5s.

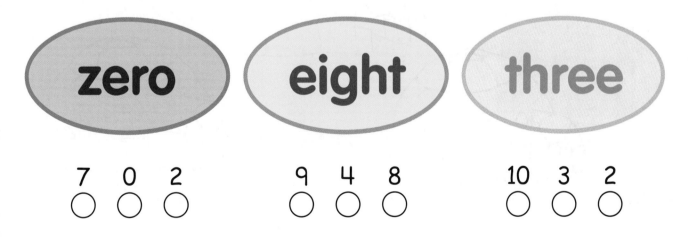

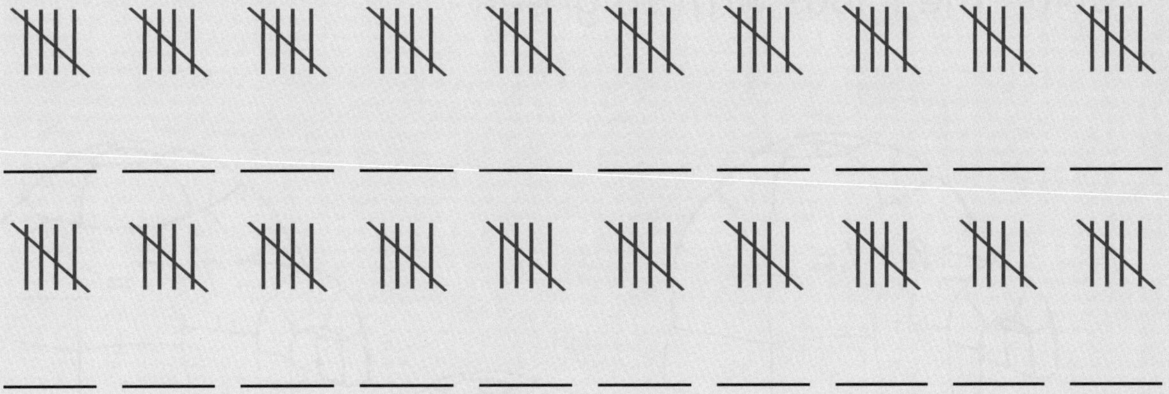

Add.

| | | | |
|---|---|---|---|
| 6 | 2 | 4 | 9 |
| 4 | 3 | 3 | 0 |
| + 3 | + 1 | + 5 | + 4 |
| ☐ | ☐ | ☐ | ☐ |

Read the word. Fill in the circle under the number.

| zero | eight | three |
|---|---|---|
| 7 ○ 0 ○ 2 ○ | 9 ○ 4 ○ 8 ○ | 10 ○ 3 ○ 2 ○ |

# Color the Igloos

**Skills:**

Addition & Subtraction to 16

Find the answers. Color the igloos with 14 blue.

Color the igloos with 15 red.

Color the igloos with 16 green.

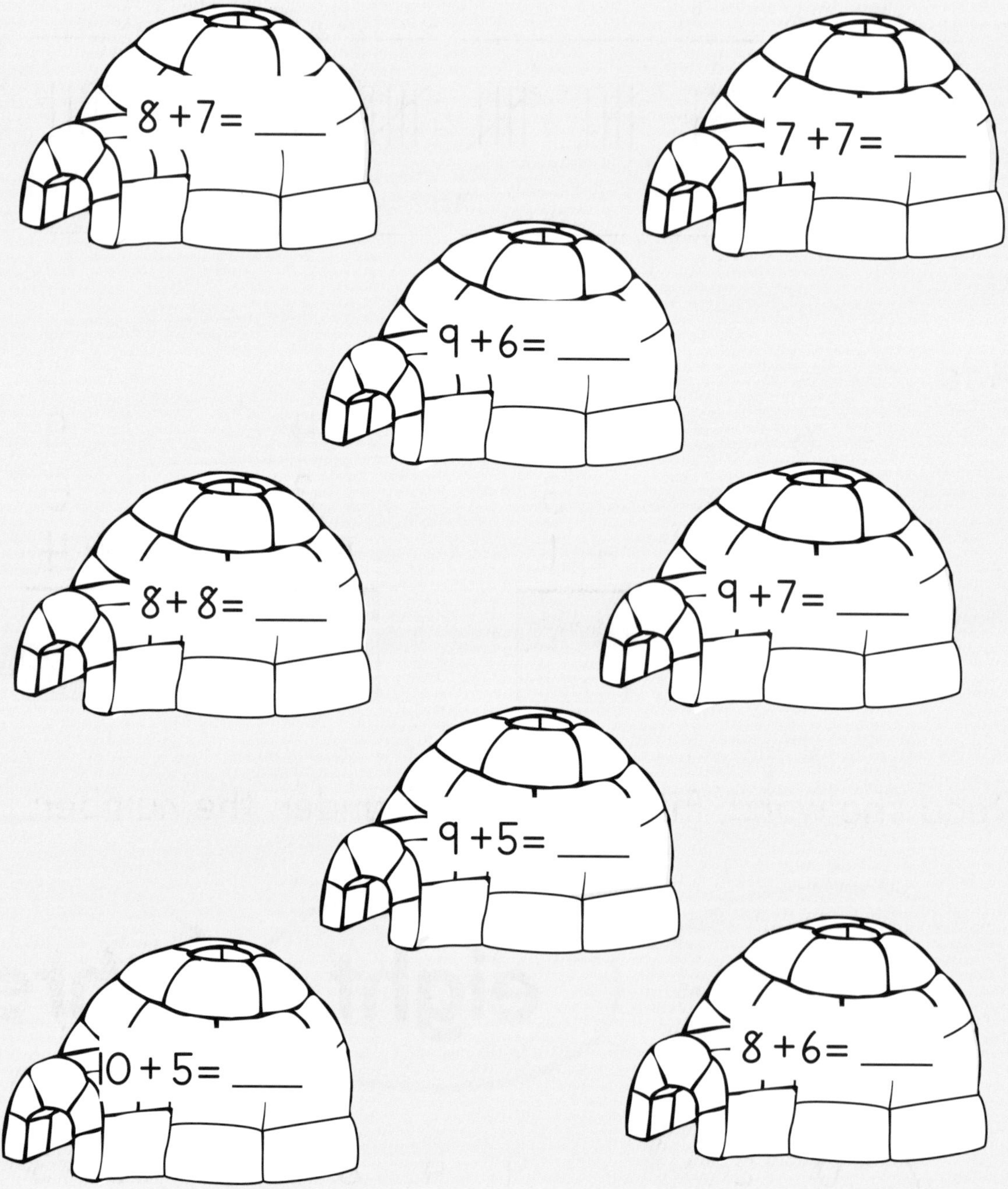


Chilly Capers

 

**Skills:**

Addition & Subtraction to 16

Use each family of numbers to make 2 addition problems and 2 subtraction problems.

___ + ___ = ___

___ + ___ = ___

___ − ___ = ___

___ − ___ = ___

___ + ___ = ___

___ + ___ = ___

___ − ___ = ___

___ − ___ = ___

___ + ___ = ___

___ + ___ = ___

___ − ___ = ___

___ − ___ = ___

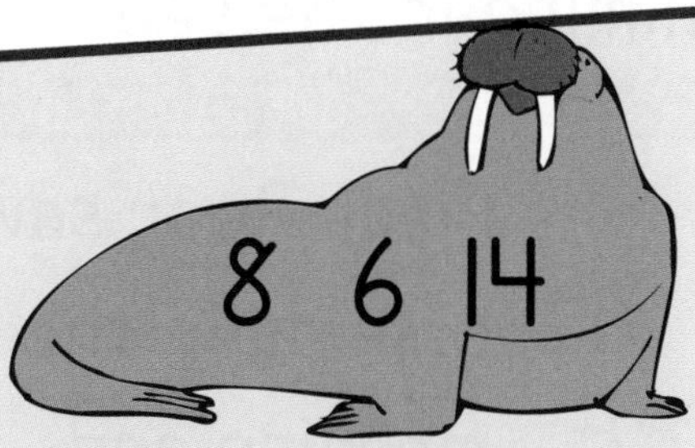


___ + ___ = ___

___ + ___ = ___

___ − ___ = ___

___ − ___ = ___

6 + 7 = ____ 13 − 6 = ____ 8 + 8 = ____

7 + 6 = ____ 13 − 7 = ____ 16 − 8 = ____

# Animals at the Poles

**Skills:**

Word Problems: Addition & Subtraction to 16

Note: You may need to help your child read the word problems.

Write the problems. Answer them.

9 penguins were swimming in the sea. 7 more penguins jumped in. How many penguins were swimming in the sea?

$\square + \square = \square$

There were ____ penguins swimming in the sea.

16 walruses were lying on the ice. 9 walruses slid back into the sea. How many walruses were still on the ice?

$\square - \square = \square$

There were ____ walruses still on the ice.

Polar Bear saw 6 seals in the morning and 9 seals in the afternoon. How many seals did Polar Bear see in all?

$\square + \square = \square$

Polar Bear saw ____ seals in all.

16 penguins were caught for the zoo. 8 of the penguins got away. How many penguins were left?

$\square - \square = \square$

There were ____ penguins left.

**Skills:**

Reading a Graph

Use the information from the graph to answer the questions.

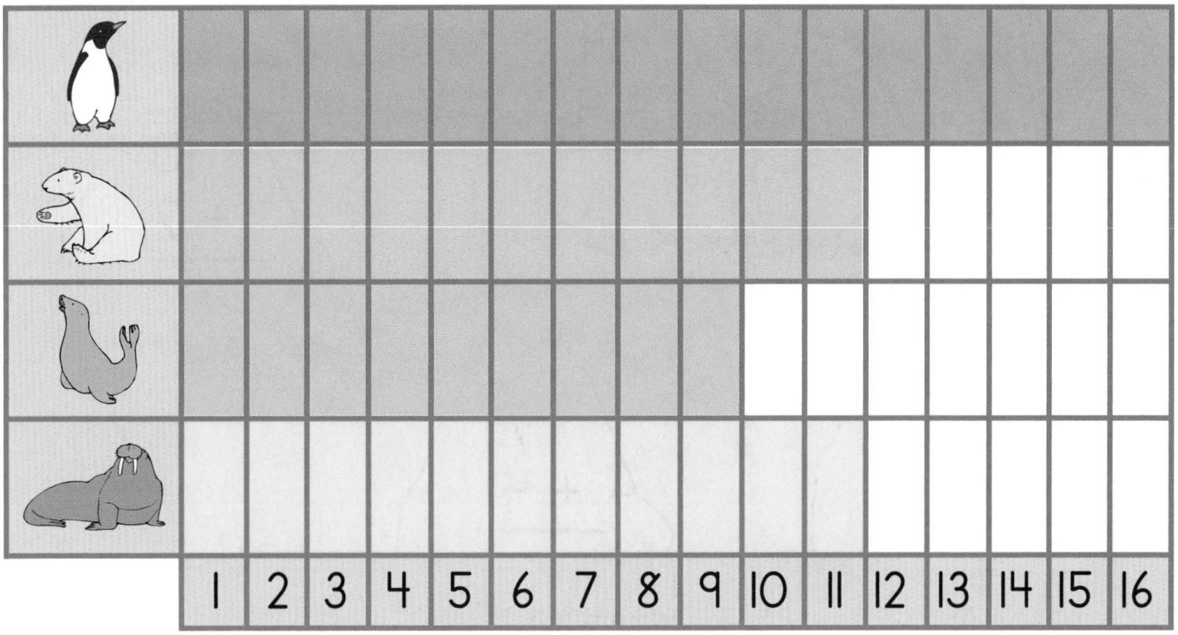


1. How many fish did each animal eat?

2. Which animal ate the most fish? 

3. Which animal ate the fewest fish? 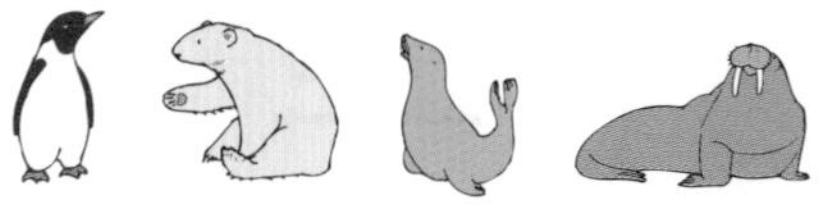

4. Polar Bear and Seal ate ____ fish in all.

5. Penguin ate ____ more fish than Walrus.

# Find the Seal

**Skills:**

Addition & Subtraction to 16

Connect the answers in order from smallest to largest.

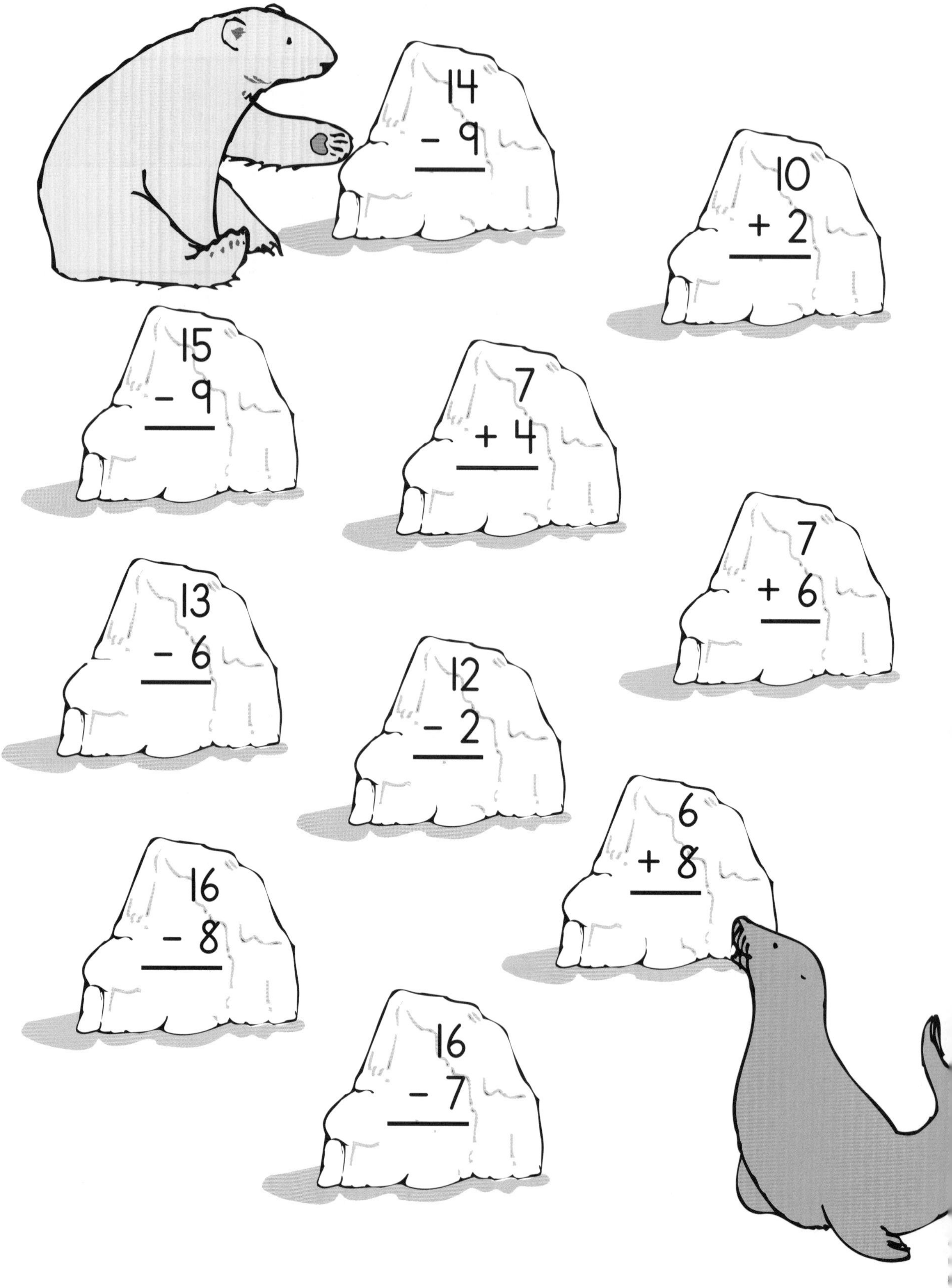


Chilly Capers

**Skills:**

Telling Time to the Half Hour

Write the time.

1 : 30     ____ : ____     ____ : ____

____ : ____     ____ : ____     ____ : ____

____ : ____     ____ : ____     ____ : ____

# Winter Gear

**Skills:**

Money—
Penny, Nickel,
Dime

Add the coins. Write the price on the tag.

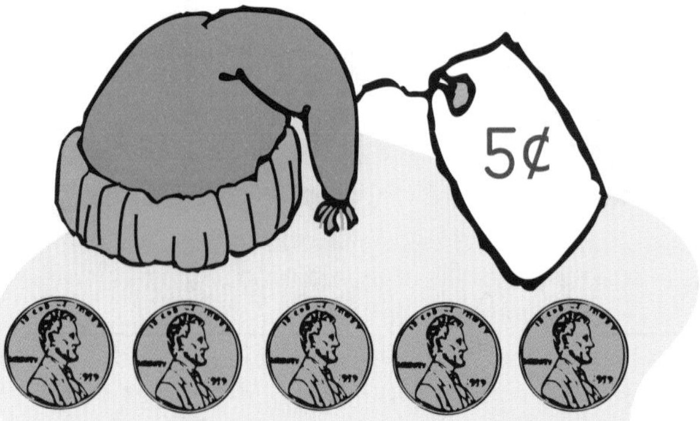


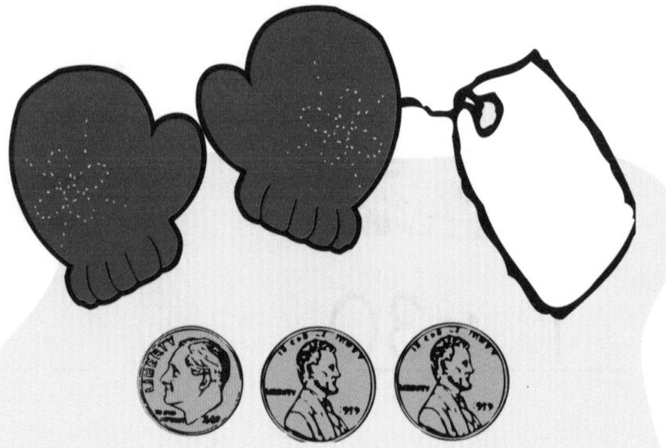

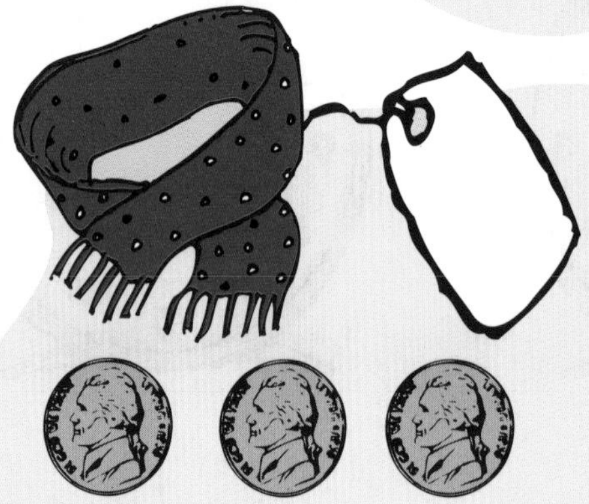

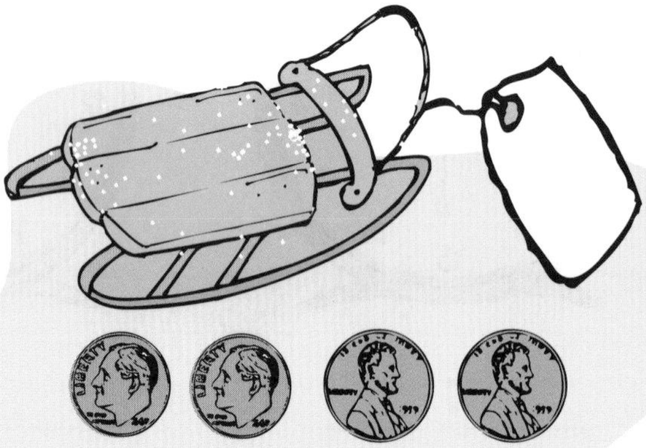

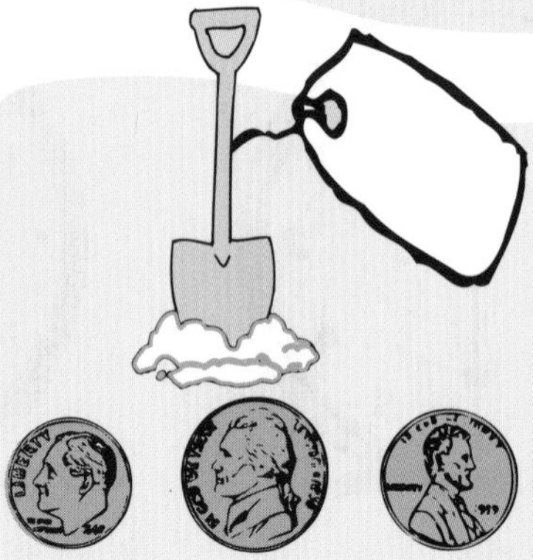

**Skills:**

Two-Digit Addition & Subtraction

Add or subtract. Do the ones first.

| tens | ones |
|---|---|
| 4 | 2 |
| + 4 | 6 |
| 8 | 8 |

$$\begin{array}{r} 15 \\ -\ 10 \\ \hline \end{array}$$

$$\begin{array}{r} 13 \\ +\ 4 \\ \hline \end{array}$$

$$\begin{array}{r} 14 \\ -\ 4 \\ \hline \end{array}$$

$$\begin{array}{r} 15 \\ +\ 13 \\ \hline \end{array}$$

$$\begin{array}{r} 58 \\ -\ 26 \\ \hline \end{array}$$

$$\begin{array}{r} 13 \\ +\ 26 \\ \hline \end{array}$$

$$\begin{array}{r} 22 \\ +\ 7 \\ \hline \end{array}$$

$$\begin{array}{r} 15 \\ -\ 15 \\ \hline \end{array}$$

# How Many Fish?

**Skills:**

Estimating

Counting by 5s, 10s

Circle the best **estimate**.

1 10

5 25

15 35

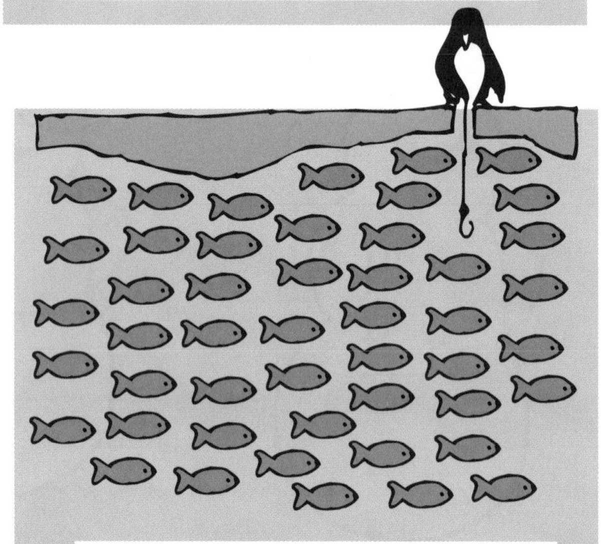

10 50

Count by 5s.

5, ____, ____, 20, ____, 30, ____, ____, ____, 50

Count by 10s.

10, ____, ____, 40, ____, ____, ____, 80, ____, ____

Note: You many need to help your child read the word problems.

Skills:

Word Problems: Addition & Subtraction to 16

Write the problems. Answer them.

The Inuit family made 15 pairs of snowshoes. 9 pairs sold at the winter market. How many pairs of snowshoes were left?

☐ pairs of snowshoes were left.

It snowed 15 inches in two days. On the first day it snowed 6 inches. How many inches did it snow on the second day?

It snowed ☐ inches on the second day.

Penguin Pete made 8 pairs of blue mittens and 8 pairs of red mittens. How many pairs of mittens did Penguin Pete make in all?

Penguin Pete made ☐ pairs of mittens.

Polar Bear hopped onto a piece of ice. She floated 8 miles to Walrus's house and then 7 more miles to Seal's house. How many miles did Polar Bear float in all?

Polar Bear floated ☐ miles in all.

# Count the Cold Things

**Skills:**
Counting by 2s

Count the snowballs by 2s. Color the 2s blue.

Count the fish by 2s.

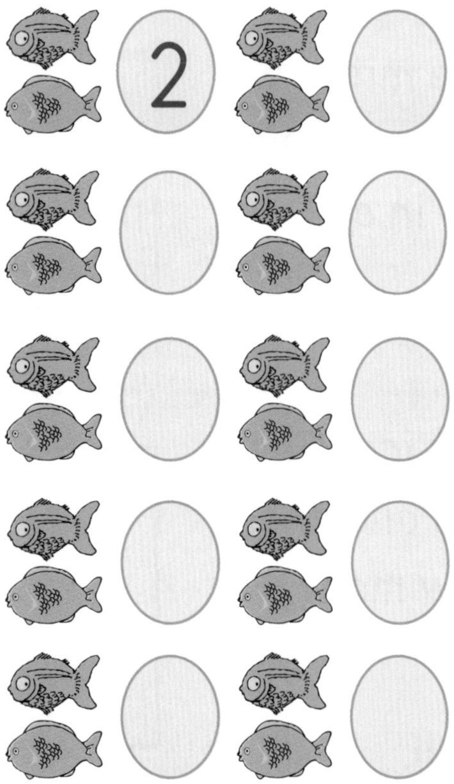


Connect the dots. Color.

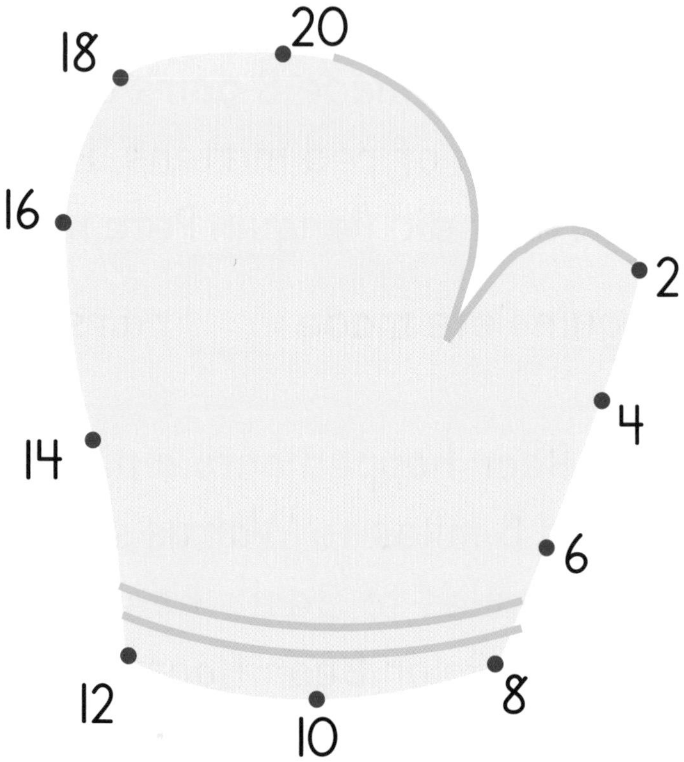


Chilly Capers

# Catch of the Day

**Skills:**

Addition & Subtraction to 16

Penguin may eat only the fish that equal (=) **15** or **16**. Help him find them. Color those fish.

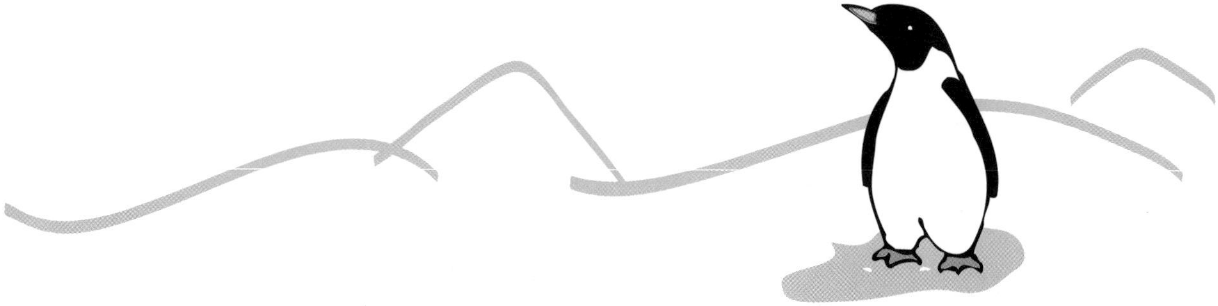

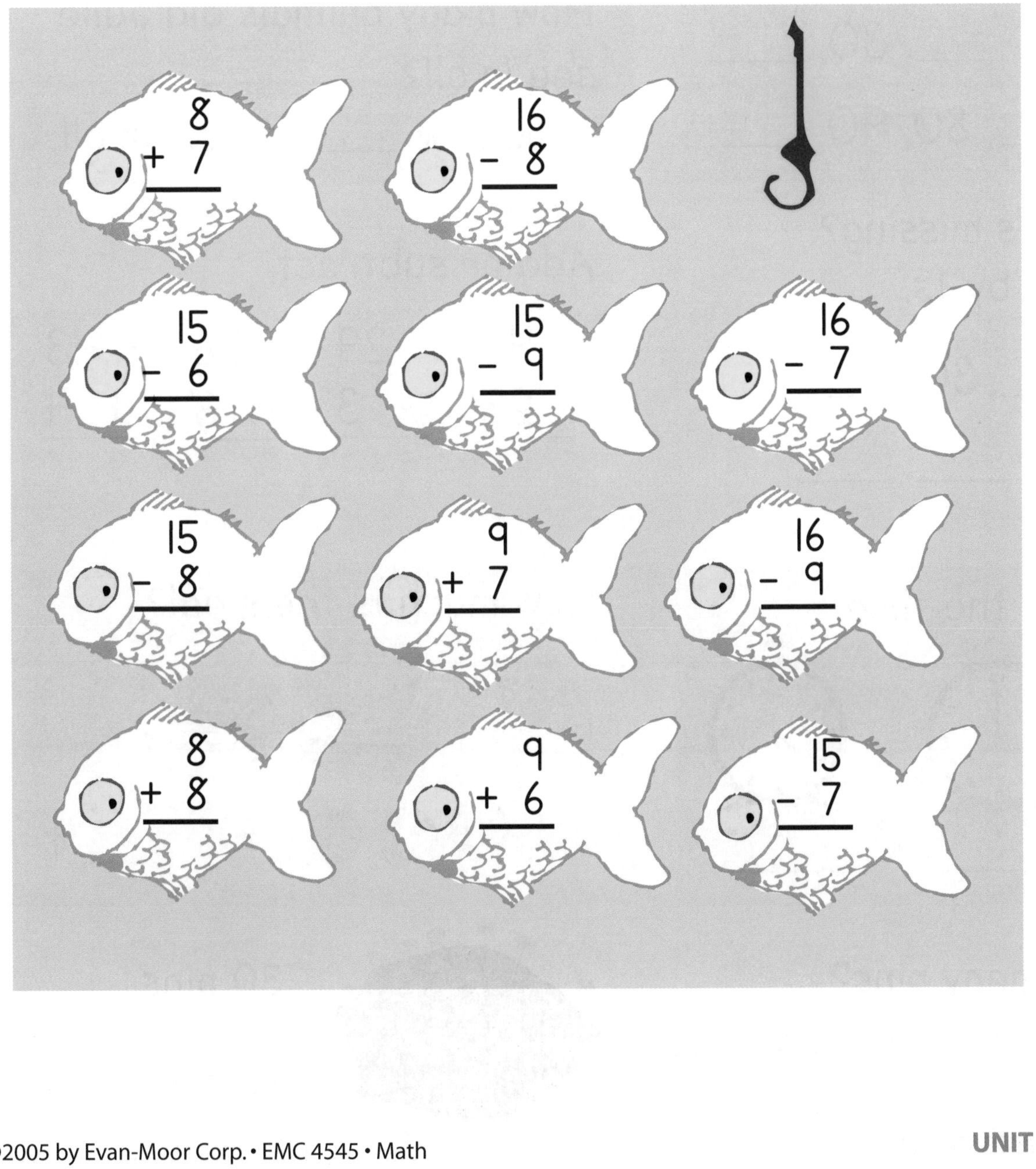


Chilly Capers

Note: Use this assessment after your child has completed through page 101. Help your child read the directions.

## TEST YOUR SKILLS

Add or subtract.

16 − 7 = ____  9 + 6 = ____  15 − 9 = ____

8 + 7 = ____  15 − 8 = ____  7 + 9 = ____

What's missing?

6, ____, 10, 12, ____

20, ____, 30, ____

____, 80, 90, ____

Julie saw 9 polar bears and 7 seals.

How many animals did Julie see in all?

Julie saw ____ animals in all.

What's missing?
Count by 1s.

____, 30, ____

49, ____, ____

Add or subtract.

| | | | |
|---|---|---|---|
| 47 | 29 | 56 | 13 |
| − 25 | − 3 | + 13 | + 4 |

Write the time.

____ : ____  ____ : ____

How much is the meal?

____¢

How many pins?
Circle the best estimate.

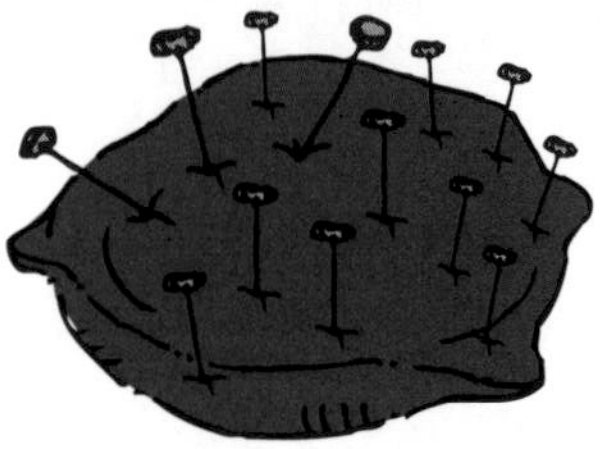

30 pins

15 pins

**Skills:**

Addition &
Subtraction
to 18

Measuring to
the Nearest
Inch

Add or subtract.

$$\begin{array}{r} 9 \\ + 8 \\ \hline \end{array}$$

$$\begin{array}{r} 8 \\ + 8 \\ \hline \end{array}$$

$$\begin{array}{r} 18 \\ - 9 \\ \hline \end{array}$$

$$\begin{array}{r} 15 \\ - 8 \\ \hline \end{array}$$

$$\begin{array}{r} 9 \\ + 7 \\ \hline \end{array}$$

$$\begin{array}{r} 16 \\ - 7 \\ \hline \end{array}$$

$$\begin{array}{r} 17 \\ - 8 \\ \hline \end{array}$$

$$\begin{array}{r} 17 \\ - 9 \\ \hline \end{array}$$

$$\begin{array}{r} 9 \\ + 9 \\ \hline \end{array}$$

$$\begin{array}{r} 16 \\ - 9 \\ \hline \end{array}$$

$$\begin{array}{r} 8 \\ + 7 \\ \hline \end{array}$$

$$\begin{array}{r} 16 \\ - 8 \\ \hline \end{array}$$

Measure each item to the nearest inch.

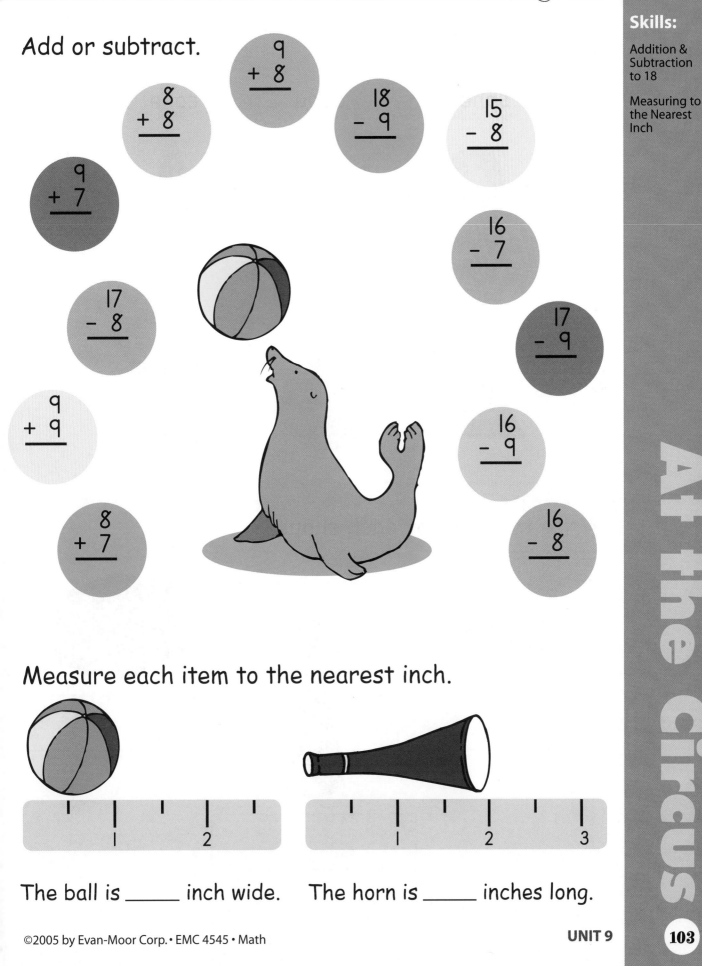

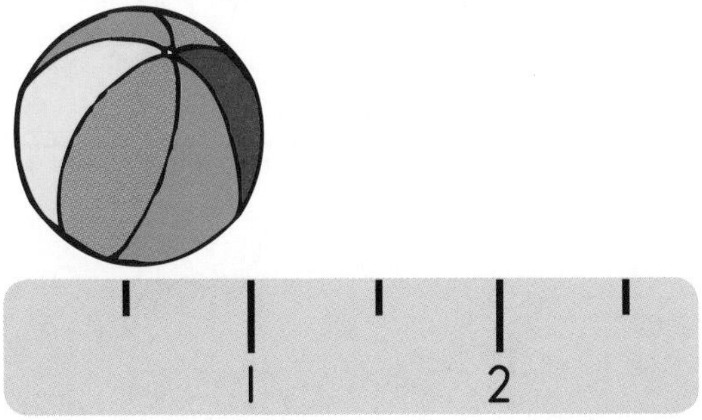

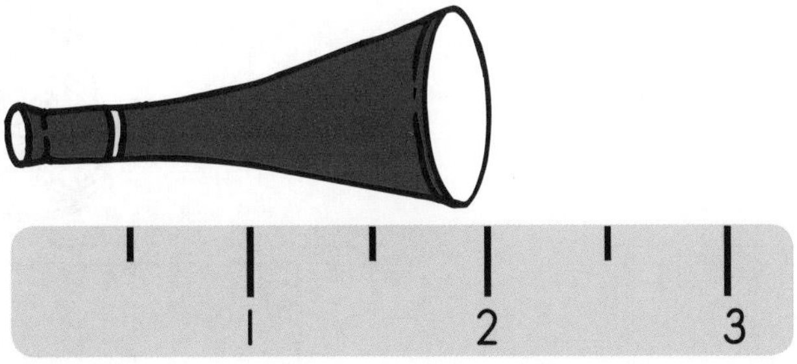

The ball is _____ inch wide.     The horn is _____ inches long.

# Shapes

**Skills:**

Identifying Geometric Shapes

At the Circus

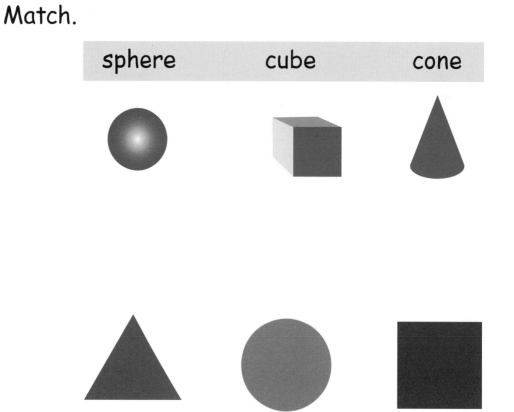

Match.

sphere cube cone

Write the name of each shape.

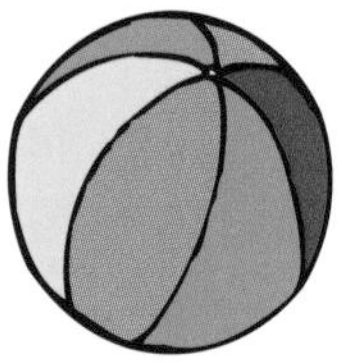

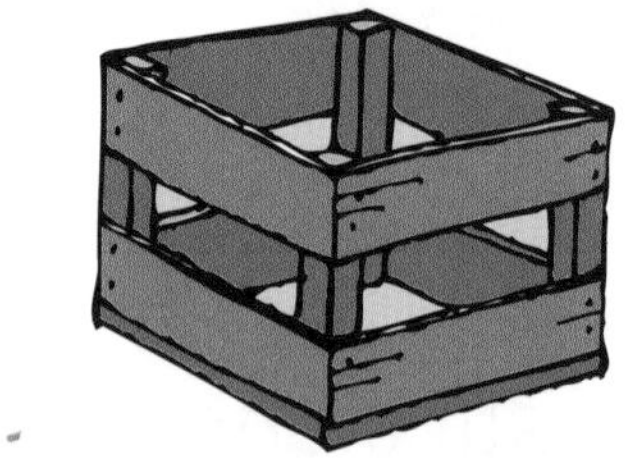

**Skills:**

Addition & Subtraction to 18



7 + ____ = 15

15 − ____ = 9

8 + ____ = 16

____ + 9 = 16

____ − 9 = 9

____ − 8 = 9

Fill your own wagon.

____ + ____ = ____

____ − ____ = ____

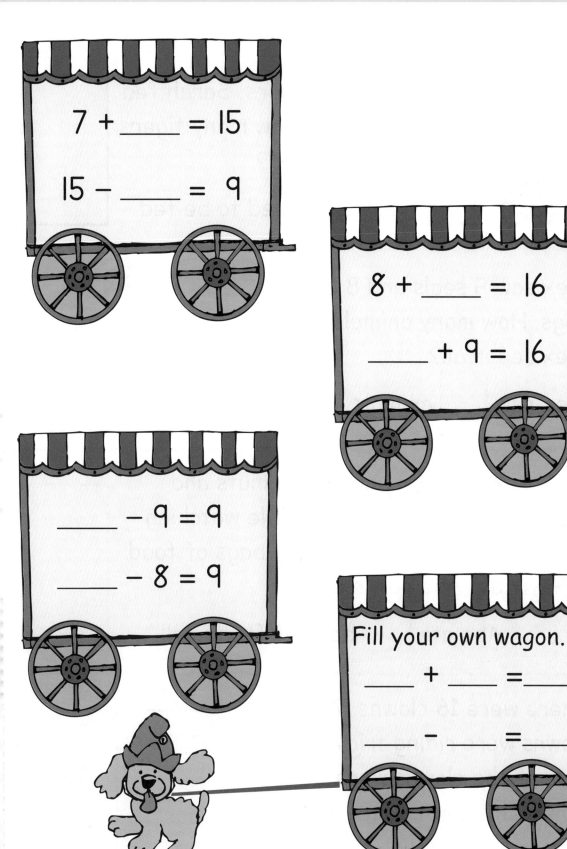

# A Day at the Circus

Note: You may need to help your child read the word problems.

There were 18 tigers. Sarah fed 9 of the tigers. How many tigers still need to be fed?

☐ tigers still need to be fed.

---

Alex saw 9 seals and 8 circus dogs. How many animals did Alex see in all?

Alex saw ☐ animals in all.

---

Abe ate 9 bags of peanuts and 5 bags of popcorn while watching the circus. How many bags of food did Abe eat in all?

Abe ate ☐ bags of food in all.

---

There were 16 clowns. 7 of the clowns were riding tricycles. The rest of the clowns were walking. How many clowns were walking?

There were ☐ clowns walking.

# How Many Centimeters?

**Skills:**

Measuring to the Nearest Centimeter

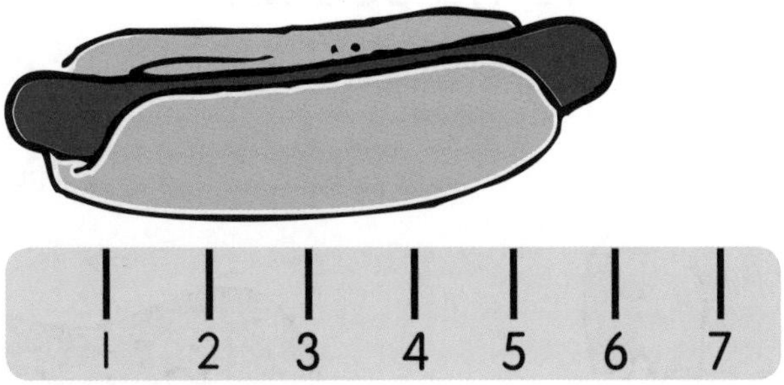


☐ centimeters

☐ centimeters

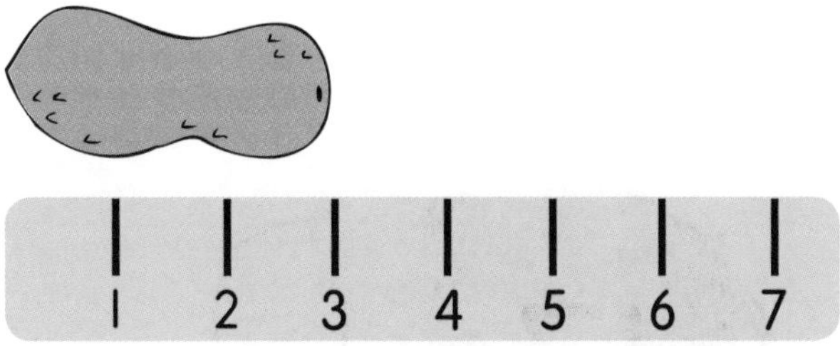


☐ centimeters

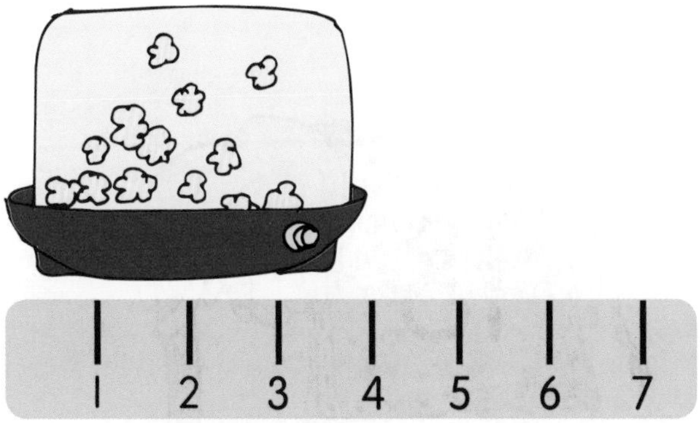


☐ centimeters

# Feed the Elephants

**Skills:**

Addition & Subtraction to 18

Match each elephant to its peanuts.

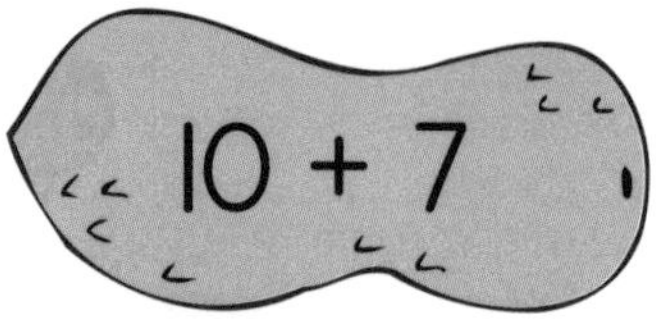

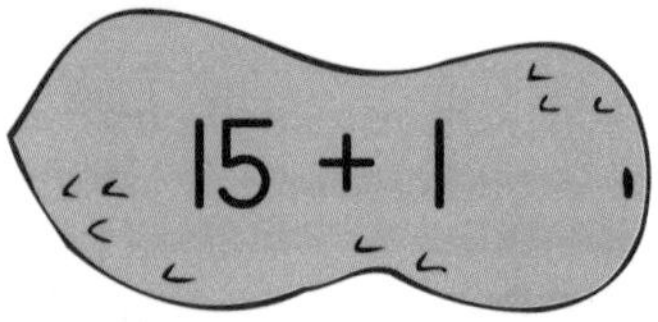


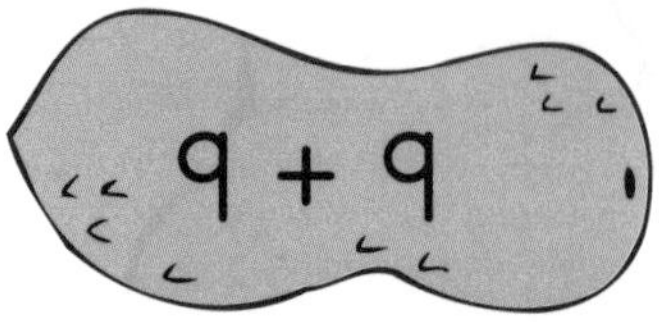


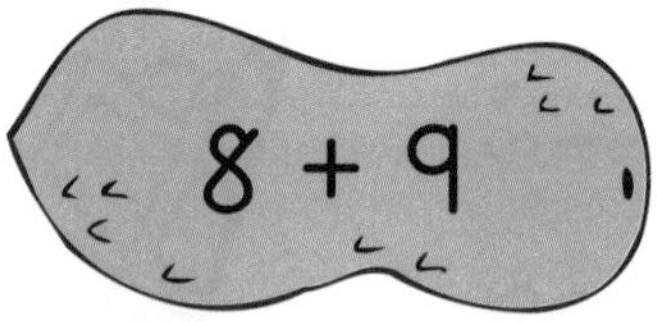


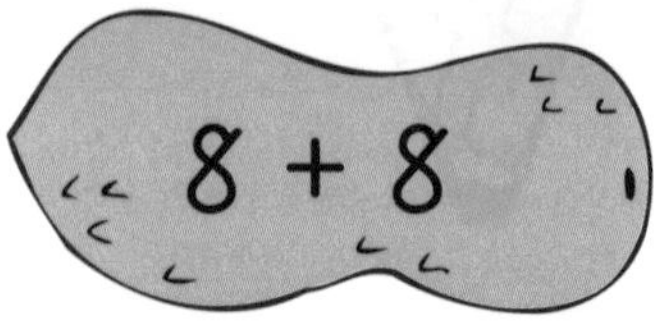


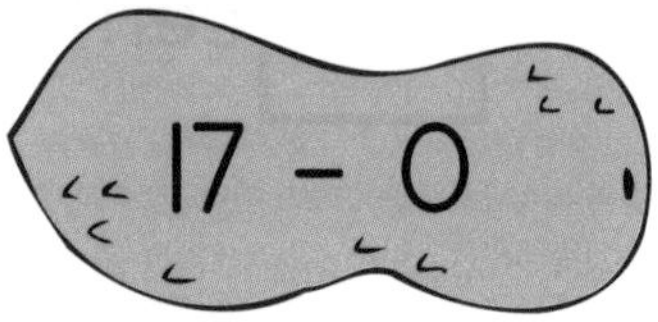


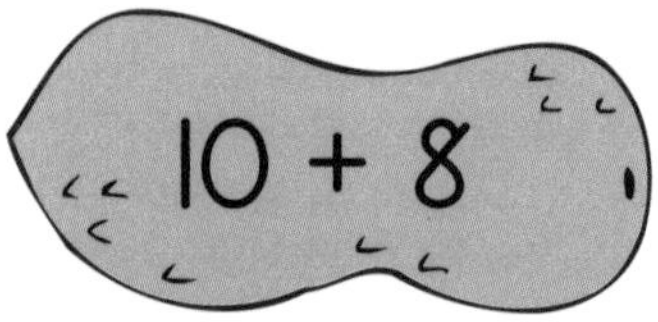


At the Circus

# When Is the Show?

**Skills:**

Telling Time to the Hour and Half Hour

At the Circus

Match the clocks to show when the circus shows begin.

# Which Is Larger?

**Skills:**

Fractions

Greater Than, Less Than

Name the fractions.
Write > or < in the circles.

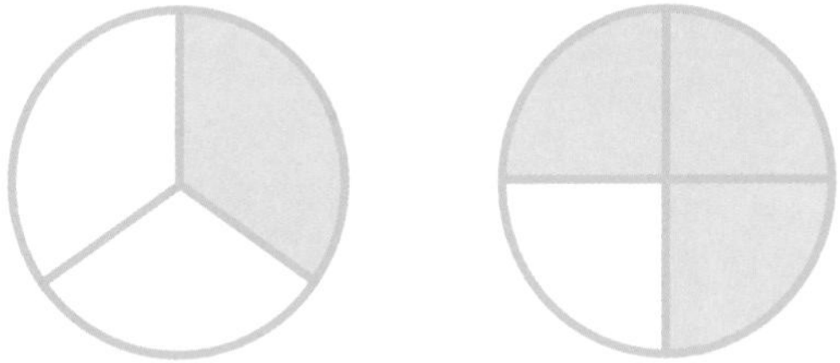

$\frac{1}{3}$ < $\frac{3}{4}$

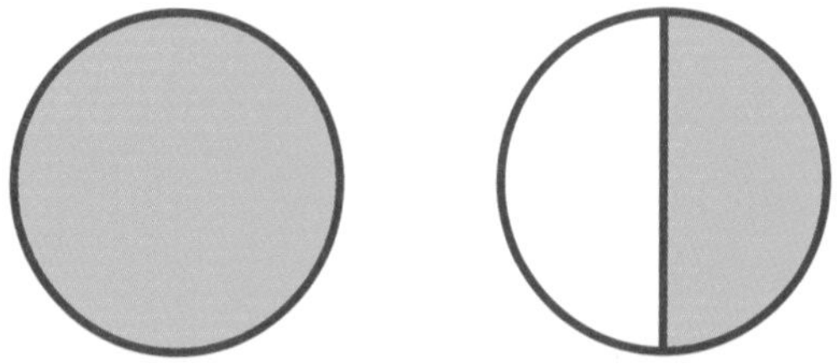

— ◯ —

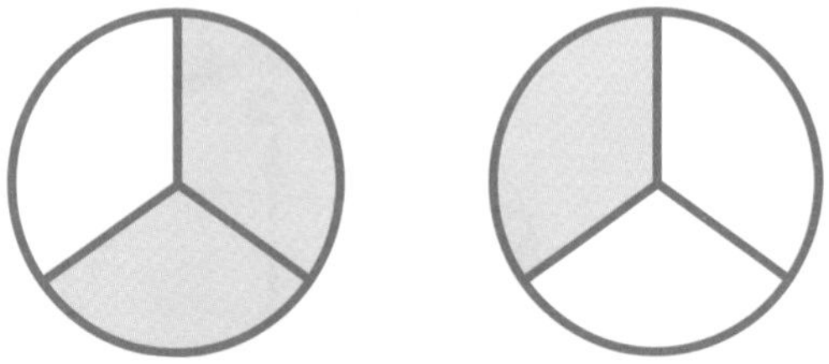

— ◯ —

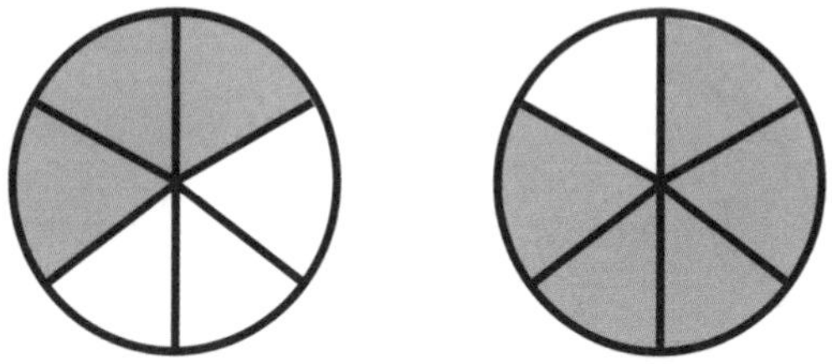

— ◯ —

Color to show the fraction.

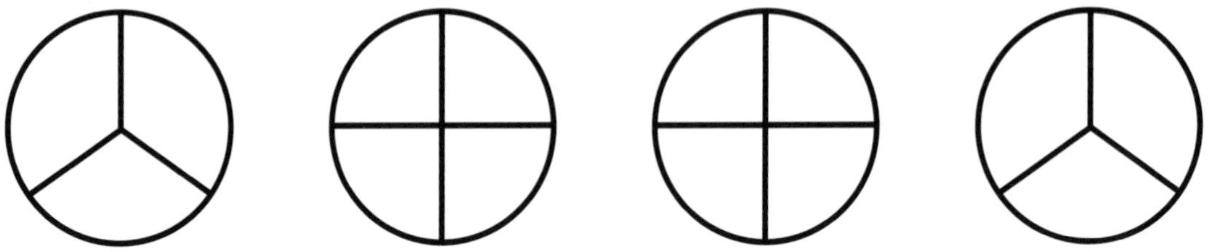

$\frac{1}{3}$ $\frac{1}{4}$ $\frac{2}{4}$ $\frac{2}{3}$

At the Circus

**Skills:**

Money—
Penny, Nickel, Dime

How much does each snack cost?

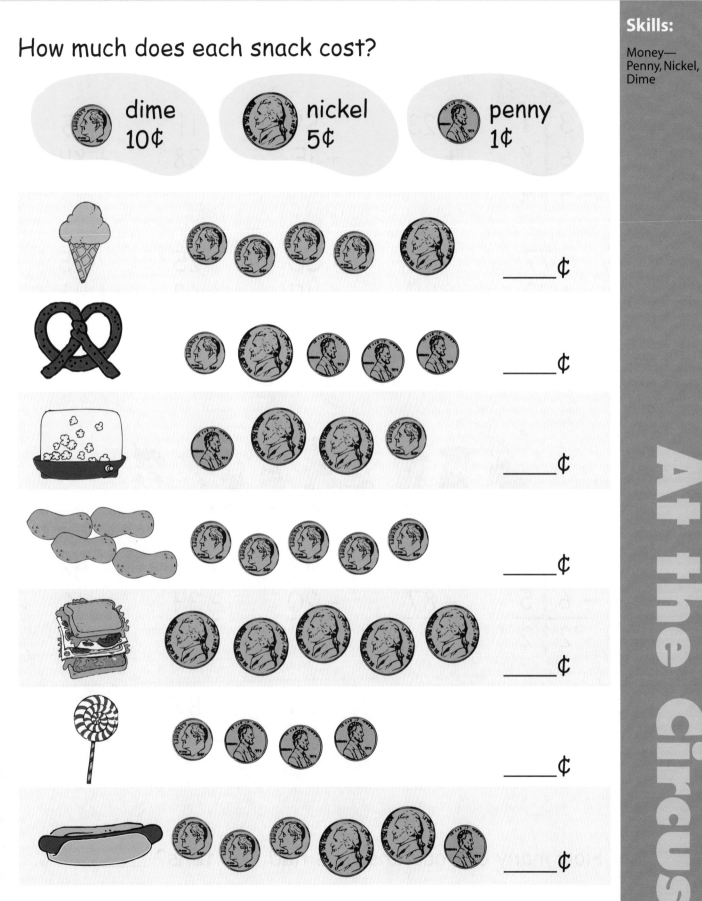

 dime 10¢

 nickel 5¢

 penny 1¢

_____¢

_____¢

_____¢

_____¢

_____¢

_____¢

_____¢

# Add and Subtract Tens and Ones

**Skills:**

Two-Digit Addition & Subtraction

Remember: Add the ones first.

| tens | ones |
|---|---|
| 3 | 1 |
| + 6 | 8 |
| 9 | 9 |

| | | | |
|---|---|---|---|
| 23 | 54 | 11 | 15 |
| + 72 | + 15 | + 38 | + 84 |

| | | | | |
|---|---|---|---|---|
| 77 | 34 | 50 | 25 | 45 |
| + 22 | + 44 | + 49 | + 63 | + 41 |

How many of your answers were the same? ______

| tens | ones |
|---|---|
| 8 | 7 |
| − 6 | 5 |
| 2 | 2 |

| | | | |
|---|---|---|---|
| 99 | 43 | 76 | 48 |
| − 87 | − 20 | − 34 | − 16 |

| | | | | |
|---|---|---|---|---|
| 79 | 80 | 79 | 87 | 22 |
| − 44 | − 40 | − 55 | − 10 | − 0 |

How many of your answers had two **tens**? ______

**Skills:**

Number Words

Place Value—Tens & Ones

Read the word. Write the number.

ten ______ four ______ eight ______

six ______ one ______ seven ______

Write the number word.

6 ________ 10 ________ 7 ________

Write the number.

☐ ten and ☐ ones = ☐

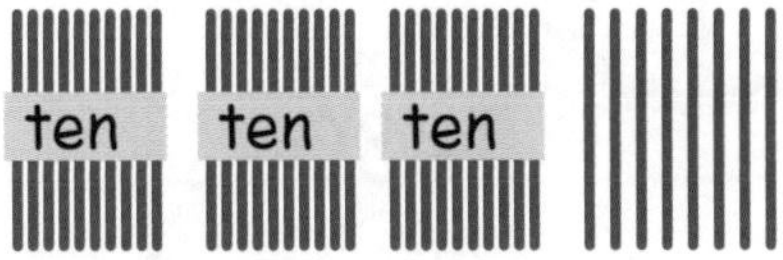


☐ tens and ☐ ones = ☐

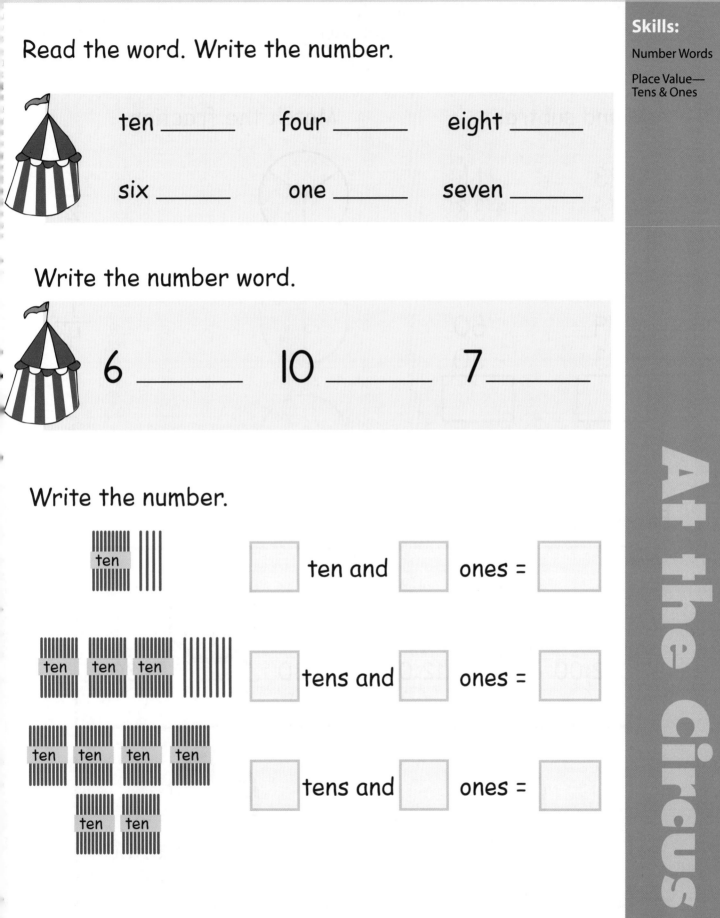

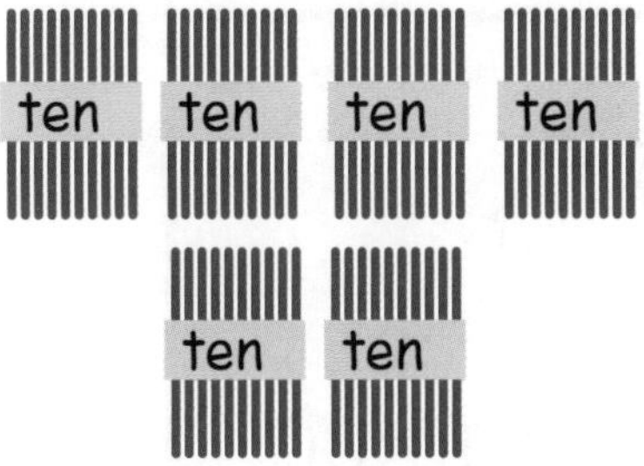


☐ tens and ☐ ones = ☐

Note: Use this assessment after your child has completed through page 113.

# TEST YOUR SKILLS

## Add and subtract.

$23 + 72 = \square$

$11 + 38 = \square$

$99 - 73 = \square$

$50 - 30 = \square$

## Match the fraction.

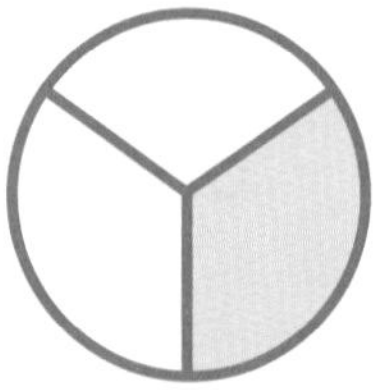

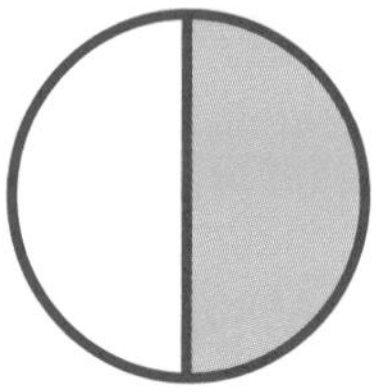

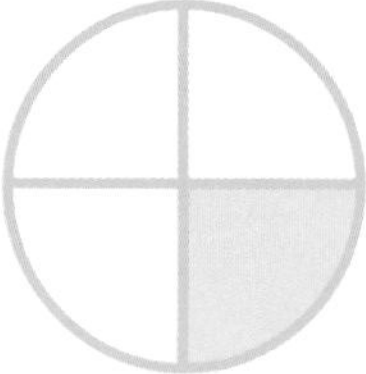

$\frac{1}{2}$

$\frac{1}{4}$

$\frac{1}{3}$

## Fill in the circle for the correct time.

2:00 ○ 12:00 ○

3:30 ○ 4:30 ○

8:30 ○ 6:30 ○

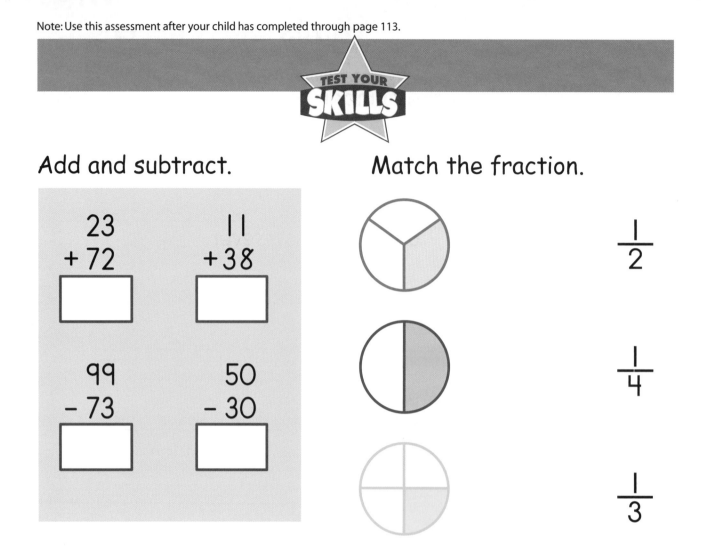

12:00 ○ 10:00 ○

**Skills:**

Addition & Subtraction to 18

Note: Unit 10 is a review of the skills practiced in Units 1 through 9.

Add and subtract.

Color the football with the largest answer brown.

| | | | |
|---|---|---|---|
| 9 − 5 | 8 + 6 | 17 − 8 | 6 + 4 |
| | 4 + 4 | 9 + 9 | 7 − 4 |
| 9 − 6 | 10 − 7 | 5 + 5 | 8 − 2 |
| 5 + 3 | | | 12 − 6 |

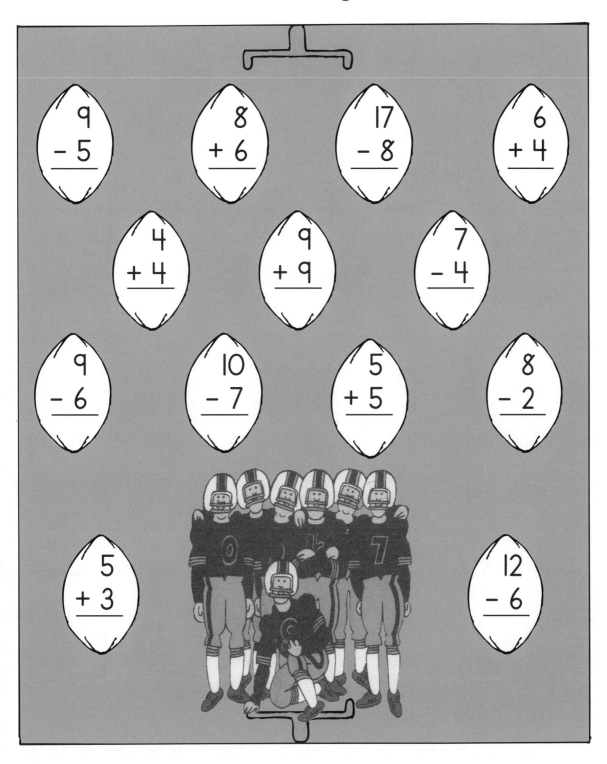

# Can You Buy It?

**Skills:**

Money—Penny, Nickel, Dime

Count your money. Circle **Yes** or **No**.

____¢

Yes No

____¢

Yes No

____¢

Yes No

____¢

Yes No

Be a Sport

Skills:

Column Addition

Use the numbers on the tennis balls to complete each problem.

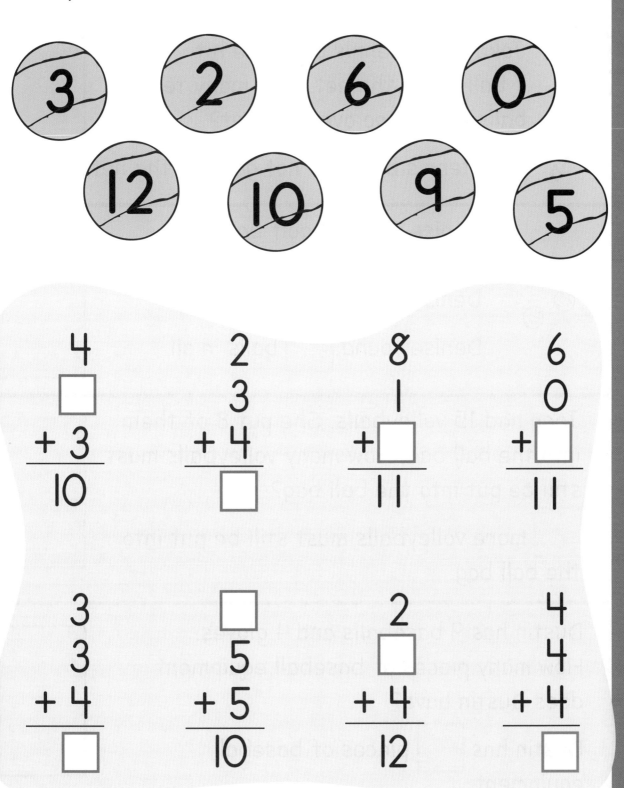

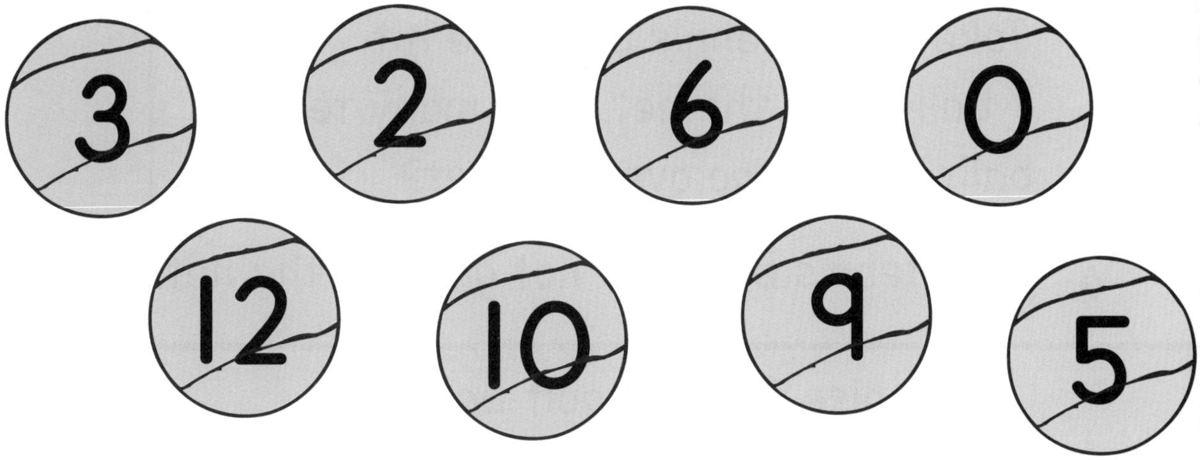


| | | | |
|---|---|---|---|
| 4 | 2 | 8 | 6 |
| ☐ | 3 | 1 | 0 |
| + 3 | + 4 | + ☐ | + ☐ |
| 10 | ☐ | 11 | 11 |

| | | | |
|---|---|---|---|
| 3 | ☐ | 2 | 4 |
| 3 | 5 | ☐ | 4 |
| + 4 | + 5 | + 4 | + 4 |
| ☐ | 10 | 12 | ☐ |

Be a Sport

# Play Ball!

**Skills:**

Word Problems: Addition and Subtraction

Note: You may need to help your child read the word problems.

Write the problems. Answer them.

Jake hit 16 tennis balls. He hit 7 balls over the net. How many tennis balls did **not** go over the net?

☐ tennis balls did **not** go over the net.

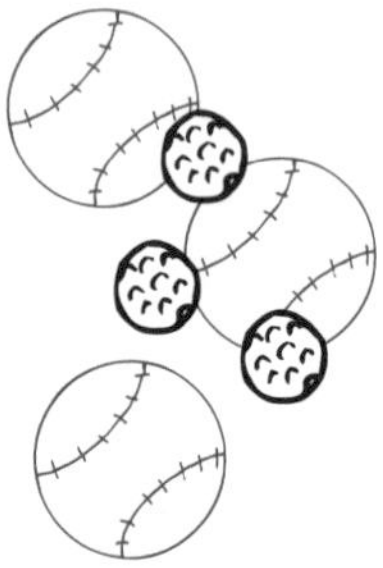

Denise found 8 golf balls and 6 baseballs. How many balls did Denise find in all?

Denise found ☐ balls in all.

Jean had 15 volleyballs. She put 8 of them into the ball bag. How many volleyballs must still be put into the ball bag?

☐ more volleyballs must still be put into the ball bag.

Dustin has 9 baseballs and 4 gloves. How many pieces of baseball equipment does Dustin have?

Dustin has ☐ pieces of baseball equipment.

**Skills:**
Addition & Subtraction to 18

Match the balls and gloves.

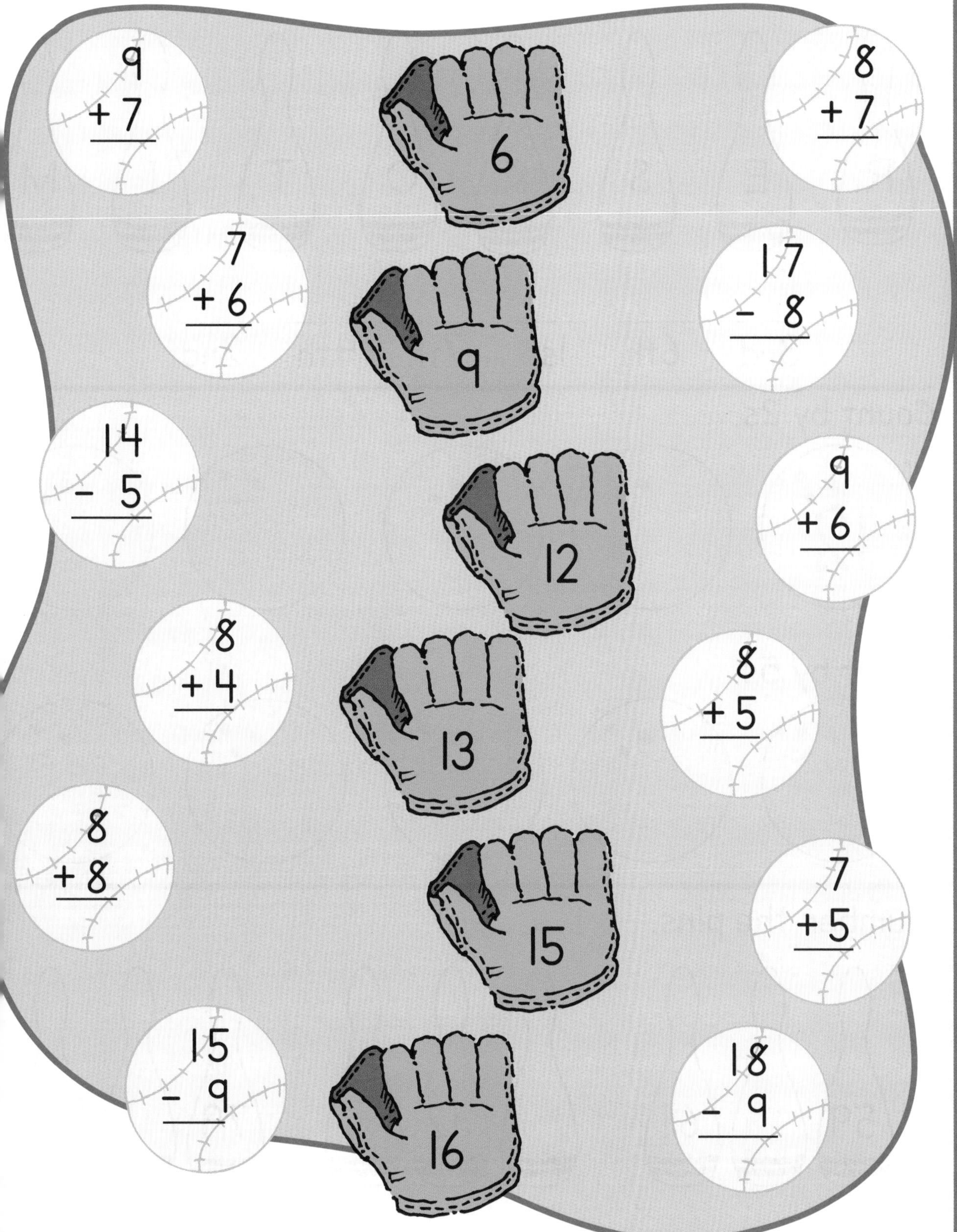

# Knock Them Down!

**Skills:**

Ordinal Numbers

Counting by 2s and 5s

Number Order

What's the bowling word?

Write the letter that goes with the number.

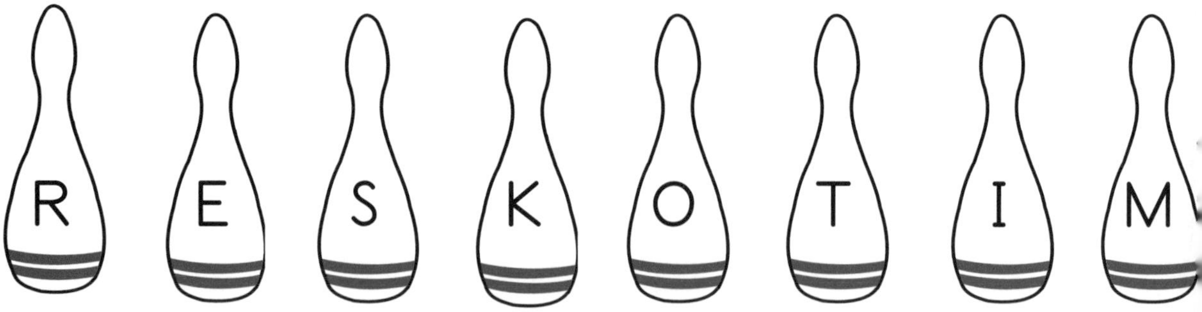


____ ____ ____ ____ ____ ____!

3rd 6th 1st 7th 4th 2nd

Count by 2s.

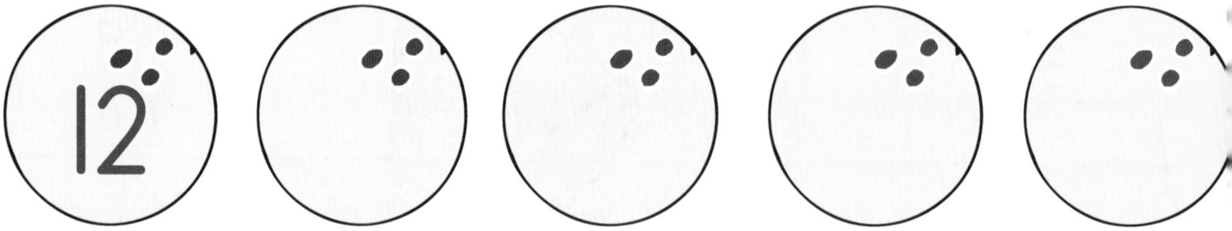


Count by 5s.

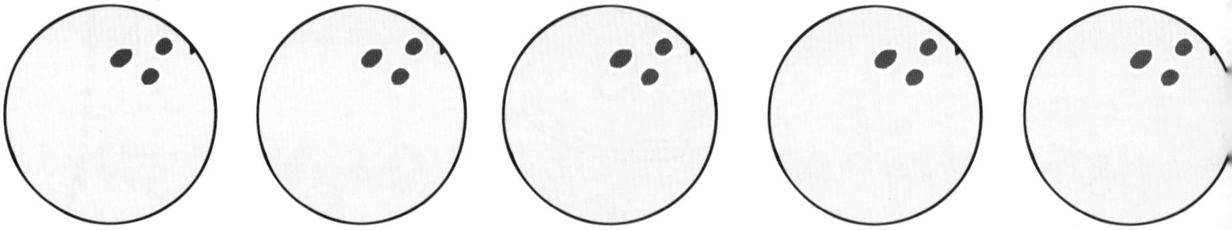

Number the pins.

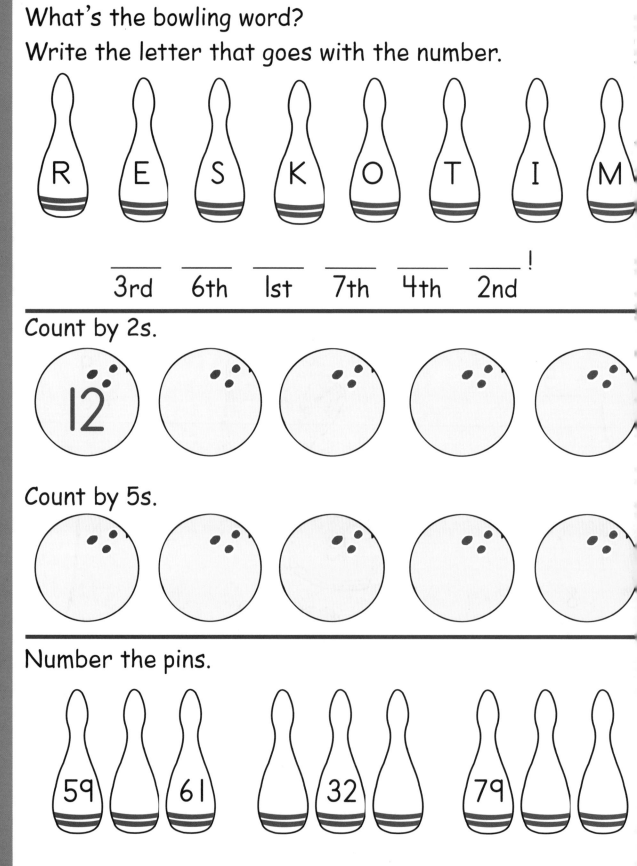

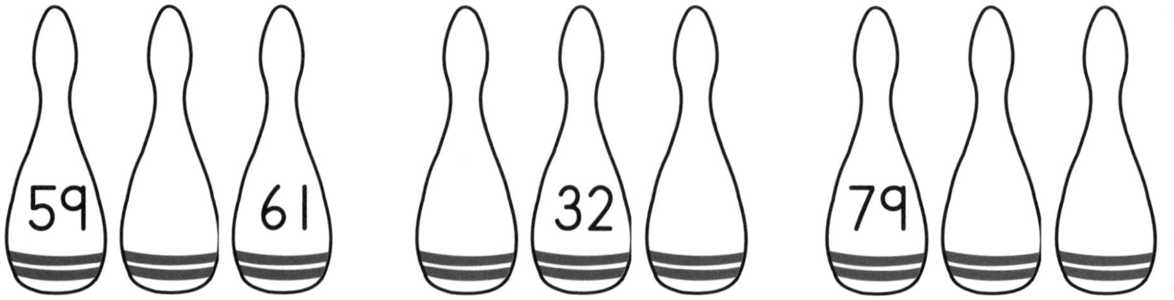


Be a Sport

**Skills:**

Fractions

Identifying Geometric Shapes

Circle the correct answers.

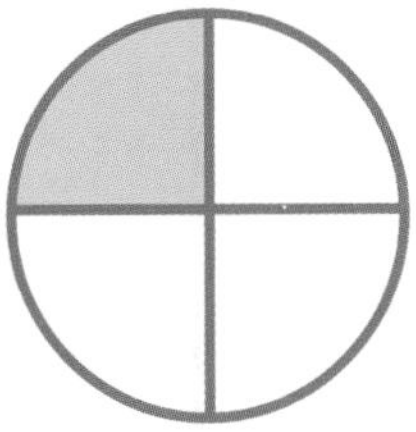

$\frac{1}{2}$ $\frac{1}{4}$

$\frac{1}{2}$ $\frac{1}{4}$

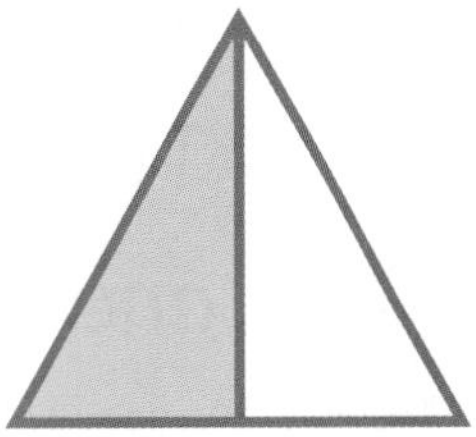

$\frac{1}{2}$ $\frac{1}{4}$

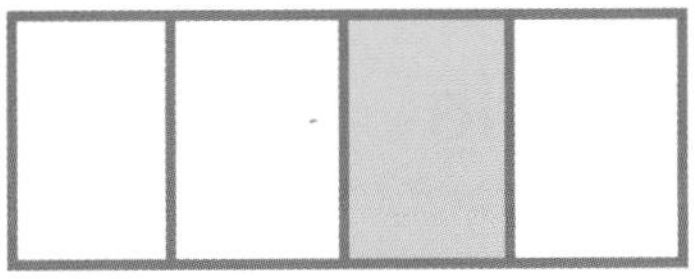

$\frac{1}{2}$ $\frac{1}{4}$

$\frac{1}{2}$ $\frac{1}{4}$

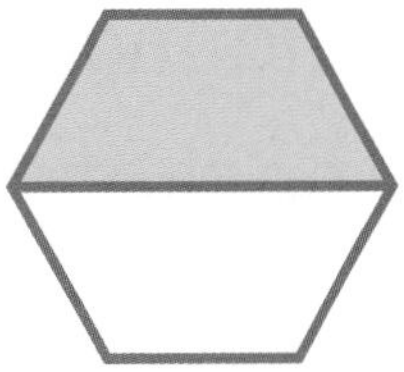

$\frac{1}{2}$ $\frac{1}{4}$

Find and mark the shapes.

# Sports for Everyone

**Skills:**

Word Problems: Addition

Note: You may need to help your child read the word problems.

Write the problems. Answer them.

The store has 23 baseball caps and 15 football helmets. How many caps and helmets are there in all?

There are ☐ caps and helmets in all.

---

Sheila made 33 baskets. Julie made 46 baskets. How many baskets did Sheila and Julie make in all?

Sheila and Julie made ☐ baskets in all.

---

Quinn shot 19 arrows at a round target. Then he shot 30 arrows at a square target. How many arrows did he shoot in all?

Quinn shot ☐ arrows in all.

---

Damian ran 14 laps this morning and 12 laps this afternoon. How many laps did Damian run in all?

Damian ran ☐ laps in all.

# Measure Inches and Centimeters

**Skills:**

Measuring to the Nearest Inch and Centimeter

Cut out the rulers. Measure the items.

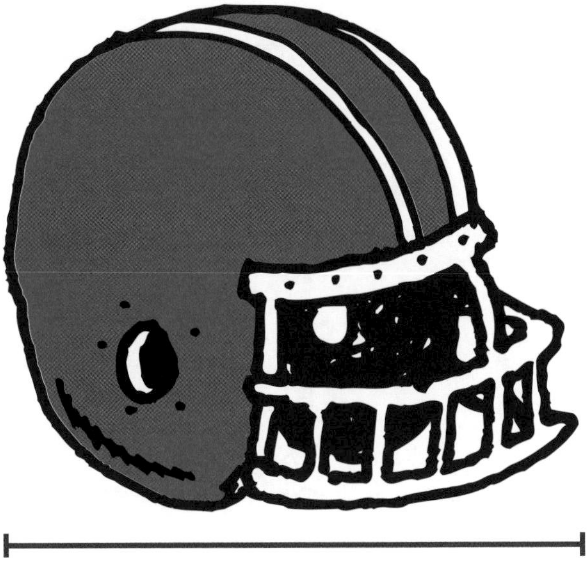

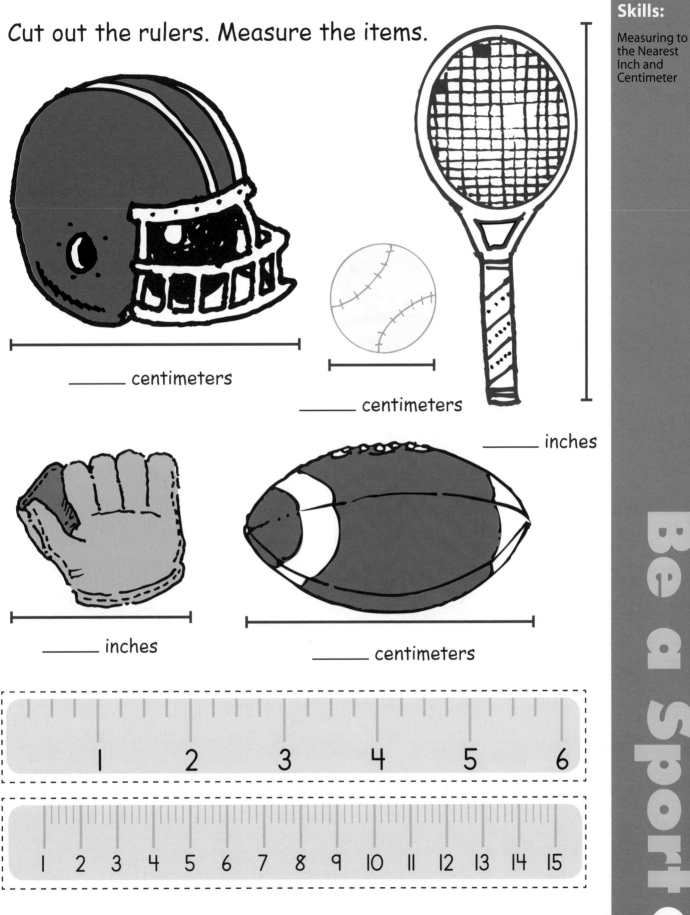

_____ centimeters

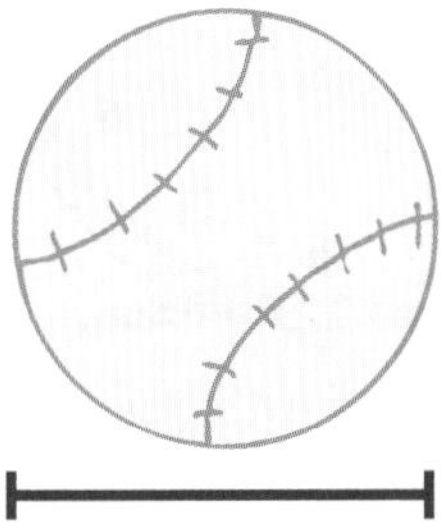

_____ centimeters

_____ inches

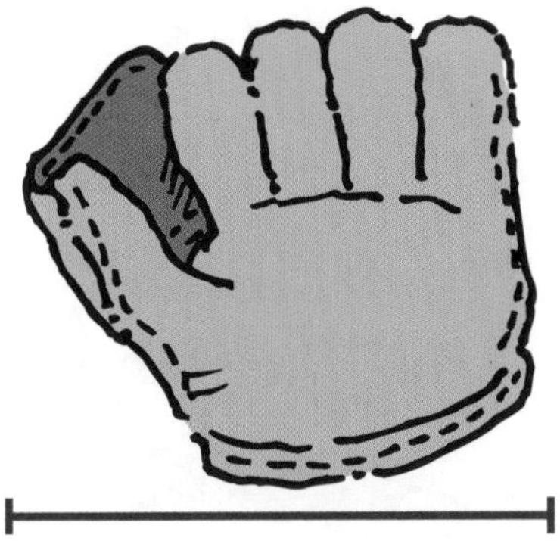

_____ inches

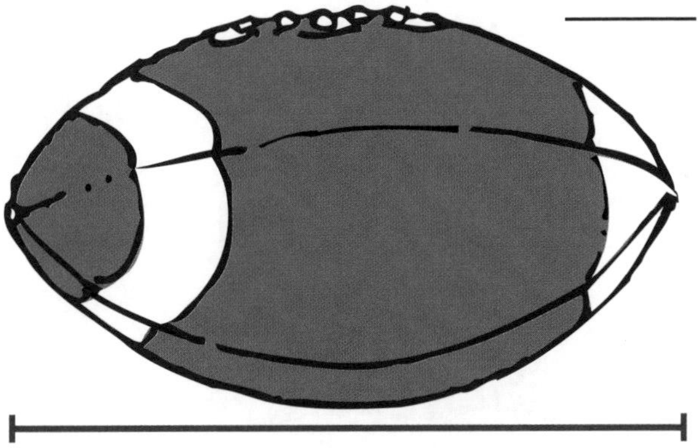

_____ centimeters

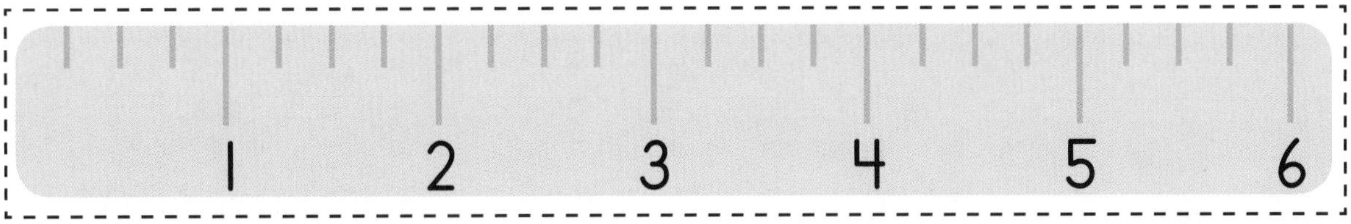


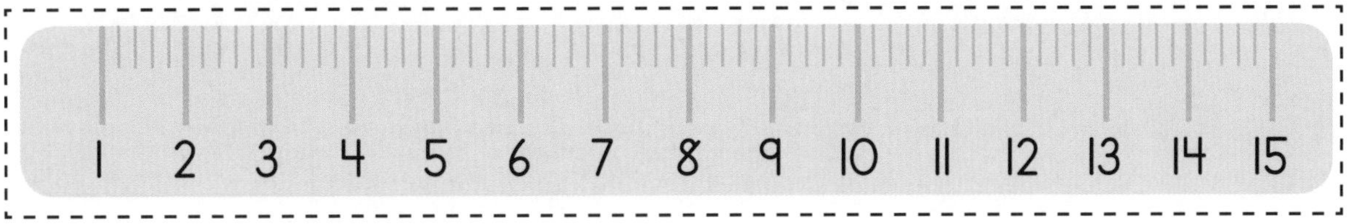


Be a Sport

# Let the Games Begin!

**Skills:**

Telling Time to the Half Hour

Write or show the time each game starts.

## Soccer Game

___ : ___

## Baseball Game

___ : ___

## Football Game

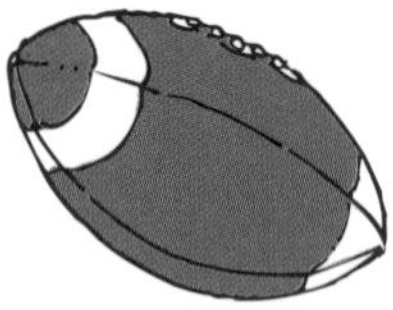

12:00

## Tennis Match

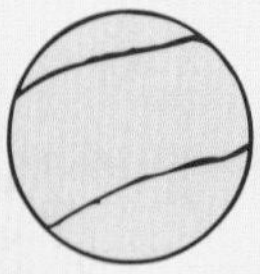

9:00

Be a Sport

# At the Sports Store

**Skills:**

Reading a Graph

Read the graph. Answer the questions.

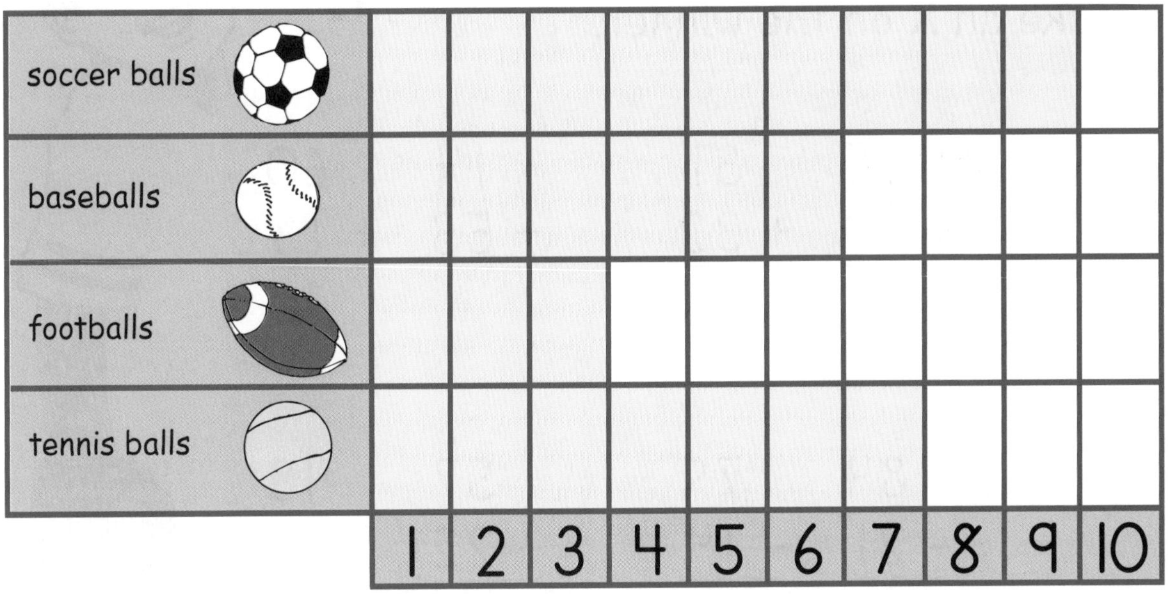


How many?

Write a statement about the graph.

______________________________

Write a question about the graph.

______________________________

# Who Won?

**Skills:**

Two-Digit Addition & Subtraction

Counting by 10s

The larger number wins.
Make an X on the winner.

$$\begin{array}{r} 25 \\ +43 \\ \hline \end{array} \qquad \begin{array}{r} 31 \\ +32 \\ \hline \end{array}$$

$$\begin{array}{r} 14 \\ +53 \\ \hline \end{array} \qquad \begin{array}{r} 60 \\ +13 \\ \hline \end{array}$$

$$\begin{array}{r} 84 \\ -21 \\ \hline \end{array} \qquad \begin{array}{r} 79 \\ -14 \\ \hline \end{array}$$

$$\begin{array}{r} 57 \\ -22 \\ \hline \end{array} \qquad \begin{array}{r} 48 \\ -16 \\ \hline \end{array}$$

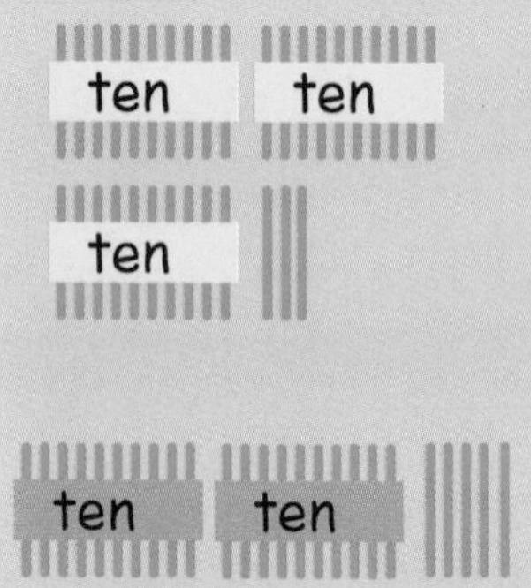


= ______

= ______

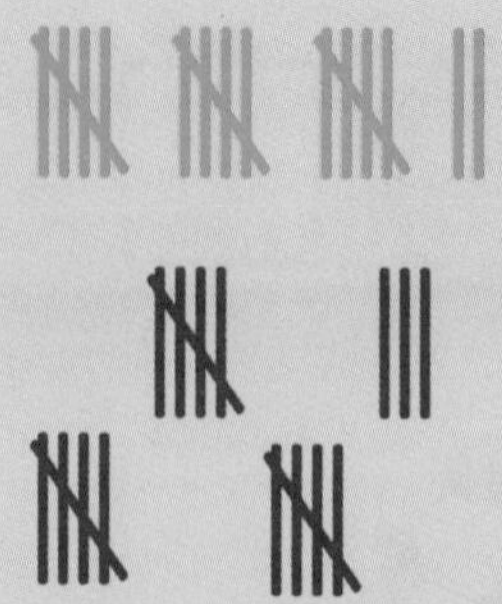

= ______

= ______

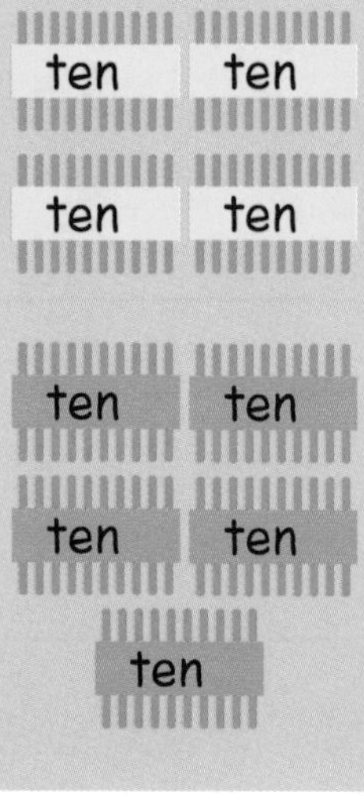


= ______

= ______

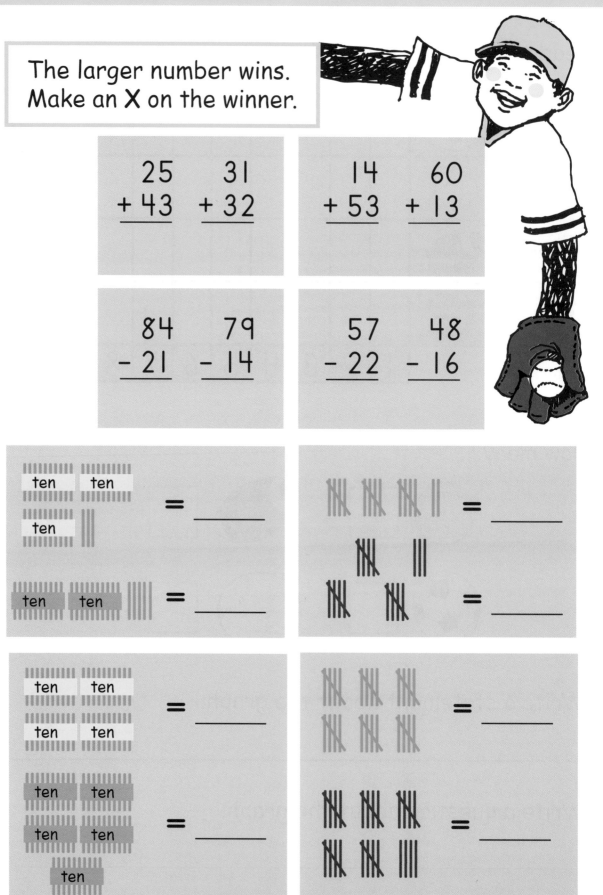

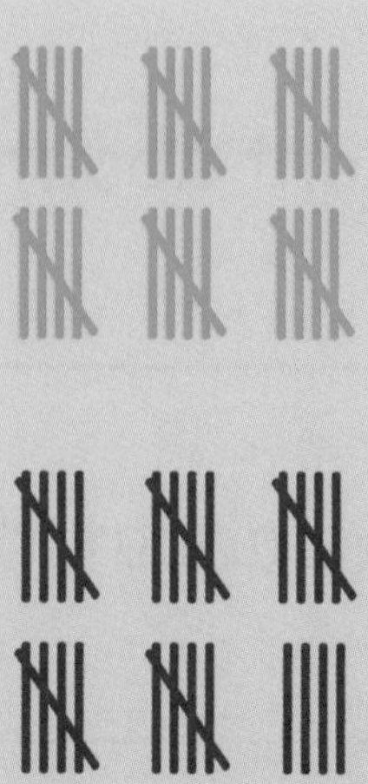

= ______

= ______

Be a Sport

Note: Use this assessment after your child has completed through page 126.

# TEST YOUR SKILLS

Add or subtract.

15 − 6 = ☐

10 − 7 = ☐

| 11 | 8 | 9 |
|---|---|---|
| − 0 | + 6 | − 9 |
| ☐ | ☐ | ☐ |

| 26 | 38 | 47 | 55 | 91 |
|---|---|---|---|---|
| + 3 | − 16 | −34 | +34 | −80 |
| ☐ | ☐ | ☐ | ☐ | ☐ |

| 5 | 2 | 15 |
|---|---|---|
| ☐ | 3 | − ☐ |
| + 2 | + 4 | 8 |
| 8 | ☐ | |

8 + 4 = ☐

☐ + 8 = 12

Count by ones.

**25,** ____, ____, ____, ____, ____, ____

Count by tens.

**30,** ____, ____, ____, ____, ____

Count by fives.

**55,** ____, ____, ____, ____, ____, ____

# TEST YOUR SKILLS

○ the 9th ★. □ the 3rd ★. X the 6th ★.

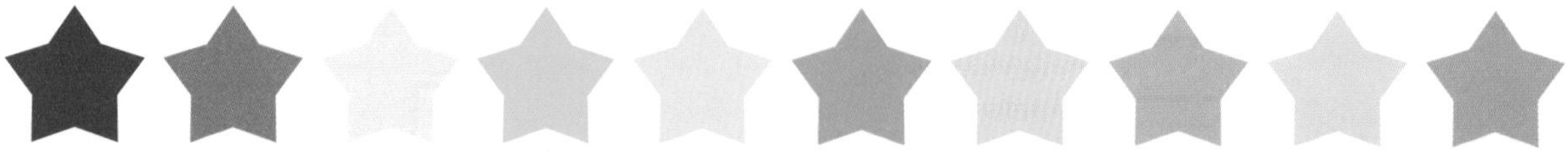

Draw the shapes. Cut each shape in $\frac{1}{2}$.

square circle triangle rectangle

Write the time.

_____:_____ _____:_____

How much money?

_______¢

_______¢

Liz made 9 cherry pies and 7 apples pies. How many pies did Liz make?

Liz made □ pies.

Adam caught 15 bugs. 6 bugs got out of the jar. How many bugs does Adam have?

Adam has □ bugs.

# Tracking Form

| Topic | Color in each page you complete. | | | | | | |
|---|---|---|---|---|---|---|---|
| Gone to the Dogs | 3 | 4 | 5 | 6 | 7 | 8 | 9 |
| | 10 | 11 | 12 | 13 | 14 | | |
| On the Farm | 15 | 16 | 17 | 18 | 19 | 20 | 21 |
| | 22 | 23 | 24 | 25 | 26 | 27 | |
| Bears Everywhere | 28 | 29 | 30 | 31 | 32 | 33 | 34 |
| | 35 | 36 | 37 | 38 | 39 | | |
| Creepy Crawlies | 40 | 41 | 42 | 43 | 44 | 45 | 46 |
| | 47 | 48 | 49 | 50 | 51 | 52 | |
| At the Zoo | 53 | 54 | 55 | 56 | 57 | 58 | 59 |
| | 60 | 61 | 62 | 63 | 64 | | |
| Camping | 65 | 66 | 67 | 68 | 69 | 70 | 71 |
| | 72 | 73 | 74 | 75 | 76 | 77 | |
| Fruity Fun | 78 | 79 | 80 | 81 | 82 | 83 | 84 |
| | 85 | 86 | 87 | 88 | 89 | | |
| Chilly Capers | 90 | 91 | 92 | 93 | 94 | 95 | 96 |
| | 97 | 98 | 99 | 100 | 101 | 102 | |
| At the Circus | 103 | 104 | 105 | 106 | 107 | 108 | 109 |
| | 110 | 111 | 112 | 113 | 114 | | |
| Be a Sport | 115 | 116 | 117 | 118 | 119 | 120 | 121 |
| | 122 | 123 | 124 | 125 | 126 | 127 | 128 |

Red numbers indicate Test Your Skills pages.

# Answer Key

## Page 3

Numbers 0, 1, 2

Trace.

0 0 0 0 0 0

1 1 1 1 1 1

2 2 2 2 2 2

Count the dogs. Write the numbers.

2 1 0

1 0 2

Gone to the Dogs

©2001 by Evan-Moor Corp. • Math Practice at Home • EMC 4516 Writing & Counting 0–2 3

## Page 4

Numbers 3, 4, 5

Trace.

3 3 3 3 3 3

4 4 4 4 4 4

5 5 5 5 5 5

Count the dogs. Match the dogs to their doghouses.

3 4 5

Gone to the Dogs

4 Writing & Counting 3–5 ©2001 by Evan-Moor Corp. • Math Practice at Home • EMC 4516

## Page 5

Numbers 6, 7, 8

Trace.

6 6 6 6 6 6

7 7 7 7 7 7

8 8 8 8 8 8

Draw the bones.

six bones eight bones

Circle the larger number on each bone.

6 (8) (8) 7 (7) 6 6 (7)

Gone to the Dogs

©2001 by Evan-Moor Corp. • Math Practice at Home • EMC 4516 Writing & Counting 6–8 5

## Page 6

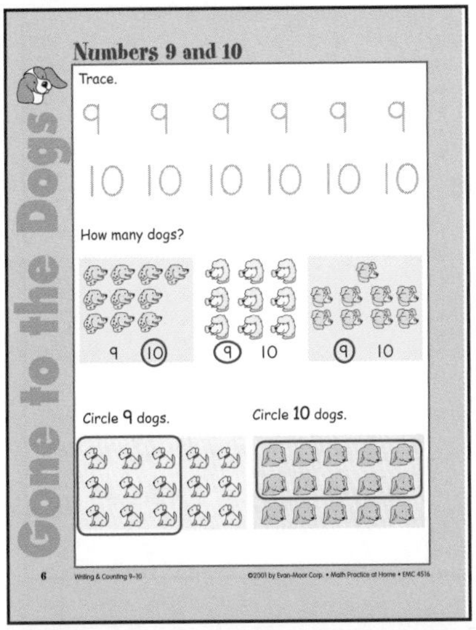

Numbers 9 and 10

Trace.

9 9 9 9 9 9

10 10 10 10 10 10

How many dogs?

9 (10) (9) 10 (9) 10

Circle 9 dogs. Circle 10 dogs.

Gone to the Dogs

6 Writing & Counting 9–10 ©2001 by Evan-Moor Corp. • Math Practice at Home • EMC 4516

## Page 7

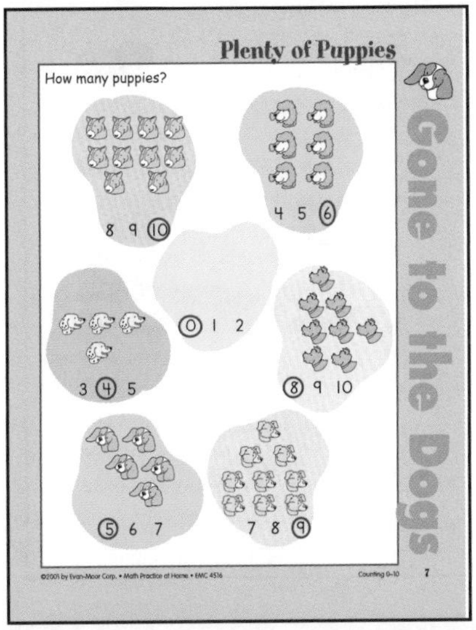

Plenty of Puppies

How many puppies?

8 9 (10) 4 5 (6)

(0) 1 2

3 (4) 5 (8) 9 10

(5) 6 7 7 8 (9)

Gone to the Dogs

©2001 by Evan-Moor Corp. • Math Practice at Home • EMC 4516 Counting 0–10 7

## Page 8

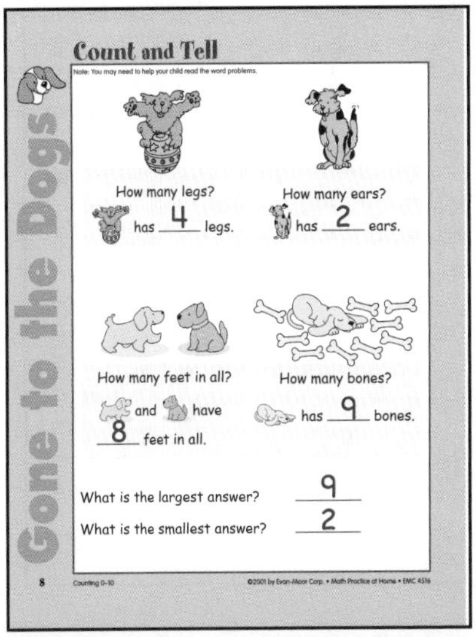

Count and Tell

Note: You may need to help your child read the word problems.

How many legs? has 4 legs.

How many ears? has 2 ears.

How many feet in all? and have 8 feet in all.

How many bones? has 9 bones.

What is the largest answer? 9

What is the smallest answer? 2

Gone to the Dogs

8 Counting 0–10 ©2001 by Evan-Moor Corp. • Math Practice at Home • EMC 4516

## Page 9

Match and Count

Note: You may need to help your child read the word problems.

4 bones were used.

6 doghouses were used.

5 cans of food were used.

3 balls were used.

What is the largest number of things used? 6

What is the smallest number of things used? 3

Gone to the Dogs

©2001 by Evan-Moor Corp. • Math Practice at Home • EMC 4516 One-to-One Correspondence 9

## Page 10

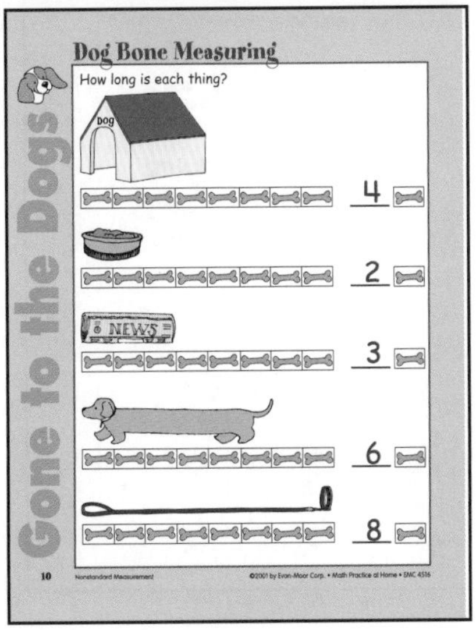

Dog Bone Measuring

How long is each thing?

DOG

4

2

NEWS

3

6

8

Gone to the Dogs

10 Nonstandard Measurement ©2001 by Evan-Moor Corp. • Math Practice at Home • EMC 4516

## Page 11

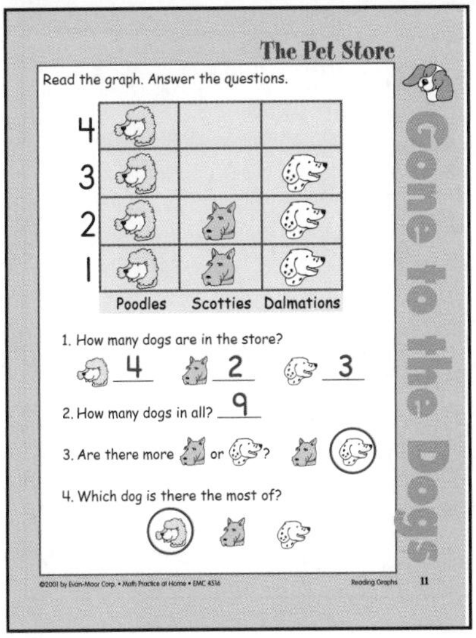

The Pet Store

Read the graph. Answer the questions.

4 3 2 1

Poodles Scotties Dalmations

1. How many dogs are in the store? 4 2 3

2. How many dogs in all? 9

3. Are there more or ?

4. Which dog is there the most of?

Gone to the Dogs

©2001 by Evan-Moor Corp. • Math Practice at Home • EMC 4516 Reading Graphs 11

## Page 12

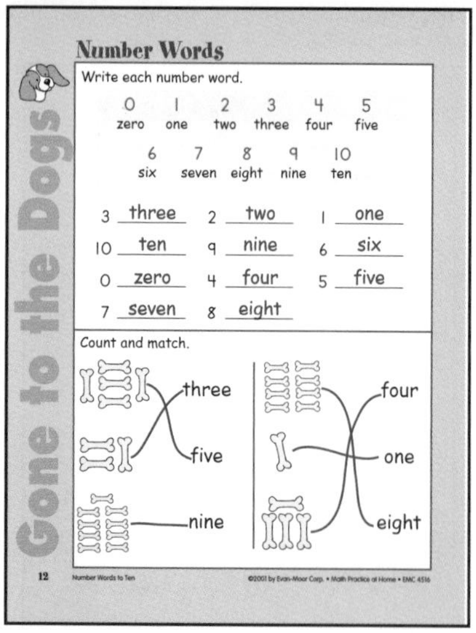
Number Words

Write each number word.

0 zero, 1 one, 2 two, 3 three, 4 four, 5 five, 6 six, 7 seven, 8 eight, 9 nine, 10 ten

3 three 2 two 1 one
10 ten 9 nine 6 six
0 zero 4 four 5 five
7 seven 8 eight

Count and match.

three five nine four one eight

Gone to the Dogs

12 Number Words to Ten ©2001 by Evan-Moor Corp. • Math Practice at Home • EMC 4516

## Page 13

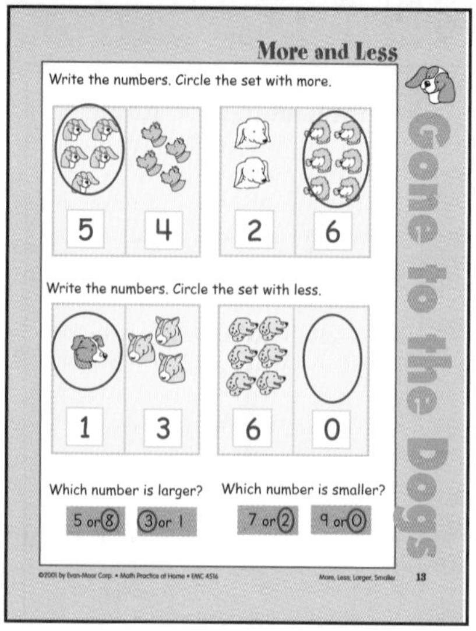
More and Less

Write the numbers. Circle the set with more.

5 4 2 6

Write the numbers. Circle the set with less.

1 3 6 0

Which number is larger? 5 or (8) (3) or 1

Which number is smaller? 7 or (2) 9 or (0)

Gone to the Dogs

©2001 by Evan-Moor Corp. • Math Practice at Home • EMC 4516 More, Less, Larger, Smaller 13

## Page 14

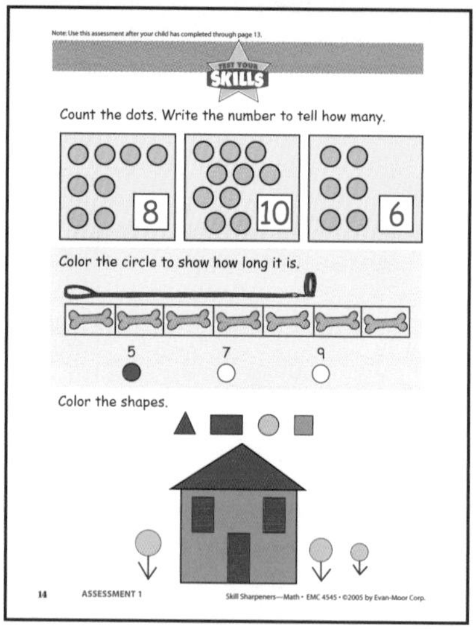
Note: Use this assessment after your child has completed through page 13.

TEST YOUR SKILLS

Count the dots. Write the number to tell how many.

8 10 6

Color the circle to show how long it is.

5 7 9

Color the shapes.

14 ASSESSMENT 1 Skill Sharpeners—Math • EMC 4545 • ©2005 by Evan-Moor Corp.

## Page 15

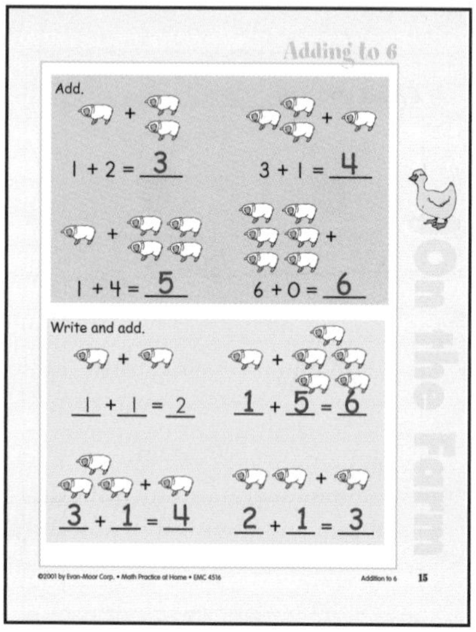
Adding to 6

Add.

1 + 2 = 3 3 + 1 = 4
1 + 4 = 5 6 + 0 = 6

Write and add.

1 + 1 = 2 1 + 5 = 6
3 + 1 = 4 2 + 1 = 3

On the Farm

©2001 by Evan-Moor Corp. • Math Practice at Home • EMC 4516 Addition to 6 15

## Page 16

What Do You See?

Add. Color.

3 = yellow 5 = brown 2 = pink 4 = green 6 = blue

5 + 1 1 + 2 3 + 2 3 + 1 2 + 3 1 + 4 2 + 2

Add.

2 + 4 = 6 3 + 2 = 5 4 + 0 = 4
3 + 3 = 6 1 + 5 = 6 4 + 1 = 5

On the Farm

16 Addition to 6 ©2001 by Evan-Moor Corp. • Math Practice at Home • EMC 4516

## Page 17

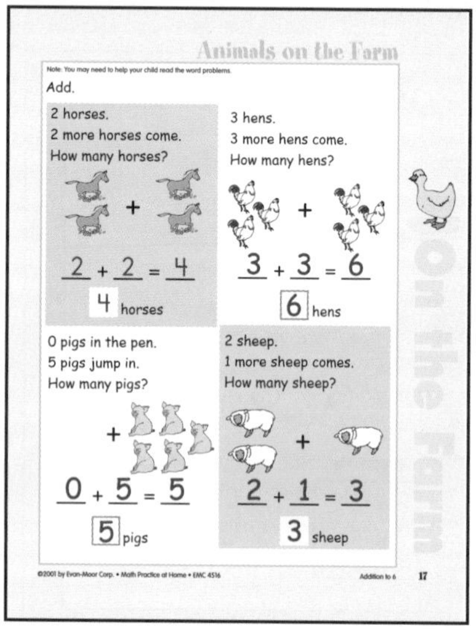
Animals on the Farm

Note: You may need to help your child read the word problems.

Add.

2 horses. 2 more horses come. How many horses? 2 + 2 = 4 4 horses

3 hens. 3 more hens come. How many hens? 3 + 3 = 6 6 hens

0 pigs in the pen. 5 pigs jump in. How many pigs? 0 + 5 = 5 5 pigs

2 sheep. 1 more sheep comes. How many sheep? 2 + 1 = 3 3 sheep

On the Farm

©2001 by Evan-Moor Corp. • Math Practice at Home • EMC 4516 Addition to 6 17

## Page 18

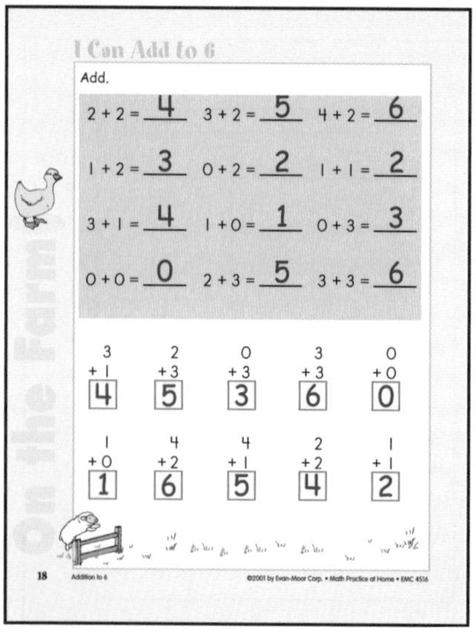
I Can Add to 6

Add.

2 + 2 = 4 3 + 2 = 5 4 + 2 = 6
1 + 2 = 3 0 + 2 = 2 1 + 1 = 2
3 + 1 = 4 1 + 0 = 1 0 + 3 = 3
0 + 0 = 0 2 + 3 = 5 3 + 3 = 6

3 + 1 = 4; 2 + 3 = 5; 0 + 3 = 3; 3 + 3 = 6; 0 + 0 = 0
1 + 0 = 1; 4 + 2 = 6; 4 + 1 = 5; 2 + 2 = 4; 1 + 1 = 2

On the Farm

18 Addition to 6 ©2001 by Evan-Moor Corp. • Math Practice at Home • EMC 4516

## Page 19

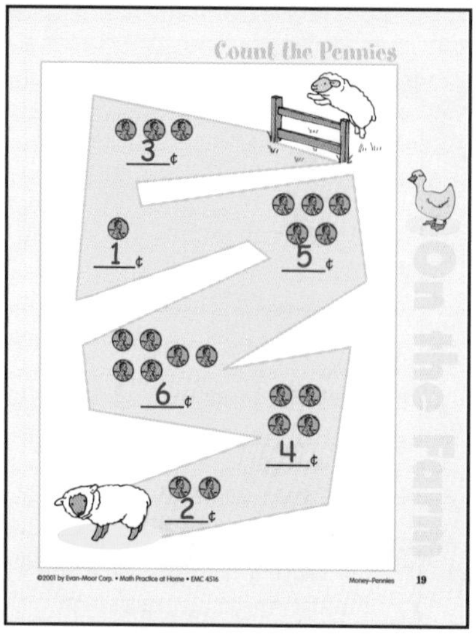
Count the Pennies

3¢ 1¢ 5¢ 6¢ 4¢ 2¢

On the Farm

©2001 by Evan-Moor Corp. • Math Practice at Home • EMC 4516 Money–Pennies 19

## Page 20

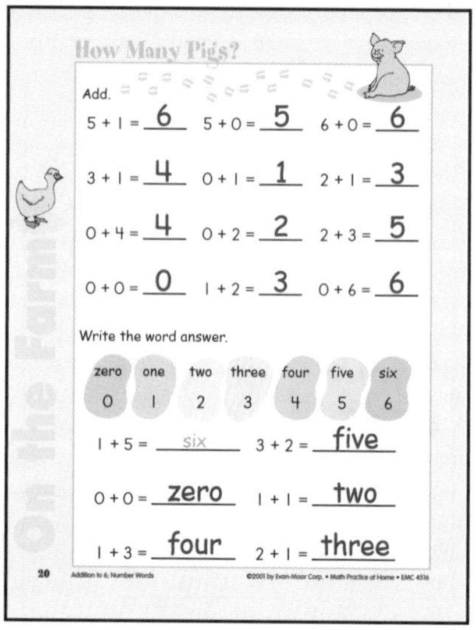
How Many Pigs?

Add.

5 + 1 = 6 5 + 0 = 5 6 + 0 = 6
3 + 1 = 4 0 + 1 = 1 2 + 1 = 3
0 + 4 = 4 0 + 2 = 2 2 + 3 = 5
0 + 0 = 0 1 + 2 = 3 0 + 6 = 6

Write the word answer.

zero 0, one 1, two 2, three 3, four 4, five 5, six 6

1 + 5 = six 3 + 2 = five
0 + 0 = zero 1 + 1 = two
1 + 3 = four 2 + 1 = three

On the Farm

20 Addition to 6; Number Words ©2001 by Evan-Moor Corp. • Math Practice at Home • EMC 4516

## Page 21

### Farm Animals Everywhere

Note: You may need to help your child read the word problems.

Add.

4 hens.
1 more hen comes.
How many hens?

4 + 1 = 5

5 hens

1 cow.
3 more cows come.
How many cows?

1 + 3 = 4

4 cows

2 chicks.
1 more chick comes.
How many chicks?

2 + 1 = 3

3 chicks

2 donkeys.
3 more donkeys come.
How many donkeys?

2 + 3 = 5

5 donkeys

On the Farm

©2001 by Evan-Moor Corp. • Math Practice at Home • EMC 4516 Addition to 6 21

## Page 22

### Pigs and Sheep

Tell how many.

1. (sheep) in the ◯? 4
2. (pig) in the ☐? 4
3. (sheep) in both the ◯ and the ☐? 1
4. (pig) in both the ◯ and the ☐? 2
5. (sheep) in the ☐ but not in the ◯? 2

On the Farm

22 Counting; Venn Diagram ©2001 by Evan-Moor Corp. • Math Practice at Home • EMC 4516

## Page 23

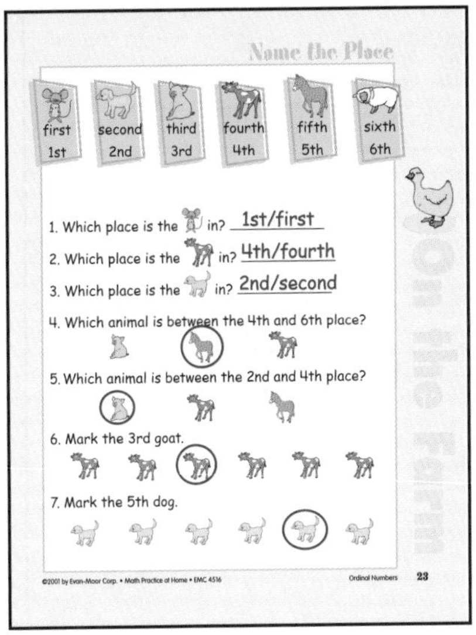
### Name the Place

first 1st, second 2nd, third 3rd, fourth 4th, fifth 5th, sixth 6th

1. Which place is the (mouse) in? 1st/first
2. Which place is the (goat) in? 4th/fourth
3. Which place is the (dog) in? 2nd/second
4. Which animal is between the 4th and 6th place?
5. Which animal is between the 2nd and 4th place?
6. Mark the 3rd goat.
7. Mark the 5th dog.

On the Farm

©2001 by Evan-Moor Corp. • Math Practice at Home • EMC 4516 Ordinal Numbers 23

## Page 24

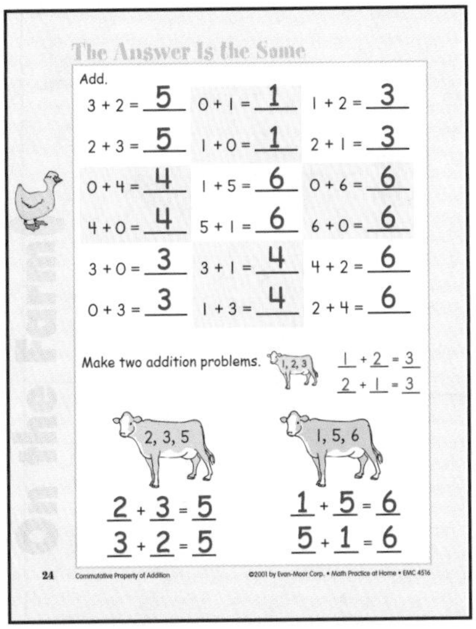
### The Answer Is the Same

Add.

| | | |
|---|---|---|
| 3 + 2 = 5 | 0 + 1 = 1 | 1 + 2 = 3 |
| 2 + 3 = 5 | 1 + 0 = 1 | 2 + 1 = 3 |
| 0 + 4 = 4 | 1 + 5 = 6 | 0 + 6 = 6 |
| 4 + 0 = 4 | 5 + 1 = 6 | 6 + 0 = 6 |
| 3 + 0 = 3 | 3 + 1 = 4 | 4 + 2 = 6 |
| 0 + 3 = 3 | 1 + 3 = 4 | 2 + 4 = 6 |

Make two addition problems. (1, 2, 3) 1 + 2 = 3, 2 + 1 = 3

(2, 3, 5) 2 + 3 = 5, 3 + 2 = 5

(1, 5, 6) 1 + 5 = 6, 5 + 1 = 6

On the Farm

24 Commutative Property of Addition ©2001 by Evan-Moor Corp. • Math Practice at Home • EMC 4516

## Page 25

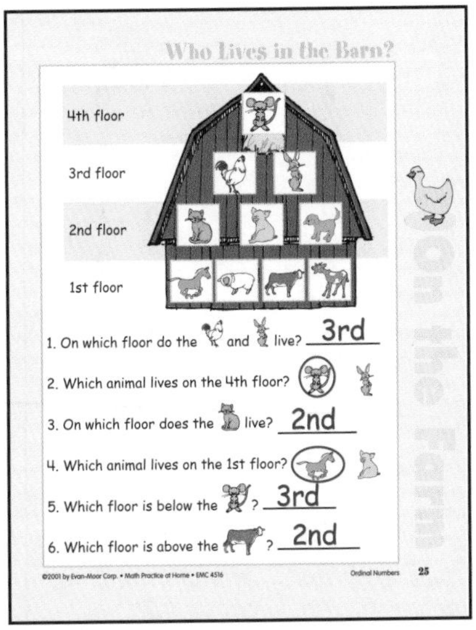
### Who Lives in the Barn?

4th floor
3rd floor
2nd floor
1st floor

1. On which floor do the (rooster) and (rabbit) live? 3rd
2. Which animal lives on the 4th floor?
3. On which floor does the (cat) live? 2nd
4. Which animal lives on the 1st floor?
5. Which floor is below the (goat)? 3rd
6. Which floor is above the (cow)? 2nd

On the Farm

©2001 by Evan-Moor Corp. • Math Practice at Home • EMC 4516 Ordinal Numbers 25

## Page 26

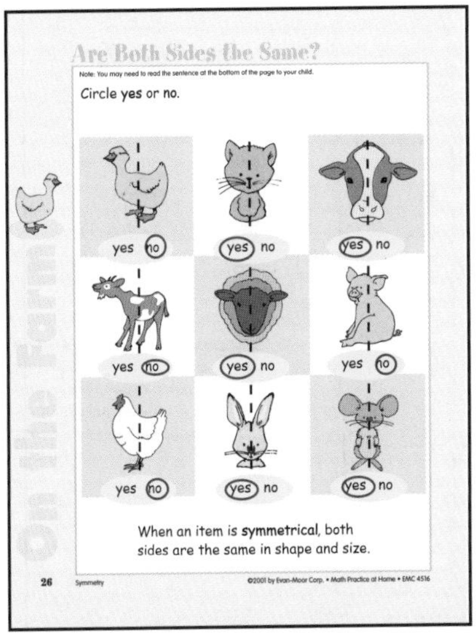
### Are Both Sides the Same?

Note: You may need to read the sentence at the bottom of the page to your child.

Circle **yes** or **no**.

yes no | yes no | yes no
yes no | yes no | yes no
yes no | yes no | yes no

When an item is **symmetrical**, both sides are the same in shape and size.

On the Farm

26 Symmetry ©2001 by Evan-Moor Corp. • Math Practice at Home • EMC 4516

## Page 27

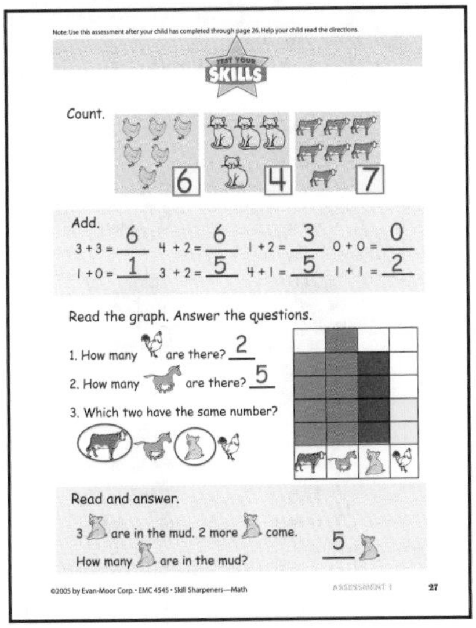
Note: Use this assessment after your child has completed through page 26. Help your child read the directions.

TEST YOUR SKILLS

Count. 6 4 7

Add.

3 + 3 = 6, 4 + 2 = 6, 1 + 2 = 3, 0 + 0 = 0
1 + 0 = 1, 3 + 2 = 5, 4 + 1 = 5, 1 + 1 = 2

Read the graph. Answer the questions.

1. How many (rooster) are there? 2
2. How many (dog) are there? 5
3. Which two have the same number?

Read and answer.

3 (pig) are in the mud. 2 more (pig) come.
How many (pig) are in the mud? 5

©2005 by Evan-Moor Corp. • EMC 4545 • Skill Sharpeners—Math ASSESSMENT 1 27

## Page 28

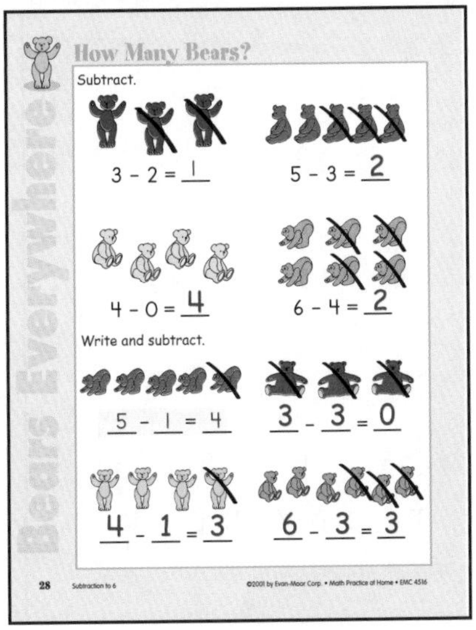
### How Many Bears?

Subtract.

3 - 2 = 1
5 - 3 = 2
4 - 0 = 4
6 - 4 = 2

Write and subtract.

5 - 1 = 4
3 - 3 = 0
4 - 1 = 3
6 - 3 = 3

Bears Everywhere

28 Subtraction to 6 ©2001 by Evan-Moor Corp. • Math Practice at Home • EMC 4516

## Page 29

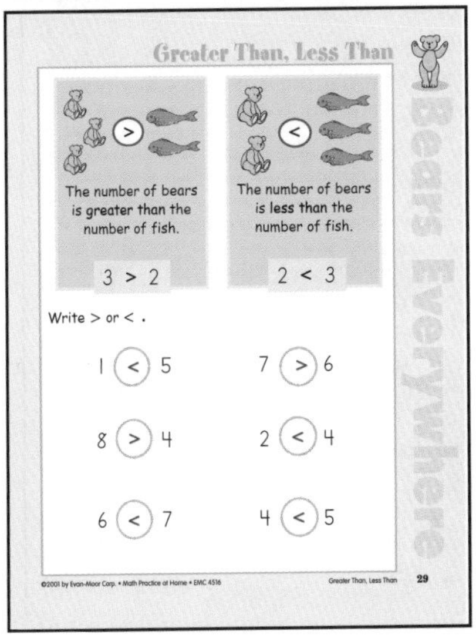
### Greater Than, Less Than

The number of bears is greater than the number of fish. 3 > 2

The number of bears is less than the number of fish. 2 < 3

Write > or < .

1 < 5 | 7 > 6
8 > 4 | 2 < 4
6 < 7 | 4 < 5

Bears Everywhere

©2001 by Evan-Moor Corp. • Math Practice at Home • EMC 4516 Greater Than, Less Than 29

## Page 30

Color the Bear
Note: You may need to read the sentence at the bottom of the page to your child.
Subtract. Color.
orange 0
brown 1
blue 2
red 3
green 4
purple 5
yellow 6
6 - 4
4 - 3
4 - 4
6 - 1
2 - 1
4 - 2
6 - 2
6 - 3
6 - 5
Subtract.
6 - 6 = 0
3 - 3 = 0
4 - 4 = 0
1 - 1 = 0
5 - 5 = 0
2 - 2 = 0
When you subtract a number from itself, you get 0.
Bears Everywhere
30 Subtraction to 6
©2001 by Evan-Moor Corp. • Math Practice at Home • EMC 4516

## Page 31

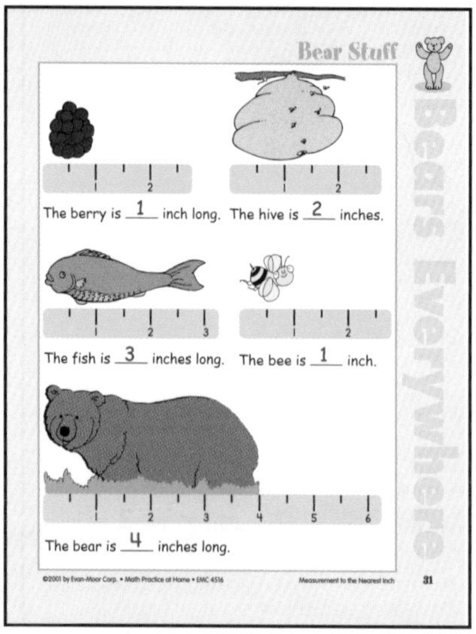

Bear Stuff
The berry is 1 inch long.
The hive is 2 inches.
The fish is 3 inches long.
The bee is 1 inch.
The bear is 4 inches long.
Bears Everywhere
©2001 by Evan-Moor Corp. • Math Practice at Home • EMC 4516
Measurement to the Nearest Inch 31

## Page 32

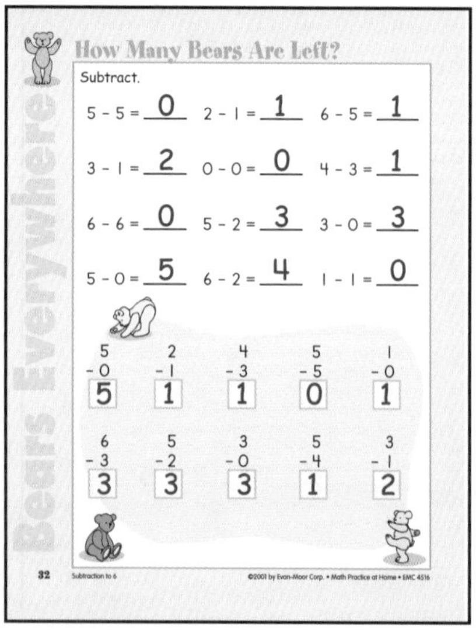

How Many Bears Are Left?
Subtract.
5 - 5 = 0
2 - 1 = 1
6 - 5 = 1
3 - 1 = 2
0 - 0 = 0
4 - 3 = 1
6 - 6 = 0
5 - 2 = 3
3 - 0 = 3
5 - 0 = 5
6 - 2 = 4
1 - 1 = 0
5 - 0 = 5
2 - 1 = 1
4 - 3 = 1
5 - 5 = 0
1 - 0 = 1
6 - 3 = 3
5 - 2 = 3
3 - 0 = 3
5 - 4 = 1
3 - 1 = 2
Bears Everywhere
32 Subtraction to 6
©2001 by Evan-Moor Corp. • Math Practice at Home • EMC 4516

## Page 33

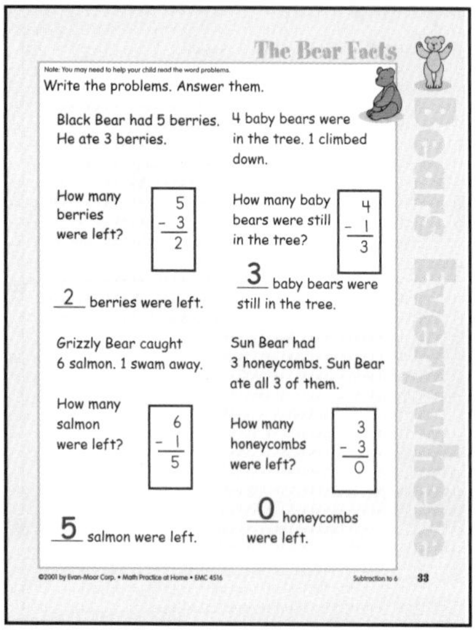

The Bear Facts
Note: You may need to help your child read the word problems.
Write the problems. Answer them.
Black Bear had 5 berries. He ate 3 berries.
How many berries were left?
5 - 3 = 2
2 berries were left.
4 baby bears were in the tree. 1 climbed down.
How many baby bears were still in the tree?
4 - 1 = 3
3 baby bears were still in the tree.
Grizzly Bear caught 6 salmon. 1 swam away.
How many salmon were left?
6 - 1 = 5
5 salmon were left.
Sun Bear had 3 honeycombs. Sun Bear ate all 3 of them.
How many honeycombs were left?
3 - 3 = 0
0 honeycombs were left.
Bears Everywhere
©2001 by Evan-Moor Corp. • Math Practice at Home • EMC 4516
Subtraction to 6 33

## Page 34

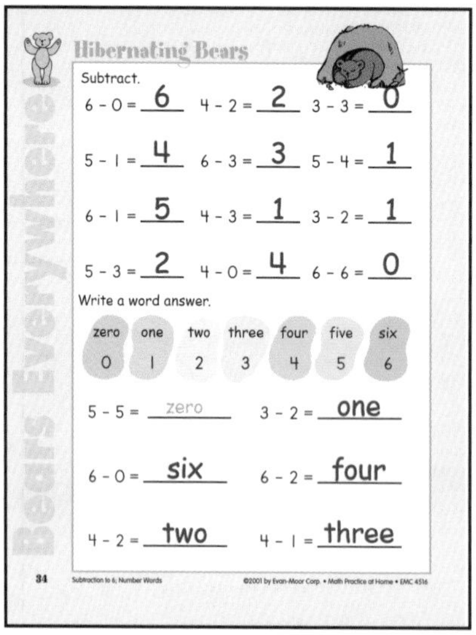

Hibernating Bears
Subtract.
6 - 0 = 6
4 - 2 = 2
3 - 3 = 0
5 - 1 = 4
6 - 3 = 3
5 - 4 = 1
6 - 1 = 5
4 - 3 = 1
3 - 2 = 1
5 - 3 = 2
4 - 0 = 4
6 - 6 = 0
Write a word answer.
zero 0
one 1
two 2
three 3
four 4
five 5
six 6
5 - 5 = zero
3 - 2 = one
6 - 0 = six
6 - 2 = four
4 - 2 = two
4 - 1 = three
Bears Everywhere
34 Subtraction to 6, Number Words
©2001 by Evan-Moor Corp. • Math Practice at Home • EMC 4516

## Page 35

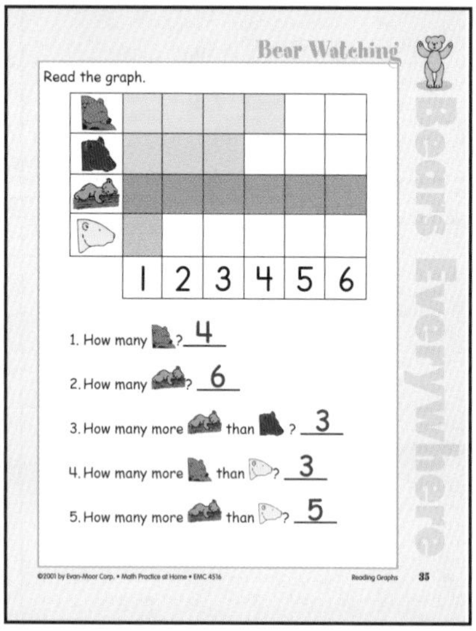

Bear Watching
Read the graph.
1 2 3 4 5 6
1. How many ? 4
2. How many ? 6
3. How many more than ? 3
4. How many more than ? 3
5. How many more than ? 5
Bears Everywhere
©2001 by Evan-Moor Corp. • Math Practice at Home • EMC 4516
Reading Graphs 35

## Page 36

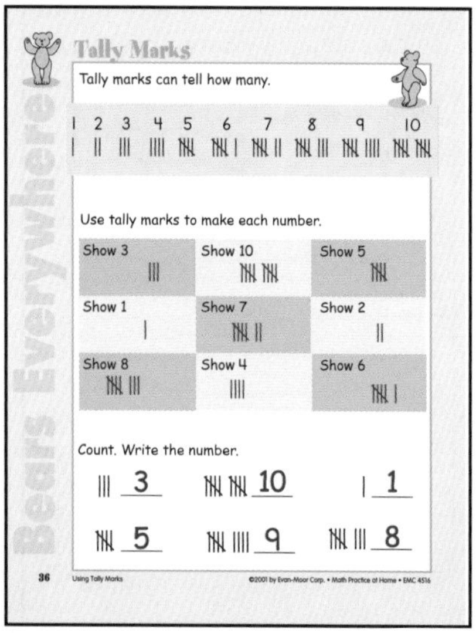

Tally Marks
Tally marks can tell how many.
1 2 3 4 5 6 7 8 9 10
Use tally marks to make each number.
Show 3
Show 10
Show 5
Show 1
Show 7
Show 2
Show 8
Show 4
Show 6
Count. Write the number.
3
10
1
5
9
8
Bears Everywhere
36 Using Tally Marks
©2001 by Evan-Moor Corp. • Math Practice at Home • EMC 4516

## Page 37

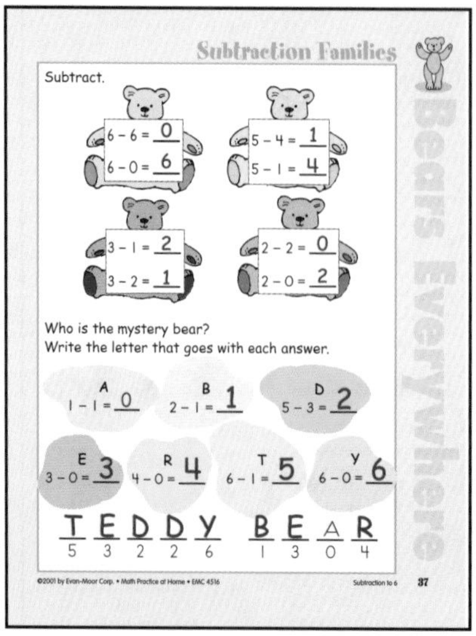

Subtraction Families
Subtract.
6 - 6 = 0
6 - 0 = 6
5 - 4 = 1
5 - 1 = 4
3 - 1 = 2
3 - 2 = 1
2 - 2 = 0
2 - 0 = 2
Who is the mystery bear?
Write the letter that goes with each answer.
A 1 - 1 = 0
B 2 - 1 = 1
D 5 - 3 = 2
E 3 - 0 = 3
R 4 - 0 = 4
T 6 - 1 = 5
Y 6 - 0 = 6
TEDDY BEAR
5 3 2 2 6 1 3 0 4
Bears Everywhere
©2001 by Evan-Moor Corp. • Math Practice at Home • EMC 4516
Subtraction to 6 37

## Page 38

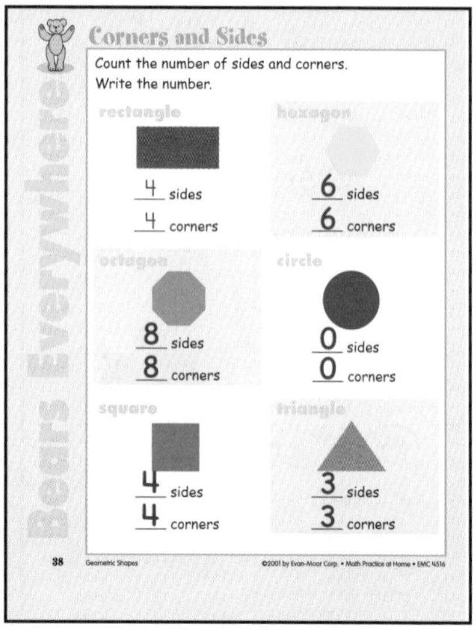

Corners and Sides
Count the number of sides and corners.
Write the number.
rectangle
4 sides
4 corners
hexagon
6 sides
6 corners
octagon
8 sides
8 corners
circle
0 sides
0 corners
square
4 sides
4 corners
triangle
3 sides
3 corners
Bears Everywhere
38 Geometric Shapes
©2001 by Evan-Moor Corp. • Math Practice at Home • EMC 4516

## Page 39

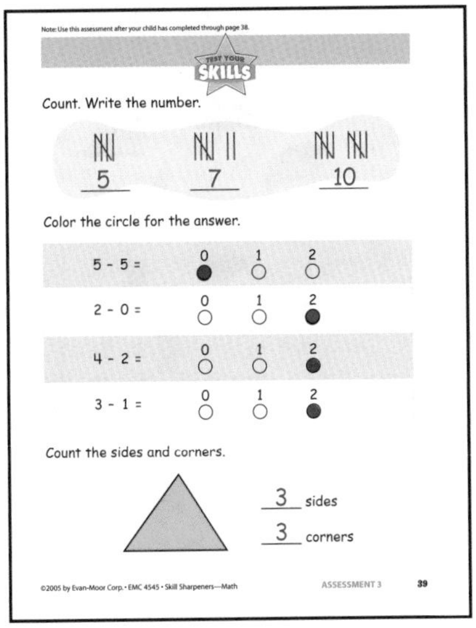
Note: Use this assessment after your child has completed through page 38.

TEST YOUR SKILLS

Count. Write the number.

5 7 10

Color the circle for the answer.

5 - 5 = 0 1 2

2 - 0 = 0 1 2

4 - 2 = 0 1 2

3 - 1 = 0 1 2

Count the sides and corners.

3 sides

3 corners

©2005 by Evan-Moor Corp. • EMC 4545 • Skill Sharpeners—Math ASSESSMENT 3 39

## Page 40

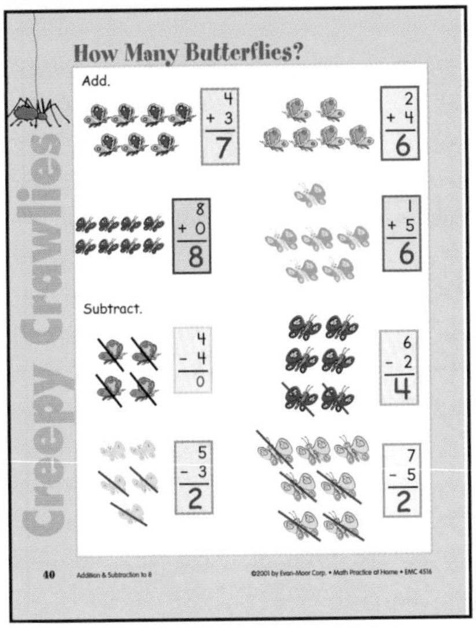
How Many Butterflies?

Add.

4 + 3 = 7

2 + 4 = 6

8 + 0 = 8

1 + 5 = 6

Subtract.

4 - 4 = 0

6 - 2 = 4

5 - 3 = 2

7 - 5 = 2

Creepy Crawlies

40 Addition & Subtraction to 8 ©2001 by Evan-Moor Corp. • Math Practice at Home • EMC 4516

## Page 41

Pretty Patterns

Circle the shape to complete each pattern.

Label the patterns.

A A B A A B A

A B C A B C A

A A B C A A B

A B B C C A B

Creepy Crawlies

©2001 by Evan-Moor Corp. • Math Practice at Home • EMC 4516 Patterns 41

## Page 42

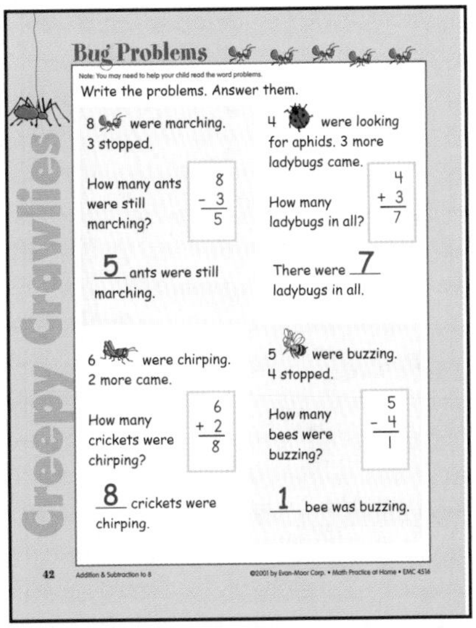
Bug Problems

Note: You may need to help your child read the word problems.

Write the problems. Answer them.

8 were marching. 3 stopped. How many ants were still marching? 8 - 3 = 5

5 ants were still marching.

4 were looking for aphids. 3 more ladybugs came. How many ladybugs in all? 4 + 3 = 7

There were 7 ladybugs in all.

6 were chirping. 2 more came. How many crickets were chirping? 6 + 2 = 8

8 crickets were chirping.

5 were buzzing. 4 stopped. How many bees were buzzing? 5 - 4 = 1

1 bee was buzzing.

Creepy Crawlies

42 Addition & Subtraction to 8 ©2001 by Evan-Moor Corp. • Math Practice at Home • EMC 4516

## Page 43

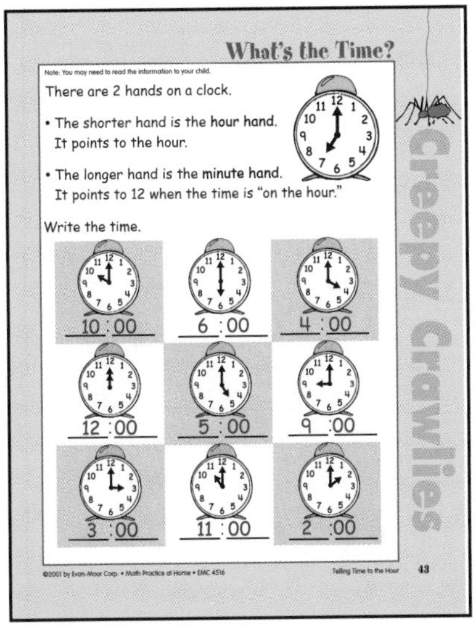
What's the Time?

Note: You may need to read the information to your child.

There are 2 hands on a clock.

- The shorter hand is the **hour hand.** It points to the hour.
- The longer hand is the **minute hand.** It points to 12 when the time is "on the hour."

Write the time.

10:00 6:00 4:00

12:00 5:00 9:00

3:00 11:00 2:00

Creepy Crawlies

©2001 by Evan-Moor Corp. • Math Practice at Home • EMC 4516 Telling Time to the Hour 43

## Page 44

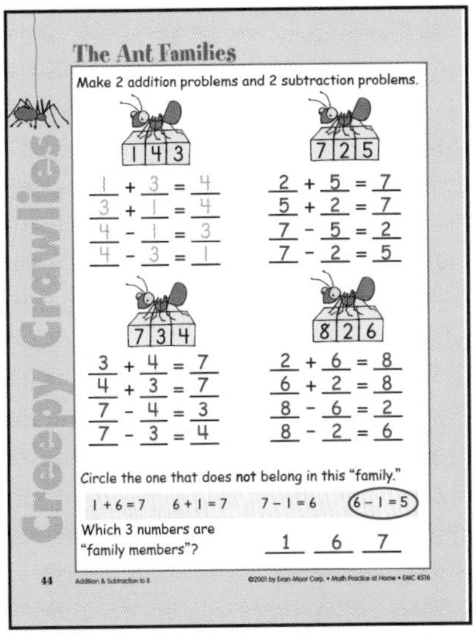
The Ant Families

Make 2 addition problems and 2 subtraction problems.

1 4 3

1 + 3 = 4

3 + 1 = 4

4 - 1 = 3

4 - 3 = 1

7 2 5

2 + 5 = 7

5 + 2 = 7

7 - 5 = 2

7 - 2 = 5

7 3 4

3 + 4 = 7

4 + 3 = 7

7 - 4 = 3

7 - 3 = 4

8 2 6

2 + 6 = 8

6 + 2 = 8

8 - 6 = 2

8 - 2 = 6

Circle the one that does **not** belong in this "family."

1 + 6 = 7 6 + 1 = 7 7 - 1 = 6 6 - 1 = 5

Which 3 numbers are "family members"? 1 6 7

Creepy Crawlies

44 Addition & Subtraction to 8 ©2001 by Evan-Moor Corp. • Math Practice at Home • EMC 4516

## Page 45

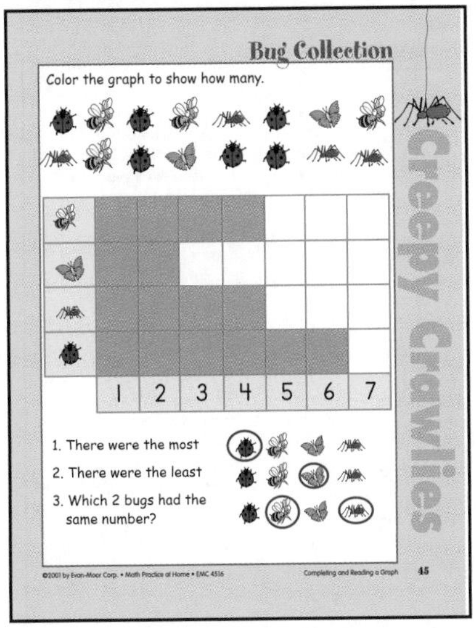
Bug Collection

Color the graph to show how many.

1 2 3 4 5 6 7

1. There were the most
2. There were the least
3. Which 2 bugs had the same number?

Creepy Crawlies

©2001 by Evan-Moor Corp. • Math Practice at Home • EMC 4516 Completing and Reading a Graph 45

## Page 46

What's Missing?

Fill in the numbers.

2 + 3 = 5

7 + 0 = 7

1 + 6 = 7

4 + 4 = 8

4 - 3 = 1

8 - 8 = 0

4 + 3 = 7

7 - 6 = 1

6 - 2 = 4

Creepy Crawlies

46 Addition & Subtraction to 8 ©2001 by Evan-Moor Corp. • Math Practice at Home • EMC 4516

## Page 47

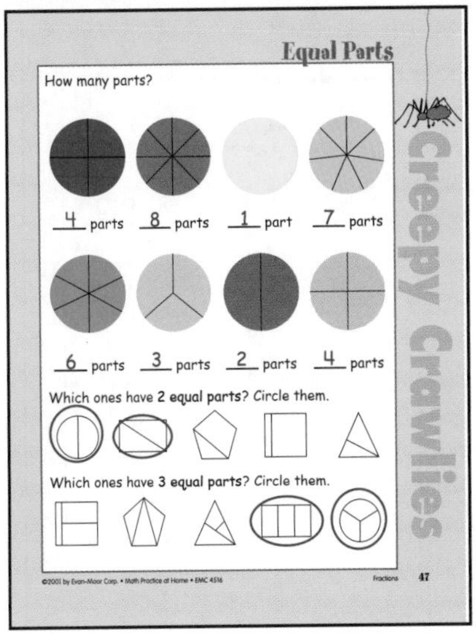
Equal Parts

How many parts?

4 parts 8 parts 1 part 7 parts

6 parts 3 parts 2 parts 4 parts

Which ones have **2** equal parts? Circle them.

Which ones have **3** equal parts? Circle them.

Creepy Crawlies

©2001 by Evan-Moor Corp. • Math Practice at Home • EMC 4516 Fractions 47

## Page 48

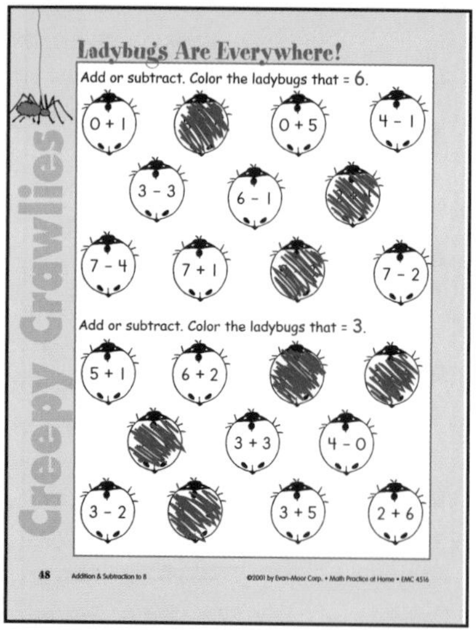
Creepy Crawlies

### Ladybugs Are Everywhere!

Add or subtract. Color the ladybugs that = 6.

0 + 1, 0 + 5, 4 - 1, 3 - 3, 6 - 1, 7 - 4, 7 + 1, 7 - 2

Add or subtract. Color the ladybugs that = 3.

5 + 1, 6 + 2, 3 + 3, 4 - 0, 3 - 2, 3 + 5, 2 + 6

48 Addition & Subtraction to 8 ©2001 by Evan-Moor Corp. • Math Practice at Home • EMC 4516

## Page 49

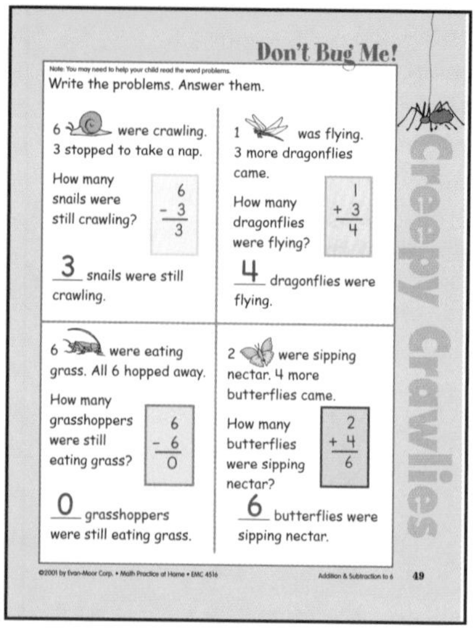
Creepy Crawlies

### Don't Bug Me!

Note: You may need to help your child read the word problems.

Write the problems. Answer them.

6 were crawling. 3 stopped to take a nap. How many snails were still crawling? 6 − 3 = 3. 3 snails were still crawling.

1 was flying. 3 more dragonflies came. How many dragonflies were flying? 1 + 3 = 4. 4 dragonflies were flying.

6 were eating grass. All 6 hopped away. How many grasshoppers were still eating grass? 6 − 6 = 0. 0 grasshoppers were still eating grass.

2 were sipping nectar. 4 more butterflies came. How many butterflies were sipping nectar? 2 + 4 = 6. 6 butterflies were sipping nectar.

©2001 by Evan-Moor Corp. • Math Practice at Home • EMC 4516 Addition & Subtraction to 6 49

## Page 50

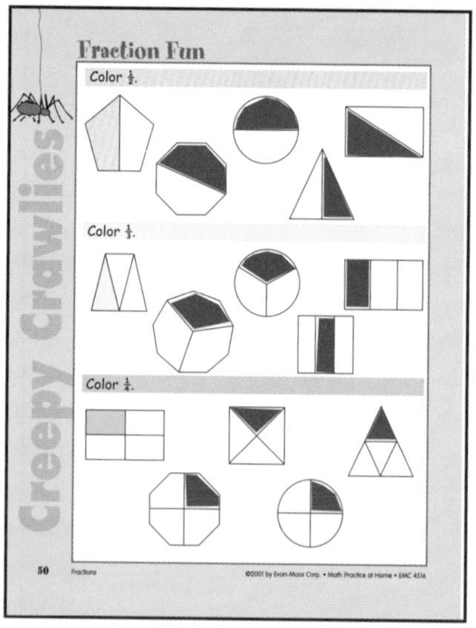
Creepy Crawlies

### Fraction Fun

Color $\frac{1}{2}$.

Color $\frac{1}{3}$.

Color $\frac{1}{4}$.

50 Fractions ©2001 by Evan-Moor Corp. • Math Practice at Home • EMC 4516

## Page 51

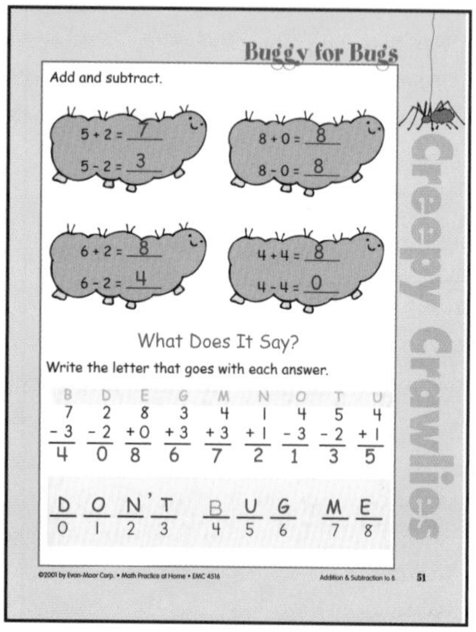
Creepy Crawlies

### Buggy for Bugs

Add and subtract.

5 + 2 = 7, 5 − 2 = 3, 8 + 0 = 8, 8 − 0 = 8, 6 + 2 = 8, 6 − 2 = 4, 4 + 4 = 8, 4 − 4 = 0

What Does It Say?

Write the letter that goes with each answer.

| B | D | E | G | M | N | O | T | U |
|---|---|---|---|---|---|---|---|---|
| 7 − 3 = 4 | 2 − 2 = 0 | 8 + 0 = 8 | 3 + 3 = 6 | 4 + 3 = 7 | 1 + 1 = 2 | 4 − 3 = 1 | 5 − 2 = 3 | 4 + 1 = 5 |

D O N'T B U G M E
0 1 2 3 4 5 6 7 8

©2001 by Evan-Moor Corp. • Math Practice at Home • EMC 4516 Addition & Subtraction to 8 51

## Page 52

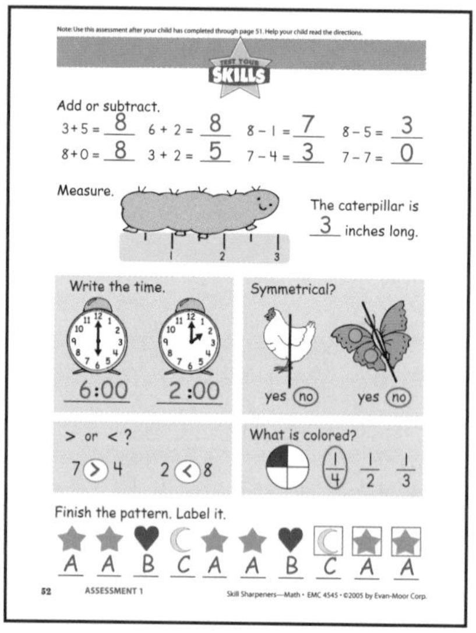
Note: Use this assessment after your child has completed through page 51. Help your child read the directions.

Test Your Skills

Add or subtract.

3 + 5 = 8, 6 + 2 = 8, 8 − 1 = 7, 8 − 5 = 3, 8 + 0 = 8, 3 + 2 = 5, 7 − 4 = 3, 7 − 7 = 0

Measure. The caterpillar is 3 inches long.

Write the time. 6:00 2:00

Symmetrical? yes (no) yes (no)

> or <? 7 > 4 2 < 8

What is colored? $\frac{1}{4}$ $\frac{1}{2}$ $\frac{1}{3}$

Finish the pattern. Label it. A A B C A A B C A A

52 ASSESSMENT 1 Skill Sharpeners—Math • EMC 4545 • ©2005 by Evan-Moor Corp.

## Page 53

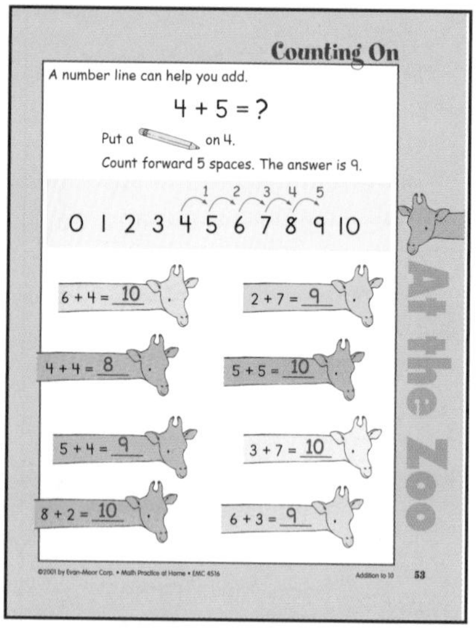
At the Zoo

### Counting On

A number line can help you add.

4 + 5 = ?

Put a pencil on 4. Count forward 5 spaces. The answer is 9.

0 1 2 3 4 5 6 7 8 9 10

6 + 4 = 10, 2 + 7 = 9, 4 + 4 = 8, 5 + 5 = 10, 5 + 4 = 9, 3 + 7 = 10, 8 + 2 = 10, 6 + 3 = 9

©2001 by Evan-Moor Corp. • Math Practice at Home • EMC 4516 Addition to 10 53

## Page 54

At the Zoo

### Counting Back

A number line can help you subtract.

9 − 3 = ?

Put a pencil on 9. Count back 3 spaces. The answer is 6.

0 1 2 3 4 5 6 7 8 9 10

10 − 5 = 5, 9 − 9 = 0, 10 − 2 = 8, 9 − 5 = 4, 10 − 8 = 2, 9 − 6 = 3, 10 − 9 = 1, 9 − 2 = 7, 10 − 4 = 6

Write the answers in order from smallest to greatest.

0, 1, 2, 3, 4, 5, 6, 7, 8

54 Subtraction to 10 ©2001 by Evan-Moor Corp. • Math Practice at Home • EMC 4516

## Page 55

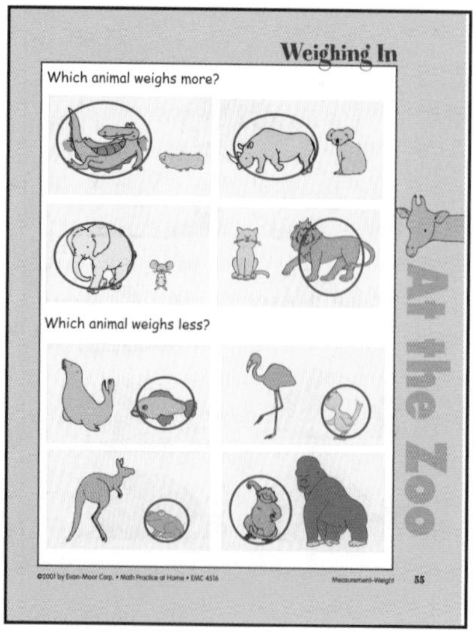
At the Zoo

### Weighing In

Which animal weighs more?

Which animal weighs less?

©2001 by Evan-Moor Corp. • Math Practice at Home • EMC 4516 Measurement—Weight 55

## Page 56

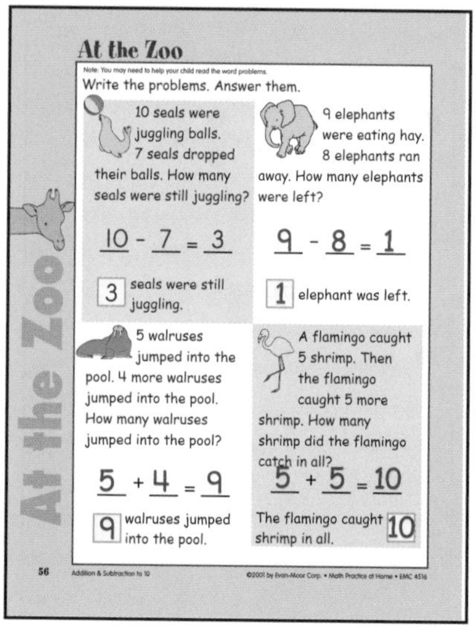
At the Zoo

### At the Zoo

Note: You may need to help your child read the word problems.

Write the problems. Answer them.

10 seals were juggling balls. 7 seals dropped their balls. How many seals were still juggling? 10 − 7 = 3. 3 seals were still juggling.

9 elephants were eating hay. 8 elephants ran away. How many elephants were left? 9 − 8 = 1. 1 elephant was left.

5 walruses jumped into the pool. 4 more walruses jumped into the pool. How many walruses jumped into the pool? 5 + 4 = 9. 9 walruses jumped into the pool.

A flamingo caught 5 shrimp. Then the flamingo caught 5 more shrimp. How many shrimp did the flamingo catch in all? 5 + 5 = 10. The flamingo caught 10 shrimp in all.

56 Addition & Subtraction to 10 ©2001 by Evan-Moor Corp. • Math Practice at Home • EMC 4516

## Page 57

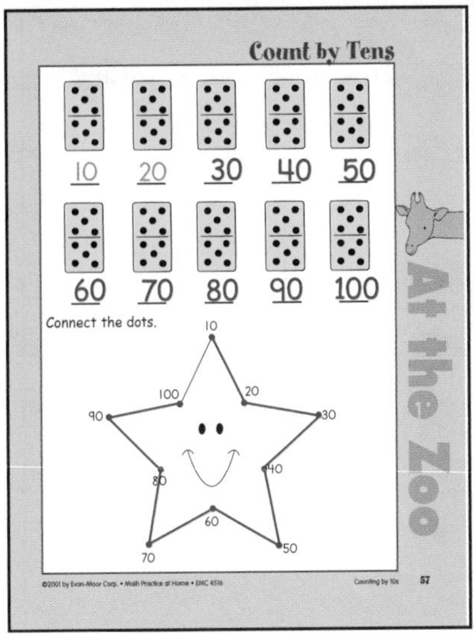


## Page 58

## Page 59

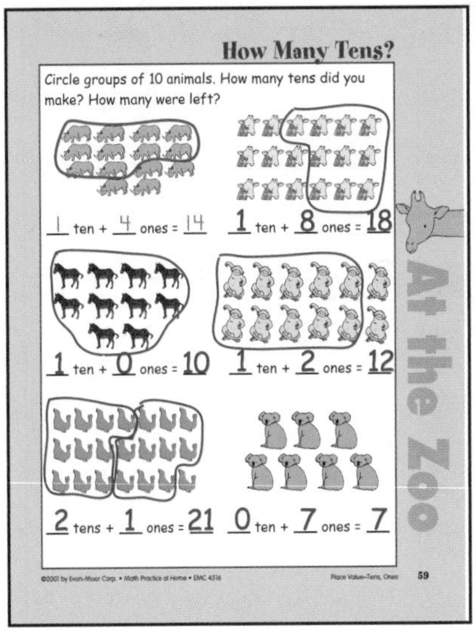


## Page 60

## Page 61

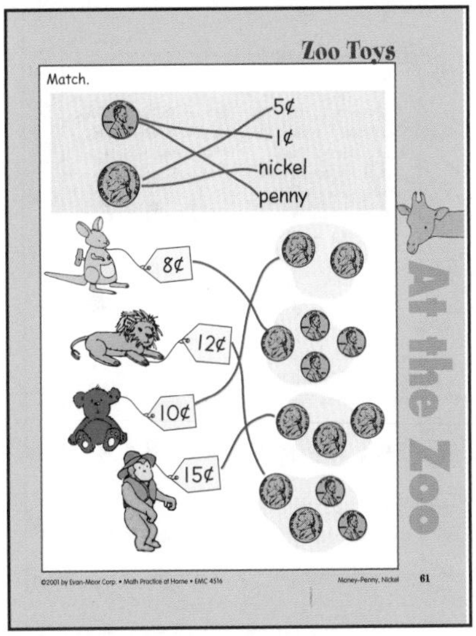


## Page 62

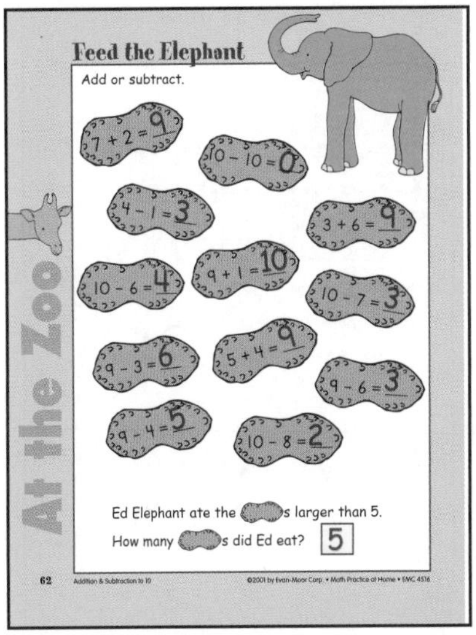


## Page 63

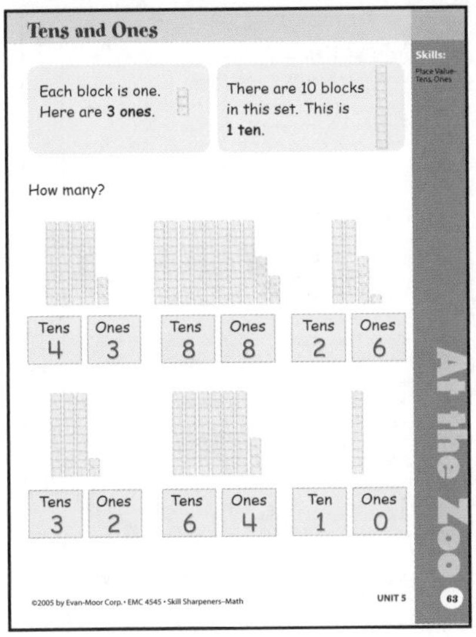


## Page 64

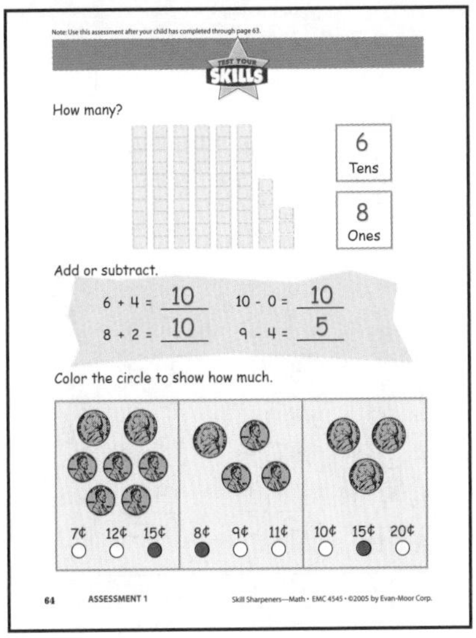


## Page 65

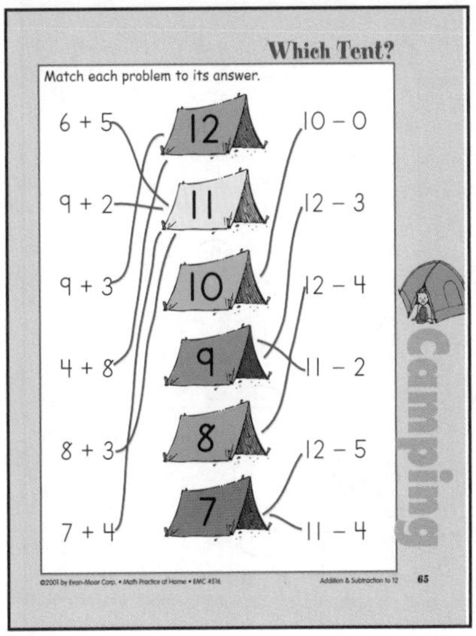

## Page 66

**Number Families**

Number families have 2 addition problems and 2 subtraction problems made from 3 numbers.

3 numbers: 7, 5, 12
2 addition problems: 7 + 5 = 12, 5 + 7 = 12
2 subtraction problems: 12 − 7 = 5, 12 − 5 = 7

Complete each number family.

8, 3, 11: 8 + 3 = 11; 3 + 8 = 11; 11 − 3 = 8; 11 − 8 = 3
9, 2, 11: 9 + 2 = 11; 2 + 9 = 11; 11 − 2 = 9; 11 − 9 = 2
8, 4, 12: 8 + 4 = 12; 4 + 8 = 12; 12 − 4 = 8; 12 − 8 = 4
9, 3, 12: 9 + 3 = 12; 3 + 9 = 12; 12 − 3 = 9; 12 − 9 = 3

Camping

66 Addition & Subtraction to 12 ©2001 by Evan-Moor Corp. • Math Practice at Home • EMC 4516

## Page 67

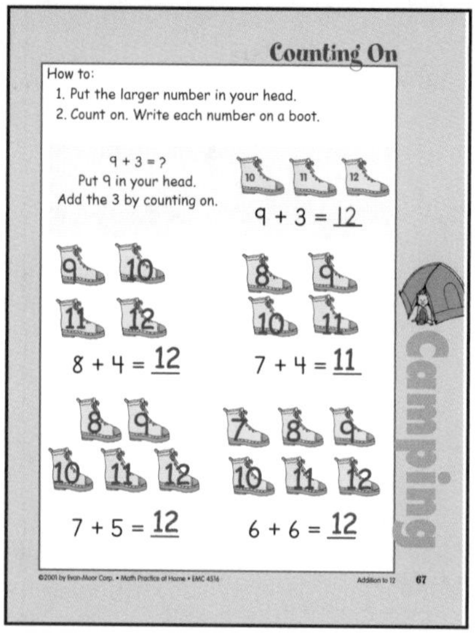
**Counting On**

How to:
1. Put the larger number in your head.
2. Count on. Write each number on a boot.

9 + 3 = ? Put 9 in your head. Add the 3 by counting on. 10, 11, 12. 9 + 3 = 12

9, 10, 11, 12: 8 + 4 = 12
8, 9, 10, 11: 7 + 4 = 11
8, 9, 10, 11, 12: 7 + 5 = 12
7, 8, 9, 10, 11, 12: 6 + 6 = 12

Camping

©2001 by Evan-Moor Corp. • Math Practice at Home • EMC 4516 Addition to 12 67

## Page 68

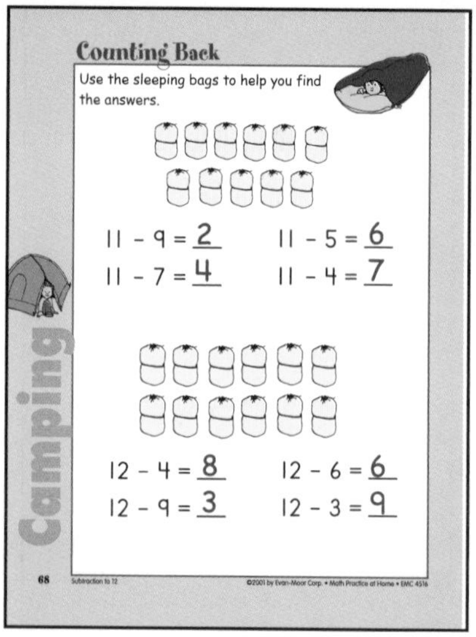
**Counting Back**

Use the sleeping bags to help you find the answers.

11 − 9 = 2; 11 − 5 = 6
11 − 7 = 4; 11 − 4 = 7

12 − 4 = 8; 12 − 6 = 6
12 − 9 = 3; 12 − 3 = 9

Camping

68 Subtraction to 12 ©2001 by Evan-Moor Corp. • Math Practice at Home • EMC 4516

## Page 69

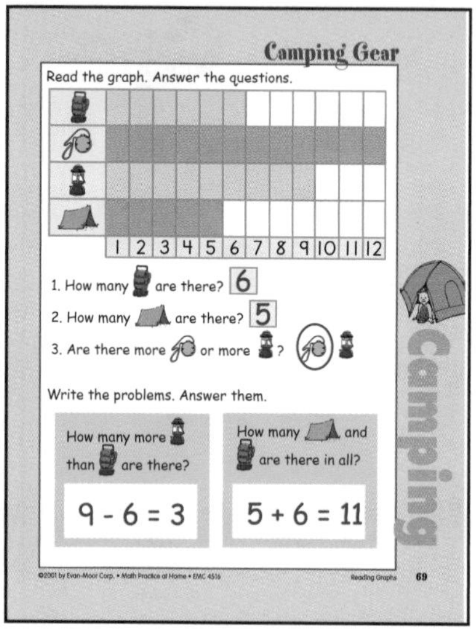
**Camping Gear**

Read the graph. Answer the questions.

1 2 3 4 5 6 7 8 9 10 11 12

1. How many are there? 6
2. How many are there? 5
3. Are there more or more ?

Write the problems. Answer them.

How many more than are there? 9 − 6 = 3
How many and are there in all? 5 + 6 = 11

Camping

©2001 by Evan-Moor Corp. • Math Practice at Home • EMC 4516 Reading Graphs 69

## Page 70

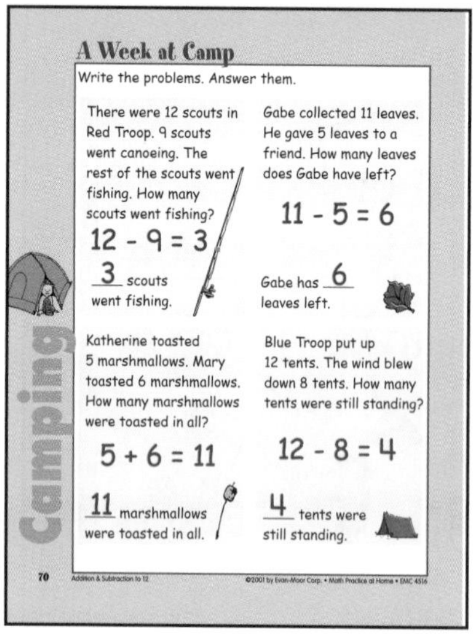
**A Week at Camp**

Write the problems. Answer them.

There were 12 scouts in Red Troop. 9 scouts went canoeing. The rest of the scouts went fishing. How many scouts went fishing? 12 − 9 = 3. 3 scouts went fishing.

Gabe collected 11 leaves. He gave 5 leaves to a friend. How many leaves does Gabe have left? 11 − 5 = 6. Gabe has 6 leaves left.

Katherine toasted 5 marshmallows. Mary toasted 6 marshmallows. How many marshmallows were toasted in all? 5 + 6 = 11. 11 marshmallows were toasted in all.

Blue Troop put up 12 tents. The wind blew down 8 tents. How many tents were still standing? 12 − 8 = 4. 4 tents were still standing.

Camping

70 Addition & Subtraction to 12 ©2001 by Evan-Moor Corp. • Math Practice at Home • EMC 4516

## Page 71

**Mystery Message**

Write the letter that goes with each number.

A: 12 − 7 = 5; F: 12 − 11 = 1; K: 8 + 3 = 11; M: 2 + 1 = 3
N: 10 − 6 = 4; O: 7 − 7 = 0; R: 3 + 9 = 12; S: 7 + 1 = 8
T: 12 − 2 = 10; U: 11 − 9 = 2; W: 0 + 6 = 6; Y: 11 − 4 = 7

S T A Y (8 10 5 7) A W A Y (5 6 5 7)
F R O M (1 12 0 3)
S K U N K S! (8 11 2 4 11 8)

Camping

©2001 by Evan-Moor Corp. • Math Practice at Home • EMC 4516 Addition & Subtraction to 12 71

## Page 72

**Fill Them Up!**

Would you use a spoon or a cup to fill the containers?

spoon (cup) — spoon (cup) — (spoon) cup
spoon (cup) — (spoon) cup — spoon (cup)
spoon (cup) — (spoon) cup — spoon (cup)

Camping

72 Liquid Measurement ©2001 by Evan-Moor Corp. • Math Practice at Home • EMC 4516

## Page 73

**Two-Digit Numbers**

Add or subtract the ones first.
Then add or subtract the tens.

27 + 30 = 57 (Start on the ones side.)
98 − 25 = 73
13 + 31 = 44
64 − 30 = 34
60 + 25 = 85
37 − 27 = 10
86 − 75 = 11
71 − 51 = 20
51 + 44 = 95

Camping

©2001 by Evan-Moor Corp. • Math Practice at Home • EMC 4516 Adding & Subtracting Two-Digit Numbers 73

## Page 74

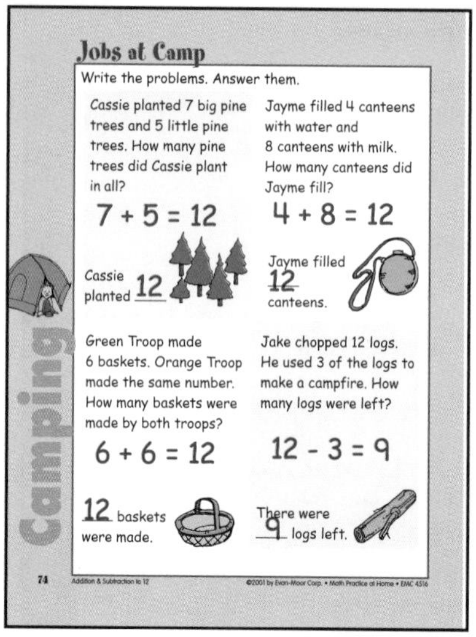
**Jobs at Camp**

Write the problems. Answer them.

Cassie planted 7 big pine trees and 5 little pine trees. How many pine trees did Cassie plant in all? 7 + 5 = 12. Cassie planted 12.

Jayme filled 4 canteens with water and 8 canteens with milk. How many canteens did Jayme fill? 4 + 8 = 12. Jayme filled 12 canteens.

Green Troop made 6 baskets. Orange Troop made the same number. How many baskets were made by both troops? 6 + 6 = 12. 12 baskets were made.

Jake chopped 12 logs. He used 3 of the logs to make a campfire. How many logs were left? 12 − 3 = 9. There were 9 logs left.

Camping

74 Addition & Subtraction to 12 ©2001 by Evan-Moor Corp. • Math Practice at Home • EMC 4516

## Page 75

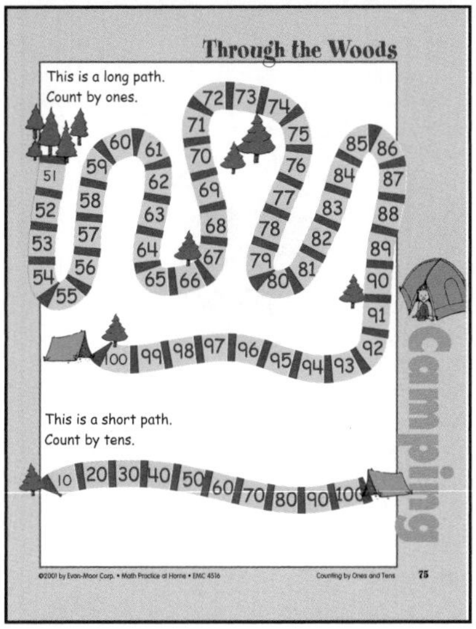

### Through the Woods

This is a long path.
Count by ones.

51 52 53 54 55 56 57 58 59 60 61 62 63 64 65 66 67 68 69 70 71 72 73 74 75 76 77 78 79 80 81 82 83 84 85 86 87 88 89 90 91 92 93 94 95 96 97 98 99 100

This is a short path.
Count by tens.

10 20 30 40 50 60 70 80 90 100

Camping

©2001 by Evan-Moor Corp. • Math Practice at Home • EMC 4516 — Counting by Ones and Tens — 75

## Page 76

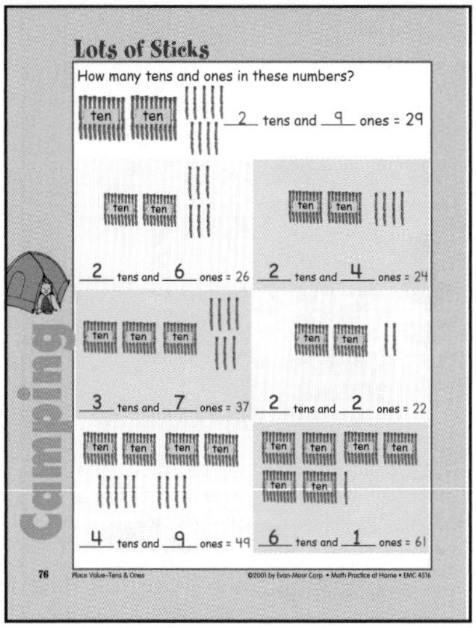

### Lots of Sticks

How many tens and ones in these numbers?

2 tens and 9 ones = 29

2 tens and 6 ones = 26 — 2 tens and 4 ones = 24

3 tens and 7 ones = 37 — 2 tens and 2 ones = 22

4 tens and 9 ones = 49 — 6 tens and 1 ones = 61

Camping

76 — Place Value—Tens & Ones — ©2001 by Evan-Moor Corp. • Math Practice at Home • EMC 4516

## Page 77

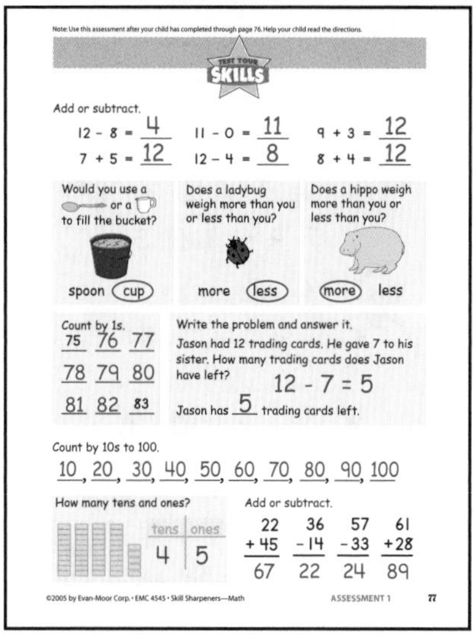

Note: Use this assessment after your child has completed through page 76. Help your child read the directions.

TEST YOUR SKILLS

Add or subtract.

12 − 8 = 4 — 11 − 0 = 11 — 9 + 3 = 12
7 + 5 = 12 — 12 − 4 = 8 — 8 + 4 = 12

Would you use a spoon or a cup to fill the bucket? spoon (cup)
Does a ladybug weigh more than you or less than you? more (less)
Does a hippo weigh more than you or less than you? (more) less

Count by 1s.
75 76 77
78 79 80
81 82 83

Write the problem and answer it.
Jason had 12 trading cards. He gave 7 to his sister. How many trading cards does Jason have left?
12 − 7 = 5
Jason has 5 trading cards left.

Count by 10s to 100.
10, 20, 30, 40, 50, 60, 70, 80, 90, 100

How many tens and ones?
tens 4, ones 5

Add or subtract.
22 + 45 = 67 — 36 − 14 = 22 — 57 − 33 = 24 — 61 + 28 = 89

©2005 by Evan-Moor Corp. • EMC 4545 • Skill Sharpeners—Math — ASSESSMENT 1 — 77

## Page 78

### A Good Crop

Find the answer that is the same as 3 + 3 + 3.
Color that apple red. Color the other apples yellow.

Fruity Fun

78 — Addition & Subtraction to 14 — ©2001 by Evan-Moor Corp. • Math Practice at Home • EMC 4516

## Page 79

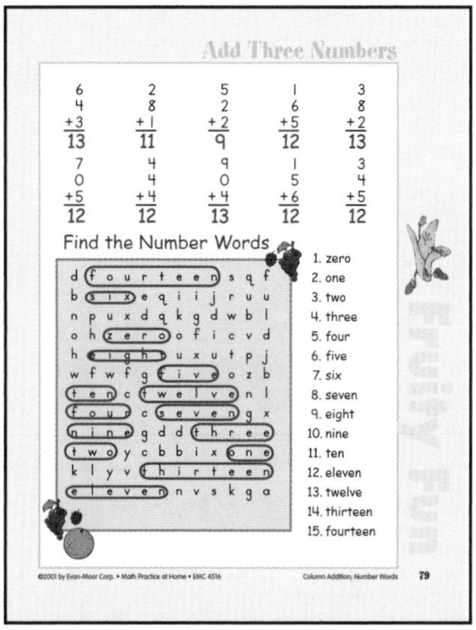

### Add Three Numbers

6 + 4 + 3 = 13 — 2 + 8 + 1 = 11 — 5 + 2 + 2 = 9 — 1 + 6 + 5 = 12 — 3 + 8 + 2 = 13
7 + 0 + 5 = 12 — 4 + 4 + 4 = 12 — 9 + 0 + 4 = 13 — 1 + 5 + 6 = 12 — 3 + 4 + 5 = 12

Find the Number Words

1. zero
2. one
3. two
4. three
5. four
6. five
7. six
8. seven
9. eight
10. nine
11. ten
12. eleven
13. twelve
14. thirteen
15. fourteen

Fruity Fun

©2001 by Evan-Moor Corp. • Math Practice at Home • EMC 4516 — Column Addition; Number Words — 79

## Page 80

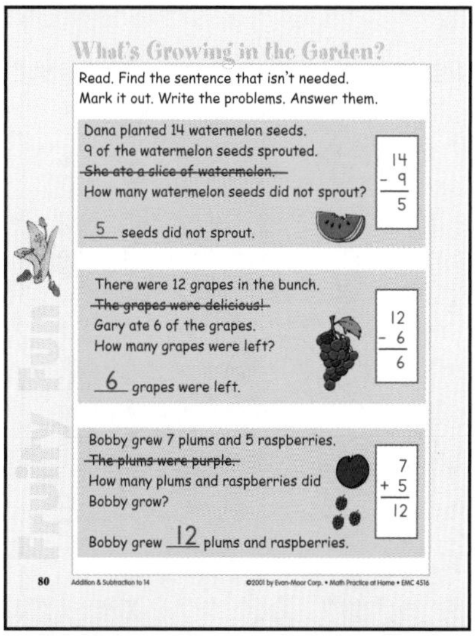

### What's Growing in the Garden?

Read. Find the sentence that isn't needed.
Mark it out. Write the problems. Answer them.

Dana planted 14 watermelon seeds.
9 of the watermelon seeds sprouted.
~~She ate a slice of watermelon.~~
How many watermelon seeds did not sprout?
5 seeds did not sprout. — 14 − 9 = 5

There were 12 grapes in the bunch.
~~The grapes were delicious!~~
Gary ate 6 of the grapes.
How many grapes were left?
6 grapes were left. — 12 − 6 = 6

Bobby grew 7 plums and 5 raspberries.
~~The plums were purple.~~
How many plums and raspberries did Bobby grow?
Bobby grew 12 plums and raspberries. — 7 + 5 = 12

Fruity Fun

80 — Addition & Subtraction to 14 — ©2001 by Evan-Moor Corp. • Math Practice at Home • EMC 4516

## Page 81

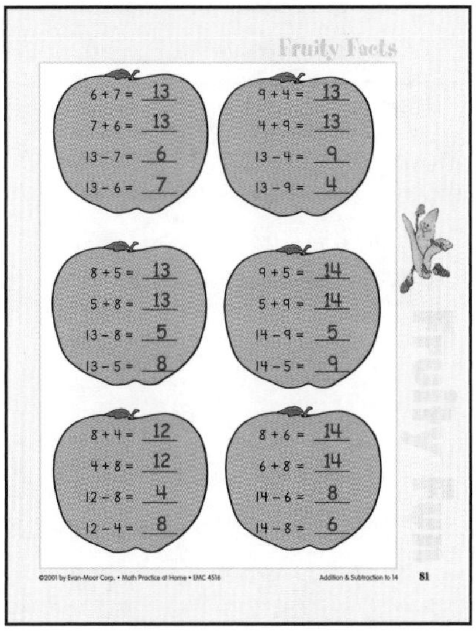

### Fruity Facts

6 + 7 = 13; 7 + 6 = 13; 13 − 7 = 6; 13 − 6 = 7
9 + 4 = 13; 4 + 9 = 13; 13 − 4 = 9; 13 − 9 = 4
8 + 5 = 13; 5 + 8 = 13; 13 − 8 = 5; 13 − 5 = 8
9 + 5 = 14; 5 + 9 = 14; 14 − 9 = 5; 14 − 5 = 9
8 + 4 = 12; 4 + 8 = 12; 12 − 8 = 4; 12 − 4 = 8
8 + 6 = 14; 6 + 8 = 14; 14 − 6 = 8; 14 − 8 = 6

Fruity Fun

©2001 by Evan-Moor Corp. • Math Practice at Home • EMC 4516 — Addition & Subtraction to 14 — 81

## Page 82

### All About June

Look at the calendar. Answer the questions.

JUNE

1. What is the name of this month? June
2. How many days are in this month? 30
3. Flag Day is on what day? 14
4. There is a birthday on Thursday or June 10
5. There is a soccer game on Friday or June 25
6. How many Tuesdays are in this month? 5
7. How many Saturdays are in this month? 4

Fruity Fun

82 — Reading a Calendar — ©2001 by Evan-Moor Corp. • Math Practice at Home • EMC 4516

## Page 83

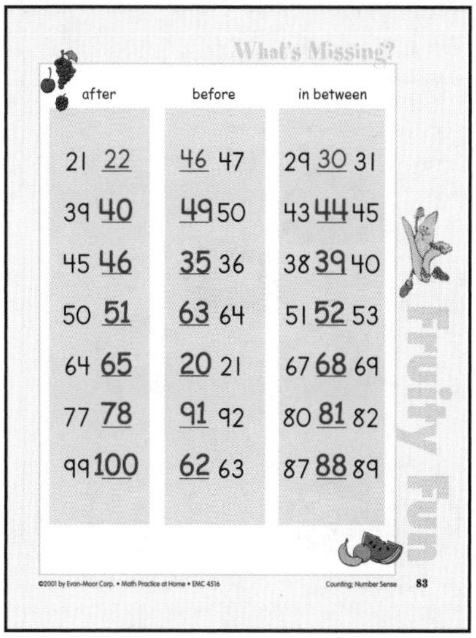

### What's Missing?

| after | before | in between |
| --- | --- | --- |
| 21 22 | 46 47 | 29 30 31 |
| 39 40 | 49 50 | 43 44 45 |
| 45 46 | 35 36 | 38 39 40 |
| 50 51 | 63 64 | 51 52 53 |
| 64 65 | 20 21 | 67 68 69 |
| 77 78 | 91 92 | 80 81 82 |
| 99 100 | 62 63 | 87 88 89 |

Fruity Fun

©2001 by Evan-Moor Corp. • Math Practice at Home • EMC 4516 — Counting; Number Sense — 83

## Page 84

### Talking Fruit

Barry Banana has a message for you.
Write the letter that goes with each number.

EAT (6 5 8)
FIVE (14 12 9 6)
FRUITS (14 3 7 12 8 4)
A DAY! (5 13 5 11)

| A | D | E | F | I |
|---|---|---|---|---|
| 14 − 9 = 5 | 8 + 5 = 13 | 13 − 7 = 6 | 7 + 7 = 14 | 9 + 3 = 12 |

| R | S | T | U | V | Y |
|---|---|---|---|---|---|
| 11 − 8 = 3 | 13 − 9 = 4 | 13 − 5 = 8 | 14 − 7 = 7 | 14 − 5 = 9 | 7 + 4 = 11 |

Fruity Fun

84 Addition & Subtraction to 14 ©2001 by Evan-Moor Corp. • Math Practice at Home • EMC 4516

## Page 85

### Farmer Fred's Fruit

Skills: Completing and Reading a Graph

Farmer Fred likes to keep track of the fruit he sells at his stand. Here is what he sold last Saturday.

8 bags of cherries
10 watermelons
7 baskets of berries
5 pears

Color the graph to show what Farmer Fred sold.

| | 1 | 2 | 3 | 4 | 5 | 6 | 7 | 8 | 9 | 10 |
|---|---|---|---|---|---|---|---|---|---|---|
| cherries | ■ | ■ | ■ | ■ | ■ | ■ | ■ | ■ | | |
| berries | ■ | ■ | ■ | ■ | ■ | ■ | ■ | | | |
| watermelons | ■ | ■ | ■ | ■ | ■ | ■ | ■ | ■ | ■ | ■ |
| pears | ■ | ■ | ■ | ■ | ■ | | | | | |

1. How many more watermelons sold than pears? 5
2. Which fruit sold the smallest amount? pears
3. How many bags of cherries and baskets of berries? 15

Fruity Fun

©2005 by Evan-Moor Corp. • EMC 4545 • Skill Sharpeners—Math UNIT 7 85

## Page 86

### A Yummy Snack

Add and subtract. Color.

red 7, yellow 5, blue 8, green 10

14 − 6 = 8
9 + 1 = 10
12 − 4 = 8
13 − 6 = 7
14 − 6 = 8
11 − 3 = 8
14 − 9 = 5
6 + 2 = 8
13 − 8 = 5
11 − 6 = 5
7 + 1 = 8
5 + 3 = 8

Fruity Fun

86 Addition & Subtraction to 14 ©2001 by Evan-Moor Corp. • Math Practice at Home • EMC 4516

## Page 87

### Count by Fives

Count by 5s.

5 10 15 20 25
30 35 40 45 50

Connect the dots.

Fruity Fun

©2001 by Evan-Moor Corp. • Math Practice at Home • EMC 4516 Counting by 5s 87

## Page 88

### Greater Than, Less Than

> = greater than   < = less than
8 > 7   7 < 8

7 < 12   13 < 20   18 > 9
5 < 15   14 > 4   10 > 0

Add or subtract. Write > or < in the ◯.

| | |
|---|---|
| 9 + 5 > 12 + 1 (14, 13) | 8 + 5 > 5 + 6 (13, 11) |
| 3 + 7 < 6 + 6 (10, 12) | 5 + 4 < 8 + 3 (9, 11) |
| 13 − 8 < 11 − 4 (5, 7) | 14 − 7 < 5 + 4 (7, 9) |
| 7 + 6 > 14 − 5 (13, 9) | 12 − 7 > 11 − 7 (5, 4) |

Fruity Fun

88 Greater Than, Less Than ©2001 by Evan-Moor Corp. • Math Practice at Home • EMC 4516

## Page 89

Note: Use this assessment after your child has completed through page 88.

TEST YOUR SKILLS

Count by 5s.

5 10 15 20 25 30 35 40 45 50
55 60 65 70 75 80 85 90 95 100

Add.

| 6 + 4 + 3 | 2 + 3 + 1 | 4 + 3 + 5 | 9 + 0 + 4 |
|---|---|---|---|
| 13 | 6 | 12 | 13 |

Read the word. Color the circle under the number.

zero: 7 ○ 0 ● 2 ○
eight: 9 ○ 4 ○ 8 ●
three: 10 ○ 3 ● 2 ○

©2005 by Evan-Moor Corp. • EMC 4545 • Skill Sharpeners—Math ASSESSMENT 1 89

## Page 90

### Color the Igloos

Find the answers. Color the igloos with 14 blue.
Color the igloos with 15 red.
Color the igloos with 16 green.

8 + 7 = 15
7 + 7 = 14
9 + 6 = 15
8 + 8 = 16
9 + 7 = 16
9 + 5 = 14
10 + 5 = 15
8 + 6 = 14

Chilly Capers

90 Addition & Subtraction to 16 ©2001 by Evan-Moor Corp. • Math Practice at Home • EMC 4516

## Page 91

### Meet the Walrus Families

Use each family of numbers to make 2 addition problems and 2 subtraction problems.

| 9 6 15 | 7 8 15 |
|---|---|
| 9 + 6 = 15 | 7 + 8 = 15 |
| 6 + 9 = 15 | 8 + 7 = 15 |
| 15 − 6 = 9 | 15 − 7 = 8 |
| 15 − 9 = 6 | 15 − 8 = 7 |

| 9 7 16 | 8 6 14 |
|---|---|
| 9 + 7 = 16 | 8 + 6 = 14 |
| 7 + 9 = 16 | 6 + 8 = 14 |
| 16 − 7 = 9 | 14 − 6 = 8 |
| 16 − 9 = 7 | 14 − 8 = 6 |

6 + 7 = 13   13 − 6 = 7   8 + 8 = 16
7 + 6 = 13   13 − 7 = 6   16 − 8 = 8

Chilly Capers

©2001 by Evan-Moor Corp. • Math Practice at Home • EMC 4516 Addition & Subtraction to 16 91

## Page 92

### Animals at the Poles

Note: You may need to help your child read the word problems.

Write the problems. Answer them.

9 penguins were swimming in the sea. 7 more penguins jumped in. How many penguins were swimming in the sea?
9 + 7 = 16
There were 16 penguins swimming in the sea.

16 walruses were lying on the ice. 9 walruses slid back into the sea. How many walruses were still on the ice?
16 − 9 = 7
There were 7 walruses still on the ice.

Polar Bear saw 6 seals in the morning and 9 seals in the afternoon. How many seals did Polar Bear see in all?
6 + 9 = 15
Polar Bear saw 15 seals in all.

16 penguins were caught for the zoo. 8 of the penguins got away. How many penguins were left?
16 − 8 = 8
There were 8 penguins left.

Chilly Capers

92 Addition & Subtraction to 16 ©2001 by Evan-Moor Corp. • Math Practice at Home • EMC 4516

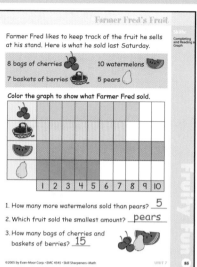

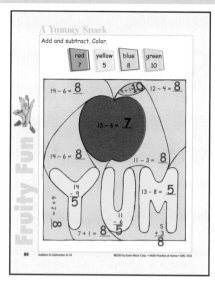

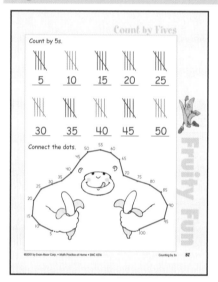

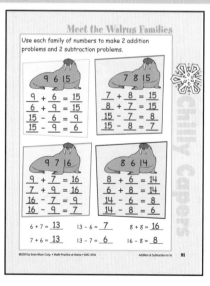

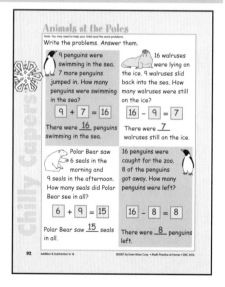

## Page 93

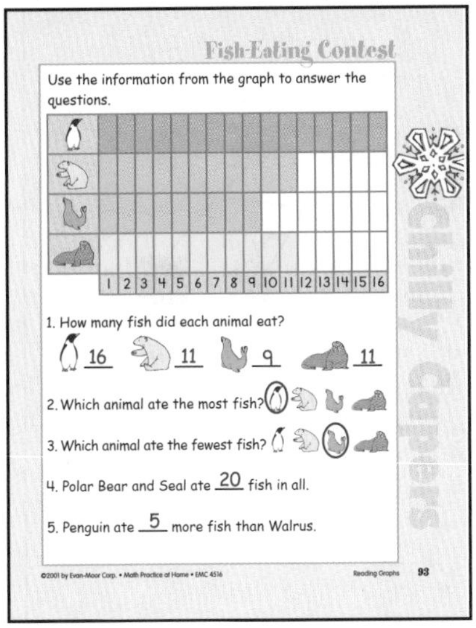

Fish-Eating Contest

Use the information from the graph to answer the questions.

1 2 3 4 5 6 7 8 9 10 11 12 13 14 15 16

1. How many fish did each animal eat? 16 11 9 11

2. Which animal ate the most fish?

3. Which animal ate the fewest fish?

4. Polar Bear and Seal ate 20 fish in all.

5. Penguin ate 5 more fish than Walrus.

©2001 by Evan-Moor Corp. • Math Practice at Home • EMC 4516 Reading Graphs 93

## Page 94

Find the Seal

Connect the answers in order from smallest to largest.

14 − 9 = 5; 10 + 2 = 12; 15 − 9 = 6; 7 + 4 = 11; 7 + 6 = 13; 13 − 6 = 7; 12 − 2 = 10; 6 + 8 = 14; 16 − 8 = 8; 16 − 7 = 9

94 Addition & Subtraction to 16 ©2001 by Evan-Moor Corp. • Math Practice at Home • EMC 4516

## Page 95

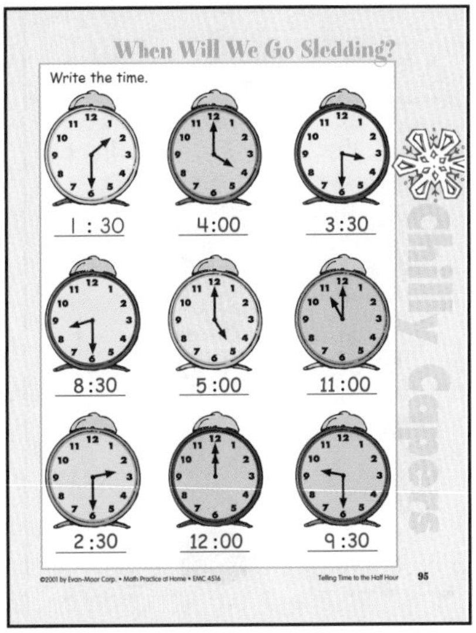

When Will We Go Sledding?

Write the time.

1:30 4:00 3:30

8:30 5:00 11:00

2:30 12:00 9:30

©2001 by Evan-Moor Corp. • Math Practice at Home • EMC 4516 Telling Time to the Half Hour 95

## Page 96

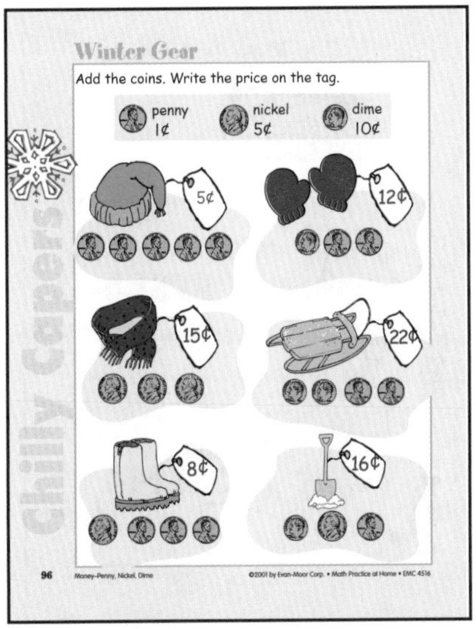

Winter Gear

Add the coins. Write the price on the tag.

penny 1¢ nickel 5¢ dime 10¢

5¢ 12¢ 15¢ 22¢ 8¢ 16¢

96 Money–Penny, Nickel, Dime ©2001 by Evan-Moor Corp. • Math Practice at Home • EMC 4516

## Page 97

Let It Snow!

Add or subtract. Do the ones first.

tens ones 42 + 46 = 88; 15 − 10 = 5; 13 + 4 = 17

14 − 4 = 10; 15 + 13 = 28; 58 − 26 = 32

13 + 26 = 39; 22 + 7 = 29; 15 − 15 = 0

©2001 by Evan-Moor Corp. • Math Practice at Home • EMC 4516 Two-Digit Addition & Subtraction 97

## Page 98

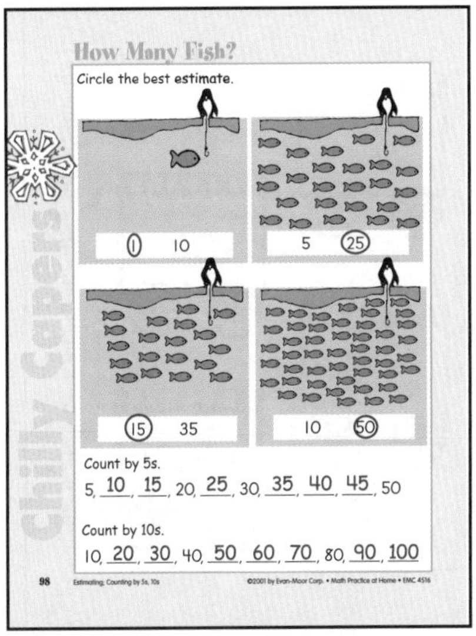

How Many Fish?

Circle the best estimate.

1 10 5 25

15 35 10 50

Count by 5s.

5, 10, 15, 20, 25, 30, 35, 40, 45, 50

Count by 10s.

10, 20, 30, 40, 50, 60, 70, 80, 90, 100

98 Estimating; Counting by 5s, 10s ©2001 by Evan-Moor Corp. • Math Practice at Home • EMC 4516

## Page 99

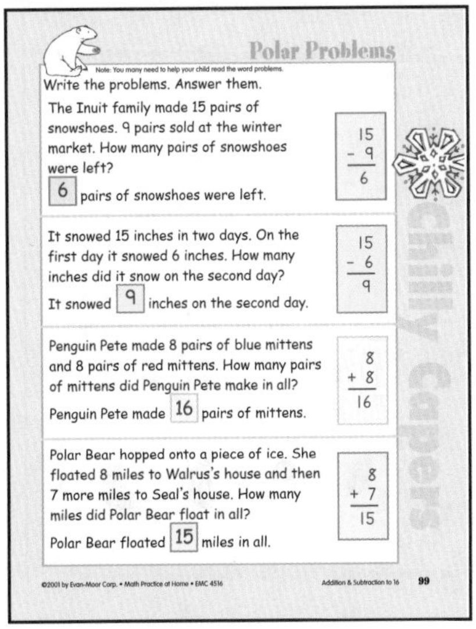

Polar Problems

Note: You many need to help your child read the word problems.

Write the problems. Answer them.

The Inuit family made 15 pairs of snowshoes. 9 pairs sold at the winter market. How many pairs of snowshoes were left? 6 pairs of snowshoes were left. 15 − 9 = 6

It snowed 15 inches in two days. On the first day it snowed 6 inches. How many inches did it snow on the second day? It snowed 9 inches on the second day. 15 − 6 = 9

Penguin Pete made 8 pairs of blue mittens and 8 pairs of red mittens. How many pairs of mittens did Penguin Pete make in all? Penguin Pete made 16 pairs of mittens. 8 + 8 = 16

Polar Bear hopped onto a piece of ice. She floated 8 miles to Walrus's house and then 7 more miles to Seal's house. How many miles did Polar Bear float in all? Polar Bear floated 15 miles in all. 8 + 7 = 15

©2001 by Evan-Moor Corp. • Math Practice at Home • EMC 4516 Addition & Subtraction to 16 99

## Page 100

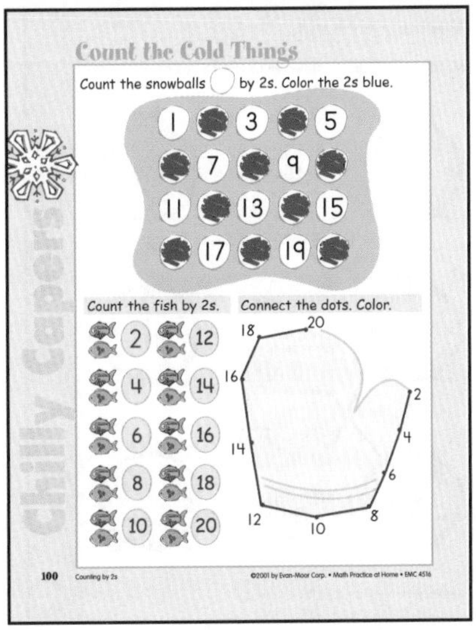

Count the Cold Things

Count the snowballs by 2s. Color the 2s blue.

1 3 5 7 9 11 13 15 17 19

Count the fish by 2s. 2 4 6 8 10 12 14 16 18 20

Connect the dots. Color. 2 4 6 8 10 12 14 16 18 20

100 Counting by 2s ©2001 by Evan-Moor Corp. • Math Practice at Home • EMC 4516

## Page 101

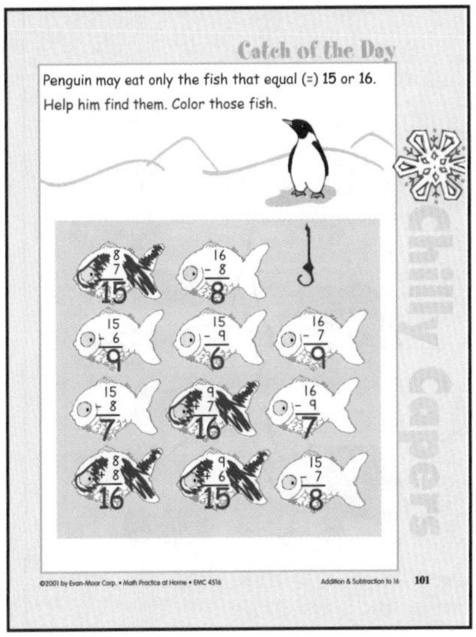

Catch of the Day

Penguin may eat only the fish that equal (=) 15 or 16. Help him find them. Color those fish.

8 + 7 = 15; 16 − 8 = 8

15 + 6 = 21; 15 − 9 = 6; 16 − 7 = 9

15 − 8 = 7; 9 + 7 = 16; 16 − 9 = 7

8 + 8 = 16; 9 + 6 = 15; 15 − 7 = 8

©2001 by Evan-Moor Corp. • Math Practice at Home • EMC 4516 Addition & Subtraction to 16 101

## Page 102

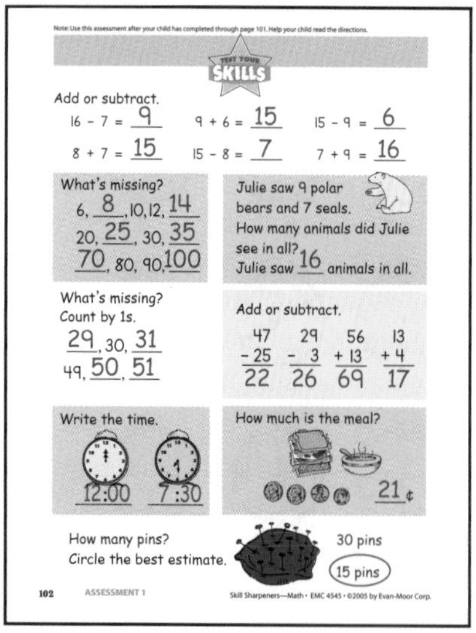
Note: Use this assessment after your child has completed through page 101. Help your child read the directions.

TEST YOUR SKILLS

Add or subtract.

16 − 7 = 9   9 + 6 = 15   15 − 9 = 6

8 + 7 = 15   15 − 8 = 7   7 + 9 = 16

What's missing?

6, 8, 10, 12, 14

20, 25, 30, 35

70, 80, 90, 100

Julie saw 9 polar bears and 7 seals. How many animals did Julie see in all?

Julie saw 16 animals in all.

What's missing? Count by 1s.

29, 30, 31

49, 50, 51

Add or subtract.

| 47 | 29 | 56 | 13 |
|---|---|---|---|
| − 25 | − 3 | + 13 | + 4 |
| 22 | 26 | 69 | 17 |

Write the time.

12:00  7:30

How much is the meal?

21¢

How many pins? Circle the best estimate.

30 pins

15 pins

102 ASSESSMENT 1  Skill Sharpeners—Math • EMC 4545 • ©2005 by Evan-Moor Corp.

## Page 103

In the Big Top

Add or subtract.

9 + 8 = 17; 18 − 9 = 9; 15 − 8 = 7; 8 + 8 = 16; 9 + 7 = 16; 16 − 7 = 9; 17 − 8 = 9; 17 − 9 = 8; 9 + 9 = 18; 16 − 9 = 7; 8 + 7 = 15; 16 − 8 = 8

Measure each item to the nearest inch.

The ball is 1 inch wide.  The horn is 2 inches long.

At the Circus

©2001 by Evan-Moor Corp. • Math Practice at Home • EMC 4516  Adding & Subtracting to 18; Measuring to the Nearest Inch  103

## Page 104

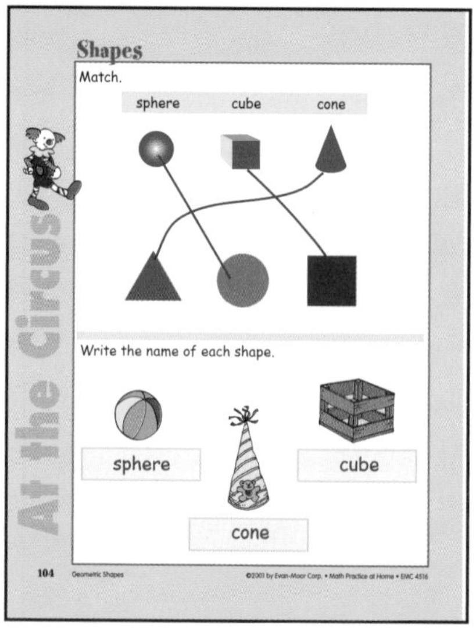
Shapes

Match.

sphere  cube  cone

Write the name of each shape.

sphere  cone  cube

At the Circus

104  Geometric Shapes  ©2001 by Evan-Moor Corp. • Math Practice at Home • EMC 4516

## Page 105

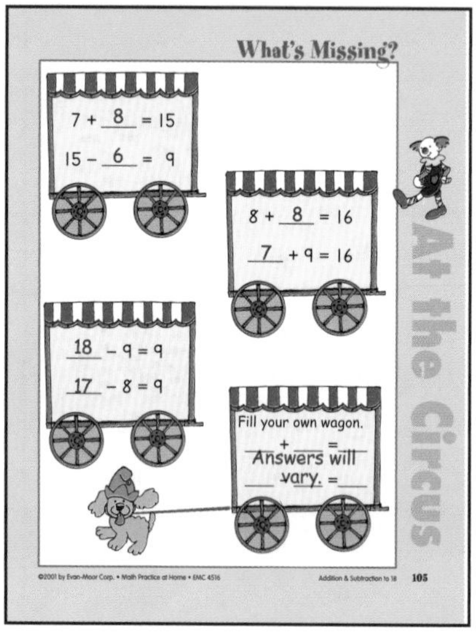
What's Missing?

7 + 8 = 15

15 − 6 = 9

8 + 8 = 16

7 + 9 = 16

18 − 9 = 9

17 − 8 = 9

Fill your own wagon.

Answers will vary.

At the Circus

©2001 by Evan-Moor Corp. • Math Practice at Home • EMC 4516  Addition & Subtraction to 18  105

## Page 106

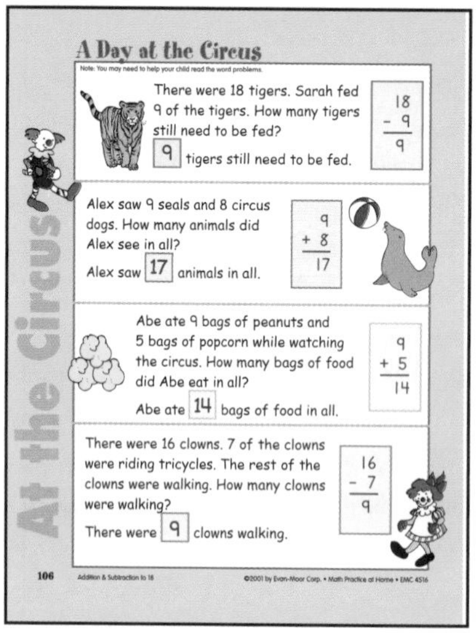
A Day at the Circus

Note: You may need to help your child read the word problems.

There were 18 tigers. Sarah fed 9 of the tigers. How many tigers still need to be fed?

18 − 9 = 9

9 tigers still need to be fed.

Alex saw 9 seals and 8 circus dogs. How many animals did Alex see in all?

9 + 8 = 17

Alex saw 17 animals in all.

Abe ate 9 bags of peanuts and 5 bags of popcorn while watching the circus. How many bags of food did Abe eat in all?

9 + 5 = 14

Abe ate 14 bags of food in all.

There were 16 clowns. 7 of the clowns were riding tricycles. The rest of the clowns were walking. How many clowns were walking?

16 − 7 = 9

There were 9 clowns walking.

At the Circus

106  Addition & Subtraction to 18  ©2001 by Evan-Moor Corp. • Math Practice at Home • EMC 4516

## Page 107

How Many Centimeters?

6 centimeters

3 centimeters

7 centimeters

4 centimeters

At the Circus

©2001 by Evan-Moor Corp. • Math Practice at Home • EMC 4516  Measuring to the Nearest Centimeter  107

## Page 108

Feed the Elephants

Match each elephant to its peanuts.

16  17  18

10 + 7; 12 + 6; 15 + 1; 9 + 9; 8 + 9; 8 + 8; 17 − 0; 10 + 8

At the Circus

108  Addition & Subtraction to 18  ©2001 by Evan-Moor Corp. • Math Practice at Home • EMC 4516

## Page 109

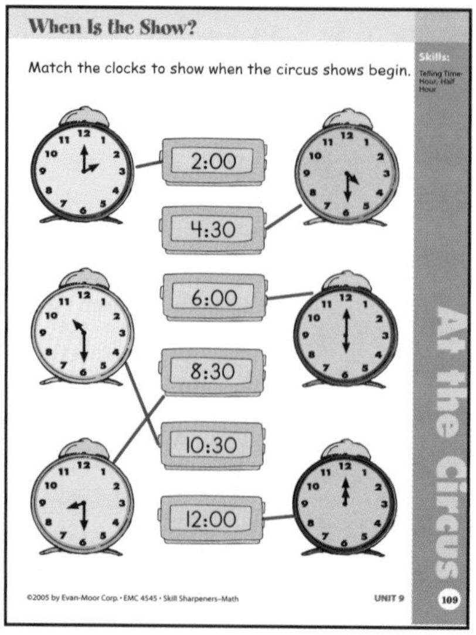
When Is the Show?

Skills: Telling Time—Hour, Half Hour

Match the clocks to show when the circus shows begin.

2:00  4:30  6:00  8:30  10:30  12:00

At the Circus

©2005 by Evan-Moor Corp. • EMC 4545 • Skill Sharpeners—Math  UNIT 9  109

## Page 110

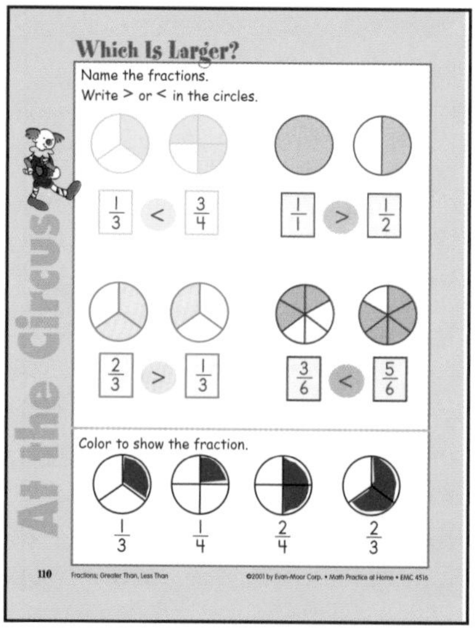
Which Is Larger?

Name the fractions.

Write > or < in the circles.

1/3 < 3/4   1/1 > 1/2

2/3 > 1/3   3/6 < 5/6

Color to show the fraction.

1/3  1/4  2/4  2/3

At the Circus

110  Fractions; Greater Than, Less Than  ©2001 by Evan-Moor Corp. • Math Practice at Home • EMC 4516

## Page 111

### At the Snack Counter

How much does each snack cost?

dime 10¢ · nickel 5¢ · penny 1¢

45 ¢

18 ¢

21 ¢

50 ¢

25 ¢

13 ¢

41 ¢

At the Circus

©2001 by Evan-Moor Corp. • Math Practice at Home • EMC 4516 — Money–Penny, Nickel, Dime 111

## Page 112

### Add and Subtract Tens and Ones

Remember: Add the ones first.

| | | | | |
|---|---|---|---|---|
| 31 + 68 = 99 | 23 + 72 = 95 | 54 + 15 = 69 | 11 + 38 = 49 | 15 + 84 = 99 |
| 77 + 22 = 99 | 34 + 44 = 78 | 50 + 49 = 99 | 25 + 63 = 88 | 45 + 41 = 86 |

How many of your answers were the same? 3

| | | | | |
|---|---|---|---|---|
| 87 − 65 = 22 | 99 − 87 = 12 | 43 − 20 = 23 | 76 − 34 = 42 | 48 − 16 = 32 |
| 79 − 44 = 35 | 80 − 40 = 40 | 79 − 55 = 24 | 87 − 10 = 77 | 22 − 0 = 22 |

How many of your answers had two **tens**? 3

At the Circus

112 Two-Digit Addition & Subtraction — ©2001 by Evan-Moor Corp. • Math Practice at Home • EMC 4516

## Page 113

### Words and Numbers

Read the word. Write the number.

ten 10 · four 4 · eight 8

six 6 · one 1 · seven 7

Write the number word.

6 six · 10 ten · 7 seven

Write the number.

1 ten and 4 ones = 14

3 tens and 8 ones = 38

6 tens and 0 ones = 60

At the Circus

©2001 by Evan-Moor Corp. • Math Practice at Home • EMC 4516 — Number Words; Place Value–Tens & Ones 113

## Page 114

Note: Use this assessment after your child has completed through page 113.

TEST YOUR SKILLS

Add and subtract.

23 + 72 = 95 · 11 + 38 = 49

99 − 73 = 26 · 50 − 30 = 20

Match the fraction.

1/2 · 1/4 · 1/3

Color the circle for the correct time.

2:00 · 12:00 (colored) · 3:30 · 4:30 (colored)

8:30 (colored) · 6:30 · 12:00 · 10:00 (colored)

114 ASSESSMENT 1 — Skill Sharpeners—Math • EMC 4545 • ©2005 by Evan-Moor Corp.

## Page 115

### Go for the Goal!

Note: Unit 10 is a review of the skills practiced in Units 1 through 9.

Add and subtract.

Color the football with the largest answer brown.

9 − 5 = 4 · 8 + 6 = 14 · 17 − 8 = 9 · 6 + 4 = 10

4 + 4 = 8 · 18 (colored) · 7 − 4 = 3

9 − 6 = 3 · 10 − 7 = 3 · 5 + 5 = 10 · 8 − 2 = 6

5 + 3 = 8 · 12 − 6 = 6

GO TEAM · Be a Sport

©2001 by Evan-Moor Corp. • Math Practice at Home • EMC 4516 — Review Addition & Subtraction to 18 115

## Page 116

### Can You Buy It?

Count your money. Circle **Yes** or **No**.

40¢ — 45 ¢ — Yes

19¢ — 16 ¢ — No

37¢ — 35 ¢ — No

28¢ — 30 ¢ — Yes

GO TEAM · Be a Sport

116 Money–Penny, Nickel, Dime — ©2001 by Evan-Moor Corp. • Math Practice at Home • EMC 4516

## Page 117

### Tennis Anyone?

Use the numbers on the tennis balls to complete each problem. Use each ball once.

3 · 2 · 6 · 0 · 12 · 10 · 9 · 5

4 + 3 + 3 = 10 · 2 + 3 + 4 = 9 · 8 + 1 + 2 = 11 · 6 + 0 + 5 = 11

3 + 3 + 4 = 10 · 0 + 5 + 5 = 10 · 2 + 6 + 4 = 12 · 4 + 4 + 4 = 12

GO TEAM · Be a Sport

©2001 by Evan-Moor Corp. • Math Practice at Home • EMC 4516 — Review Column Addition 117

## Page 118

### Play Ball!

Note: You may need to help your child read the word problems.

Write the problems. Answer them.

Jake hit 16 tennis balls. He hit 7 balls over the net. How many tennis balls did **not** go over the net? — 16 − 7 = 9

9 tennis balls did **not** go over the net.

Denise found 8 golf balls and 6 baseballs. How many balls did Denise find in all? — 8 + 6 = 14

Denise found 14 balls in all.

Jean had 15 volleyballs. She put 8 of them into the ball bag. How many volleyballs must still be put into the ball bag? — 15 − 8 = 7

7 more volleyballs must still be put into the ball bag.

Dustin has 9 baseballs and 4 gloves. How many pieces of baseball equipment does Dustin have? — 9 + 4 = 13

Dustin has 13 pieces of baseball equipment.

GO TEAM · Be a Sport

118 Review Word Problems — ©2001 by Evan-Moor Corp. • Math Practice at Home • EMC 4516

## Page 119

### Catch the Ball!

Match the balls and gloves.

9 + 7 = 16 · 7 + 6 = 13 · 14 − 5 = 9 · 8 + 4 = 12 · 8 + 8 = 16 · 15 − 9 = 6

8 + 7 = 15 · 17 − 8 = 9 · 9 + 6 = 15 · 8 + 5 = 13 · 7 + 5 = 12 · 18 − 9 = 9

Gloves: 6 · 9 · 12 · 13 · 15 · 16

GO TEAM · Be a Sport

©2001 by Evan-Moor Corp. • Math Practice at Home • EMC 4516 — Review Adding & Subtracting to 18 119

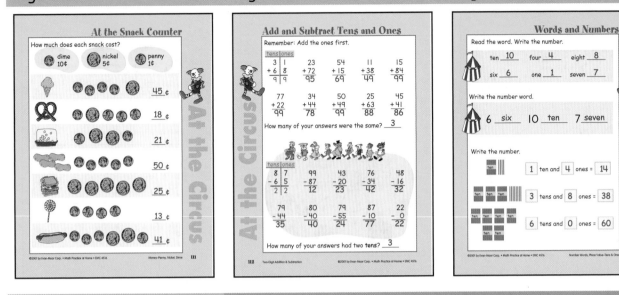

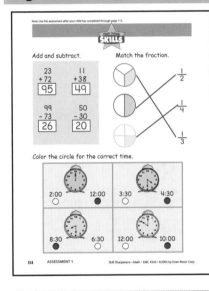

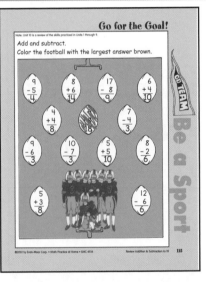

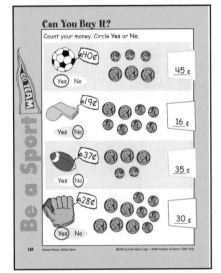

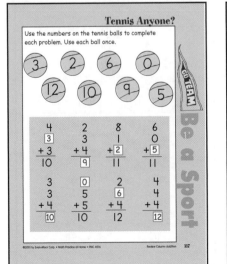

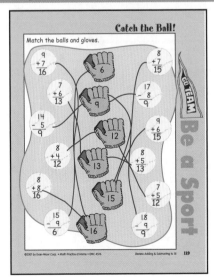

## Page 120

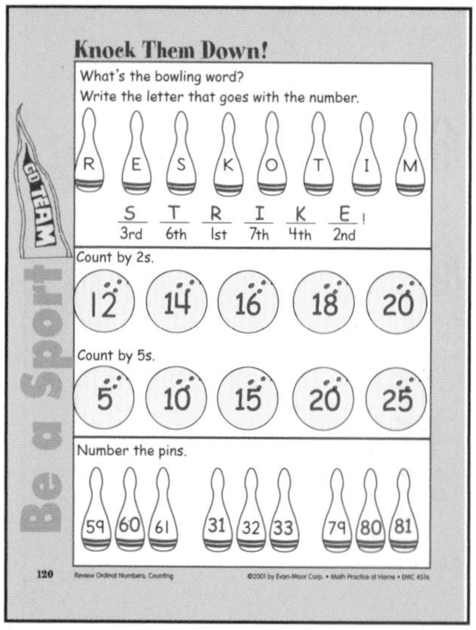

### Knock Them Down!

What's the bowling word?
Write the letter that goes with the number.

R E S K O T I M

S T R I K E !
3rd 6th 1st 7th 4th 2nd

Count by 2s.
12 14 16 18 20

Count by 5s.
5 10 15 20 25

Number the pins.
59 60 61 31 32 33 79 80 81



120 Review Ordinal Numbers, Counting ©2001 by Evan-Moor Corp. • Math Practice at Home • EMC 4516

## Page 121

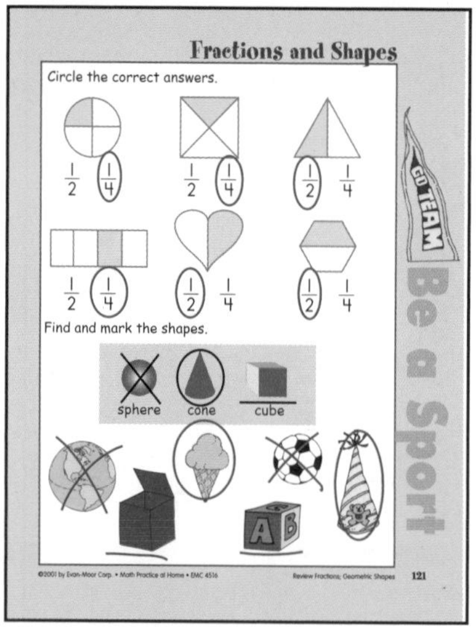

### Fractions and Shapes

Circle the correct answers.

1/2 (1/4) 1/2 (1/4) (1/2) 1/4
1/2 (1/4) (1/2) 1/4 (1/2) 1/4

Find and mark the shapes.

sphere cone cube



©2001 by Evan-Moor Corp. • Math Practice at Home • EMC 4516 Review Fractions, Geometric Shapes 121

## Page 122

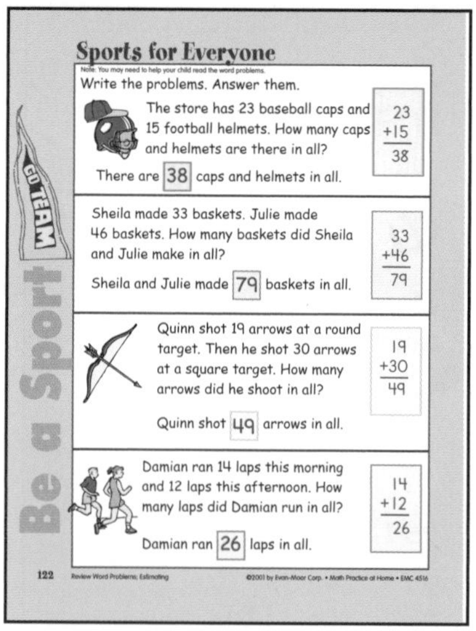

### Sports for Everyone

Note: You may need to help your child read the word problems.

Write the problems. Answer them.

The store has 23 baseball caps and 15 football helmets. How many caps and helmets are there in all?
There are 38 caps and helmets in all.
23 + 15 = 38

Sheila made 33 baskets. Julie made 46 baskets. How many baskets did Sheila and Julie make in all?
Sheila and Julie made 79 baskets in all.
33 + 46 = 79

Quinn shot 19 arrows at a round target. Then he shot 30 arrows at a square target. How many arrows did he shoot in all?
Quinn shot 49 arrows in all.
19 + 30 = 49

Damian ran 14 laps this morning and 12 laps this afternoon. How many laps did Damian run in all?
Damian ran 26 laps in all.
14 + 12 = 26



122 Review Word Problems, Estimating ©2001 by Evan-Moor Corp. • Math Practice at Home • EMC 4516

## Page 123

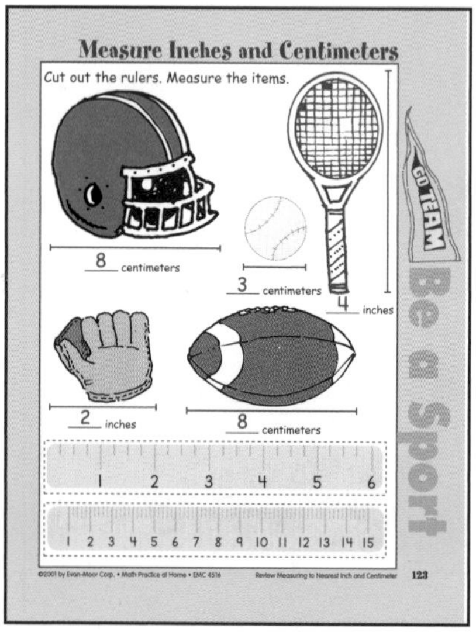

### Measure Inches and Centimeters

Cut out the rulers. Measure the items.

8 centimeters
3 centimeters
4 inches
2 inches
8 centimeters

1 2 3 4 5 6
1 2 3 4 5 6 7 8 9 10 11 12 13 14 15



©2001 by Evan-Moor Corp. • Math Practice at Home • EMC 4516 Review Measuring to Nearest Inch and Centimeter 123

## Page 124

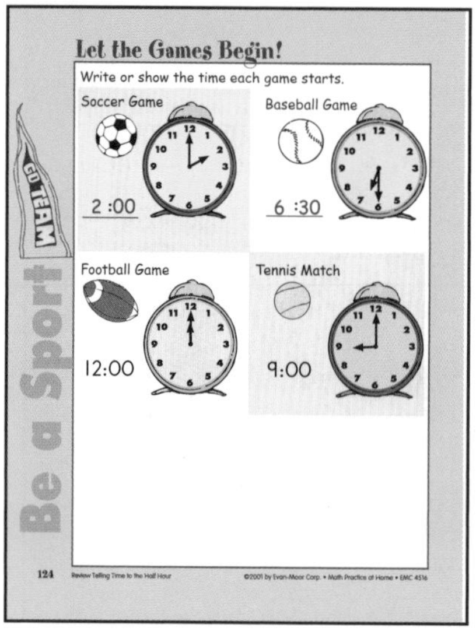

### Let the Games Begin!

Write or show the time each game starts.

Soccer Game 2:00
Baseball Game 6:30
Football Game 12:00
Tennis Match 9:00



124 Review Telling Time to the Half Hour ©2001 by Evan-Moor Corp. • Math Practice at Home • EMC 4516

## Page 125

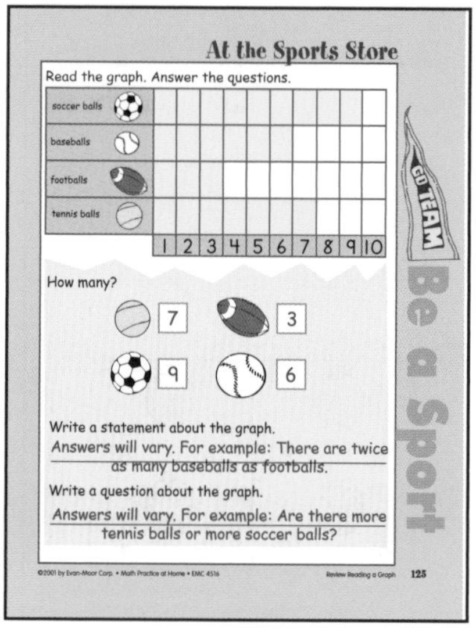

### At the Sports Store

Read the graph. Answer the questions.

soccer balls
baseballs
footballs
tennis balls
1 2 3 4 5 6 7 8 9 10

How many?
tennis balls 7, footballs 3, soccer balls 9, baseballs 6

Write a statement about the graph.
Answers will vary. For example: There are twice as many baseballs as footballs.

Write a question about the graph.
Answers will vary. For example: Are there more tennis balls or more soccer balls?



©2001 by Evan-Moor Corp. • Math Practice at Home • EMC 4516 Review Reading a Graph 125

## Page 126

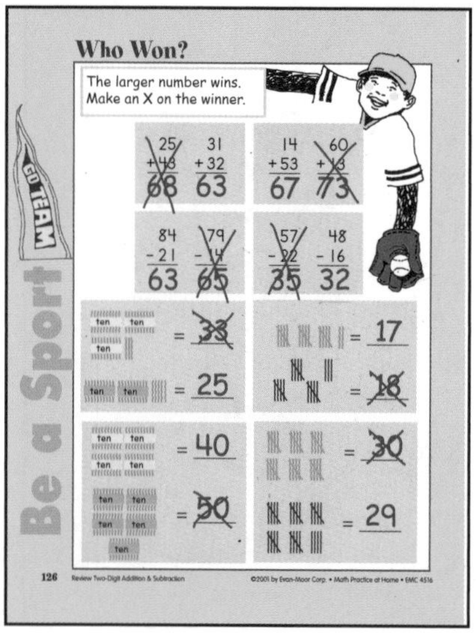

### Who Won?

The larger number wins.
Make an X on the winner.

25 + 43 = 68 (X); 31 + 32 = 63
14 + 53 = 67; 60 + 13 = 73 (X)
84 − 21 = 63; 79 − 14 = 65 (X)
57 − 22 = 35 (X); 48 − 16 = 32

= 33 (X); = 17
= 25; = 18 (X)
= 40; = 30 (X)
= 50 (X); = 29



126 Review Two-Digit Addition & Subtraction ©2001 by Evan-Moor Corp. • Math Practice at Home • EMC 4516

## Page 127

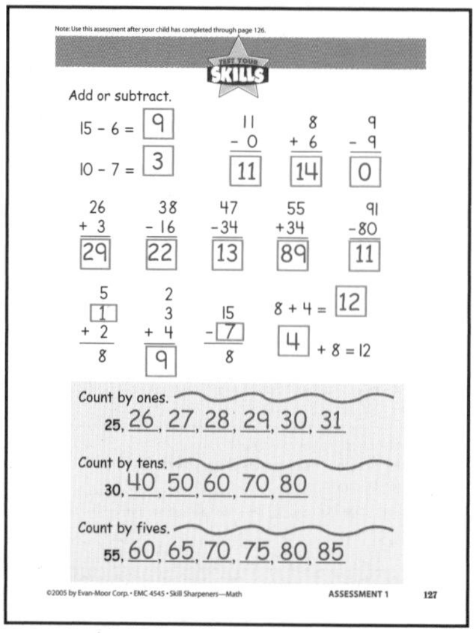

Note: Use this assessment after your child has completed through page 126.

TEST YOUR SKILLS

Add or subtract.

15 − 6 = 9
10 − 7 = 3
11 − 0 = 11
8 + 6 = 14
9 − 9 = 0

26 + 3 = 29
38 − 16 = 22
47 − 34 = 13
55 + 34 = 89
91 − 80 = 11

5 + 1 + 2 = 8
2 + 3 + 4 = 9
15 − 7 = 8
8 + 4 = 12
4 + 8 = 12

Count by ones.
25, 26, 27, 28, 29, 30, 31

Count by tens.
30, 40, 50, 60, 70, 80

Count by fives.
55, 60, 65, 70, 75, 80, 85

©2005 by Evan-Moor Corp. • EMC 4545 • Skill Sharpeners—Math ASSESSMENT 1 127

## Page 128

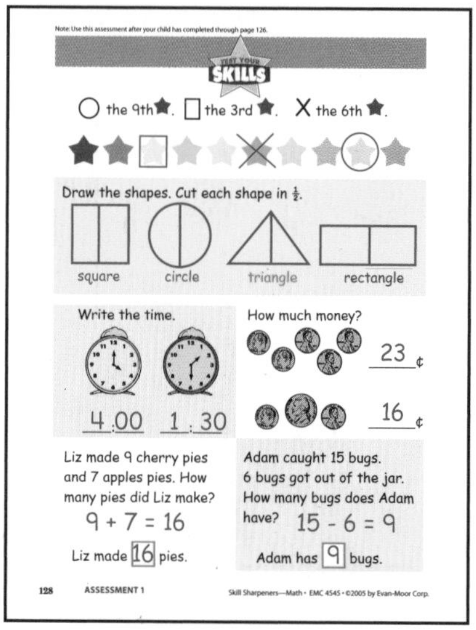

Note: Use this assessment after your child has completed through page 126.

TEST YOUR SKILLS

○ the 9th ★. □ the 3rd ★. X the 6th ★.

Draw the shapes. Cut each shape in ½.

square circle triangle rectangle

Write the time.
4:00 1:30

How much money?
23¢
16¢

Liz made 9 cherry pies and 7 apples pies. How many pies did Liz make?
9 + 7 = 16
Liz made 16 pies.

Adam caught 15 bugs. 6 bugs got out of the jar. How many bugs does Adam have?
15 − 6 = 9
Adam has 9 bugs.

128 ASSESSMENT 1 Skill Sharpeners—Math • EMC 4545 • ©2005 by Evan-Moor Corp.